STARTING TO EXPLAIN:
ESSAYS ON TWENTIETH CENTURY BRITISH AND IRISH POETRY

JOHN LUCAS

TRENT BOOKS

Published by Trent Editions 2003

Trent Editions
Department of English and Media Studies
The Nottingham Trent University
Clifton Lane.
Nottingham NG11 8NS

Printed in Great Britain by Goaters Limited, Nottingham

ISBN 1 84233 086 1

STARTING TO EXPLAIN:
ESSAYS ON TWENTIETH CENTURY BRITISH AND IRISH POETRY

Contents

FOR ANNE STEVENSON

'The great revelations all occur before the age of twenty-five … . The revelations which come later are more objective … . One becomes simultaneously humbler and more arrogant. One feels a duty and not, as before, just the desire to recognize and be recognized. Everyone over thirty-five starts to explain.'

John Berger

Acknowledgements

Acknowledgements are due to the following for essays included in this book: to the *Dark Horse* for 'A Lifetime's Catch: The Letters of WS Graham'; to *London Review of Books* for 'Accidents of Language: on Geoffrey Hill's *The Mystery of the Charity of Charles Peguy*'; to *Poetry Review* for 'Making the 1920s New', 'Edgell Rickword', 'Hard Cider and Spam: on G.S. Fraser' and 'England Made Me'; to *Stand for* 'Geoffrey Hill: *Canaan*'; to *Thumbscrew* for 'Choosing the Spartan Way'; to *The Times Literary Supplement* for 'From Severn to Somme: Ivor Gurney'. 'The Occupation of the Land: Edward Thomas's Essays' and 'Compulsions of a Codger: Roy Fuller's *New and Collected Poems*'. 'Beginning Again: Hardy's *Wessex Poems*' first appeared in the *Thomas Hardy Journal*, 1998. The essay on Lawrence's poetry formed the Introduction to my Selection of Lawrence's *Poetry and Non-Fictional Prose*, Routledge, 1990, 'Discovering England: The View from the Train' first appeared in a special issue of *Literature and History 6.2* (Autumn 1997), 'Edward Thomas, Ivor Gurney and English Socialism' first appeared in the *Ivor Gurney Journal 4* (1998), 'Poetry and Politics in the 1920s' was first published in *Poetry and Politics*, ed. Kate Flint for the English Association, 1996, '*The Poetry of Sylvia Townsend Warner*' first appeared in the Journal of the Sylvia Townsend Warner Society Journal, 2000, 'The Work of a Left-Handed Man' was first published in *The Thing About Roy Fisher*, eds. John Kerrigan and Peter Robinson, Liverpool University Press, 2000, "Appropriate Falsehoods: English Poets and American Jazz", first appeared in *The Yearbook of English Studies*, 1987, 'Seamus Heaney and the Possibilities of Poetry' was first published in *Seamus Heaney: A Collection of Critical Essays*, ed. Elmer Andrews, Macmillan,

1992, 'Speaking for England: Tony Harrison', was first published in Tony Harrison: *A Bloodaxe Critical Anthology*, ed. Neil Astley, 1991, 'New Polyolbions' was first published in *Critical Dialogues: Current Issues in English Studies in Germany and Britain*, eds. Isobel Armstrong and Hans-Werner Ludwig, the British Council/Gunter Narr Verlag, 1995.

I am grateful to Frances Banks and Carmen Glover for their expertise in typing up some of these essays and to Mahendra Solanki for casting a cold eye over several of them. Thanks also to R.J. Ellis for seeing this collection through the printers and for other kindnesses.

Preface

I was getting on for seventeen when I first thought seriously about a future career. Some of my classmates were already committed to the idea of medicine. Others fancied law, or the army, or spoke, more vaguely, of 'setting up in business'. None of these possibilities interested me. I was in love with jazz. I listened to every record I could get hold of, read whatever came to hand about the music, and gradually the conviction formed that I would devote myself to the life of a jazz musician. And so, one Saturday early in 1954, I took the £10 I had somehow scraped together to a local music shop and became the owner of a silver-plated trumpet, 'good as new'. There followed months of practice that must have driven my parents distracted – it certainly did lasting damage to their relationships with our neighbours – before I joined a band called, heaven knows why, 'The Vikings'. The band, which was of a quite spectacular incompetence, had grown out of lunch-time sessions a group of us held in the music room of our grammar school at Hampton, Middlesex. Years later I came across John Mole's verse account of similar sessions at a minor public school, where he and his 'little clique/ Dinned the music room each week'. But in 1954 I don't think it occurred to Lanky Cooper, Allan Roger, Ben Newson and others whose names I can't now recall that what we were doing might be happening elsewhere.

Except, that is, at Art Schools. One of my great friends at Hampton, Peter West, was an artist in the making who attended regular Saturday morning sessions of Life Drawing at – I think – Ealing. Peter had introduced me to the names and, mostly through postcard reproductions, the work of French Impressionists as well as Van Gogh and Cézanne, and with him I made a number of trips to London galleries. These were invariably rounded off by coffee-house discussions – an especial favourite was one in the Haymarket which featured floor tiles and a fountain – and the occasional foray into Soho's French Pub, where Peter made a point of drinking double whiskies. (I more timorously kept to half-pints of beer.) On other occasions we might call into Zwemmers, the art book-shop on the Charing Cross Road. From there you could cross to the most alluring of all coffee-bars, Bunjy's, housed in a basement of a building on Litchfield Street. It was on the staircase leading down to Bunjy's that I first saw an exhibition of Frank Auerbach's portraits, none more than twelve inches high, or so memory insists, each possessing an intensity that couldn't be dissociated from the powerful smell of newly-applied oil paint, as though the paintings had been finished off that very day.

Bunjy's was much favoured by students at the nearby St Martin's School of Art, and if while sipping your cappucino you listened in on their conversation, you soon became aware that, threading its way through their talk of art and in particular the opinions of someone called John Berger, was mention of jazz. Not jazz as in its History, or jazz its Theory, but jazz now, in London, this very night: who, including fellow students, would be playing at which pub or club, what the entrance fee was, whether the promised session would be worth the outlay, and, if so, the best means to smuggle in drink. For in those far-off, innocent and still drably conformist days, jazz was widely held to threaten decent, civilised values. Few clubs had drinks licences. Fewer still were allowed to stay open later than 10.30 pm. That Easter a front-page photograph in one tabloid newspaper had claimed to reveal how far jazz had gone in corrupting the morals of the young. A young woman was shown lying full-length under a grand piano, rendered senseless, so the caption implied, from drink (or worse) after attending an all-night jazz "rave" at Cy Laurie's club on Windmill Street. Pure hokum. The club had no grand piano. But my descents into Bunjy's soon persuaded me that jazz and art belonged together. This was the stuff dreams are made on.

I began to spend an increasing amount of time in art galleries. Not merely the Tate and the National, but those along and around Bond Street: the Marlborough, Waddington's, Cork Street. And there were others, further off but equally desirable: the Beaux Arts, the Whitechapel. It was however a quite different gallery that I have particular cause to remember. One afternoon I'd gone into Rowland, Browse and Delbanco, as it was then called, and had been bowled over by some pen and ink drawings made by an artist I'd never before heard of, Josef Herman. The drawings, of Welsh miners, made their impression because the artist had located the men's individuality, not in their faces, which were for the most part left featureless and blank, but in the way a head was tilted, a shoulder rounded, a back or knee bent. I looked at these drawings for a long time and then left, my mind full of Herman's images.

Outside, on the pavement, stood a short, fierce-looking man who was selling copies of a magazine. As soon as he spotted me he came up, greeted me as though he knew me, which he certainly didn't, and at the same time made it plain that he expected me to buy from him, pointing out in a manner which exactly blended diffidence and aggression that a shilling was little enough to pay for what he insisted were the magazine's valuable contents. I glanced at the copy he had more or less pushed into my face. *Stand.* The title meant nothing to me and I was about to walk away when the image on the cover made me look again. A miner in pit helmet and boots was in the act of fixing a long pole into the ground, watched by a dog whose back was turned to the viewer but who was very plainly part of the man's life, shared in his workaday world. Suddenly I knew I was looking at a drawing by Josef Herman. The coincidence seemed uncanny. I paid my shilling.

On the train back home I leafed through the magazine. There, I found poems printed above such unfamiliar names as Thomas Blackburn, James Reeves, Emmanuel Litvinoff and, in a translation made by Stanley Chapman, Jacques Prevert's 'Whale Hunt'. I must have at least glanced at these contributions, though half a century later I have no memory of what I thought about any of them. Little enough, I should imagine. At that period of my life I had no great interest in poetry. Prose was a different matter. If I couldn't succeed as a jazz trumpeter, there was always literary journalism. I was especially attracted to the novels of H.G. Wells and to George Orwell's essays. Shakespeare, too, was different. By the time I bought my first copy of *Stand* I'd read my way through most of the canon and had seen and been stirred by productions of at least a dozen of the plays. But for whatever reason I didn't think of Shakespeare as a poet. He was beyond all that. 'That' meant olde worlde language, fake emotion, fluted vowels, and a general air of posturing. 'That' sounded like a combination of Joyce Grenfell and the voice-over on British Gaumont News. Which, come to think of it, is a pretty accurate description of how most English actors then sounded. Yet somehow that didn't put me off Shakespeare, even though it put me off what I thought of as poetry.

Then, in *Stand*, I read this:

The goddess Fortune be praised (on her toothed wheel
I have been mincemeat these several years)
Last night, for a whole night, the unpredictable
Lay in my arms, in a tender and unquiet rest –
(I perceived the irrelevance of my former tears) –
Lay, and at dawn departed. I rose and walked the streets
Where a whitsuntide wind blew fresh, and blackbirds
Incontestably sang, and the people were beautiful.

The author's name was given as John Heath-Stubbs, although I vaguely assumed he must be the translator of a poem that had come to *Stand* from some foreign language. Nevertheless, by the time I arrived home I knew "The Unpredicted" by heart. I still do, and to my pleasure, and I hope his, I was able some twelve years ago to recite it to the poet himself when I met him during a party at the old Poetry Society headquarters at Earls Court. Why the poem made such an impact on me I can't be sure, though I do know that it had something to do with the feeling of the world new-peeled and that the word 'Incontestably' shot through me like a needle of white light. As to Jon Silkin, *Stand's* founder-editor, and in his later years a friend, I once showed him that treasured copy of *Stand* when he was staying with my wife and me, and he immediately offered to buy it back for a great deal more than the shilling I had paid for it. Naturally, I refused. I wouldn't dream of parting with it.

D.J. Enright reprinted 'The Unpredicted' in his *Oxford Book of Contemporary Poetry,* but this apart I would guess the poem has lapsed from view. Is it a good poem? I have no idea, nor do I want to know. In the Introduction to his invaluable collection of critical essays, *Troubled Thoughts, Majestic Dreams*, Dennis O'Driscoll says that his aesthetic can be summed up in the sentence, 'that there are good poets and there are bad poets and that one can tell the difference'. I imagine he'd be ready to exchange 'poets' for 'poems' and still stand by his claim. If so, I can readily agree to what he says – with this proviso: that it is no earthly use asking me to judge the worth of 'The Unpredicted'. All I can say is that my encounter with Heath Stubbs' poem threw a switch that helped to change my life. Perhaps a year after that encounter, I stumbled by chance on a copy of *The Less Deceived* and suddenly found that not only had poetry entered my world but that my world had entered poetry. Washing lines and Hall's-Distemper boards replaced the goddess Fortune. But my debt of gratitude to 'The Unpredicted' was and remains unshaken. 'And where you love you cannot break away'.

The essays that follow were all written over the past twenty or so years. Some started life as commissioned essays for books or journals, others as lectures, still others as review articles. In the interest of trying to retain a degree of homogeneity I decided to exclude any of the essays on American, Australian, and Greek poets I have written during this period. I have also excluded short notices, although with some reluctance. For ten years, from the early 1980s, I acted a poetry reviewer for the *New Statesman*, at first under the inspired editorship of Derek Mahon, later under the more relaxed but no less enjoyable regime of

Hugo Williams. It was work I took seriously, but when I came to put this book together I realised that the necessary brevity of reviews I wrote for the *Statesman*, sometimes of important collections, made it impossible for me to develop a sustained – that is, reasoned – argument, and without argument reviewing can often look like mere opinionatedness. Omitting all my *New Statesman* pieces, as well as others that over the years have appeared in such places as *Poetry Wales, Stand*, and the *TLS*, has meant going without mention of some of the contemporary poets I most admire, including Peter Porter and Anne Stevenson. I have, however, written on Peter Porter elsewhere (in *Moderns and Contemporaries* and the Introduction to Porter's own glittering collection of critical essays, *Saving From the Wreck*), and some measure of the depth of my regard for Anne Stevenson is, I hope, indicated by the fact that this book is dedicated to her.

John Lucas

'BEGINNING AGAIN': HARDY'S *WESSEX POEMS*

The publication of *Wessex Poems* at the very end of 1898 seems to have caught people by surprise. 'What induces Hardy to commit himself to verse!' Meredith wrote to a friend, and the fact that he concluded the sentence not with a question but an exclamation mark suggests that he didn't think much of the book. If so, he was speaking for others. Michael Millgate usefully runs through some of the negative, dismissive or disapproving reviews that greeted Hardy's first appearances in print as a poet; and although not all were as damning as the *Saturday Review*, which castigated the 'many slovenly, slipshod, uncouth verses, stilted in sentiment, poorly conceived and worse wrought', even the most sympathetic suggested or at least implied that while Hardy might be a true novelist he was not a natural poet.

This was not Hardy's view. In *The Life of Thomas Hardy*, which is credited to Florence Hardy and which we know to have been largely written by Hardy himself, we are told that he had not been 'a writer of novels proper … [He] had mostly aimed at keeping his narratives close to natural life and as near to poetry in their subject as the conditions would allow, and had often regretted that those conditions would not let him keep them nearer still'. There is no space here to ponder the deep implications of what Hardy might mean by that central remark about keeping narratives 'as near to poetry in their subject as the conditions would allow' – beyond, that is, remarking that key moments in the novels, such as Troy's sword play or Giles's reaching to caress the flower in Grace's bosom, have a resonance that feels to belong most naturally to the metaphoric resources of the ballad tradition, a tradition in which Hardy was steeped.

But then Hardy was steeped in all kinds and traditions of poetry.

In his great essay, 'Hardy's Virgilian Purples', Donald Davie showed how Hardy drew on the *Aeneid* for his wonderful sequence of poems prompted by Emma's death; and you cannot read very far in his poetry without recognising the extent of his knowledge of French, Italian and German poetry as well as that of his native land. Moreover, as Davie also pointed out, Hardy is formidably knowledgeable about prosodic matters. Look through the *Collected Poems* and you will see that with the possible exception of the pantoum there is scarcely a verse form, or indeed metre, that Hardy doesn't use. He said of his friend William Barnes that he sang his native woodnotes wild with a great deal of art. The same is true of Hardy himself. That is why he could write with such sardonic authority about his craft – even craftiness – as poet, why *The Life of Thomas Hardy* records him as saying that both in the reception of *Wessex Poems* and later volumes 'there was . . . as regards form, the inevitable ascription to ignorance of what was really choice after full knowledge. That the author loved the art of concealing art was undiscerned'.

Pound, as we know, *did* discern the art. He was quick to recognise Hardy's importance as a poet. 'Now *there* is a clarity,' he famously exclaimed of the *Collected Poems* and then, with pardonable exaggeration added, 'There *is* the harvest of having written 20 novels first'. Pound was wrong to think that Hardy took up poetry only when he left off writing prose fiction. He had written poems before his first novel was published; and he went on writing them throughout his novelistic career. But Pound has no doubt that Hardy is naturally a poet.

And yet when we open *Wessex Poems* and read the first poem we are hardly likely to think it either natural or clear. Under a sketch of a clock tower in whose side a sun-dial is set stands the title 'The Temporary The All', beneath that the word 'Sapphics', and beneath that the following:

> Change and chancefulness in my flowering youthtime,
> Set me sun by sun near to one unchosen;
> Wrought us fellow-like, and despite divergence,
>   Friends interlinked us.

The stiff movement of the lines, the odd neologism ('chancefulness'), the apparently clumsy and pointless alliterations – all these seem to point to Hardy as that 'apprentice at verse' which reviewers were quick to label him and which he himself emphatically denied having been at the end of the nineteenth century. He was not, he said, a beginner, although in one sense he was beginning again. For while he had written poems as a young man, in the middle period of his novel-writing he had produced 'few or none, but of late years they had been added to with great rapidity, though at first with some consternation he had found an awkwardness in getting back to an easy expression in numbers after abandoning it for so many years'. Awkwardness seems the word for 'The Temporary The All', so much so that it prompts two questions: why did Hardy publish the poem and why on earth did he put it at the head of his collection?

To offer answers to these questions bring me to my title. Hardy is obviously beginning again. He has abandoned one career and is taking up another. But for all the apparent modesty of the volume's title – it suggests the merely regional, or local – Hardy is in fact intensely ambitious. I have remarked elsewhere that I think of him as the unofficial poet laureate of the age. It is after all Hardy who in 'Drummer Hodge' writes an offbeat but more telling poem about the Boer War than any other to have come out of that dismal episode; it is Hardy who in 'The Darkling Thrush' – significantly first published in *The Times* – writes a key poem to usher in the 20th century; it is Hardy who in 'The Convergence of the Twain' writes a definitive poem about the true meaning of the sinking of the Titanic, about the blow to materialism the liner's loss implied, the pride of opulence, the vulgarity of riches the ship epitomised; and Hardy's war poems, above all 'In Time of the Breaking of Nations' and 'There Came a Great Calm', have an authority unrivalled among the work of non-combatant poets.

True, these came later than *Wessex Poems*. Yet in his first collection Hardy takes on a major contemporary issue in 'The Impercipient', where he offers to speak with authority about later 19th century pessimism, unbelief, even despair. He will later learn how to handle this authority by disguising it as diffident or personal speculation or reflection. Here, it feels bogus: I can never read the plaintive question of the would-be key lines, 'O, doth a bird deprived of wings/ Go earthbound wilfully?' without wanting to laugh out loud. A bird deprived of wings? How did it become airborne in the first place? Or, assuming that it had a full complement of wings when it took off, how did it become deprived of them? Did they suddenly fall off? Was it a case of wing fatigue? Nor does the pencil sketch of a cathedral interior do other than suggest an attempt to force grandeur onto a scene that is in truth dully conventional.

Nor, I have to say, can I feel at ease with 'The Permanent The All'. I suspect, however, that Hardy put the verses at the head of *Wessex Poems* because he wanted to indicate that he was not an apprentice. 'Sapphics' he calls them and sapphics they are. Millgate remarks that the poem 'immediately confronted readers with the kinds of problem that were to recur throughout the volume and are now recognisable as characteristically, Hardyean – the dense stresses, the strict yet unfamiliar stanza form, the inverted syntax, the archaisms and odd coinages, the profoundly pessimistic mood, unromantically and unfashionably eloquent of nonprogression and unfulfilment'. Hardly. At the end of the century nothing was more fashionable than belief in non-progression. More importantly that 'strict yet unfamiliar stanza form' isn't at all characteristic of a collection which habitually uses balladic stanzas and a wide variety of measures, most of them handled with great sophistication. Even the sonnets, while too close to the Shakespearian originals to be much more than pastiches, are accomplished pastiches. (And Hardy varies the structure, as in the four sonnets, 'She, to Him', by cunningly linking octave to sestet in a rhyme scheme that hovers between Shakespearian and Petrarchan models while being neither.)

Still, Millgate is right to suggest that the sapphics of 'The Permanent The All' would have been comparatively unfamiliar to Hardy's readers. Although Swinburne had written an especially resourceful poem called 'Sapphics', you have to go back to William Cowper's 'Lines Written

During a Period of Insanity' to find the form handled with entire ease. You certainly won't find it in the work of the then recently-appointed poet laureate, Alfred Austin. And this, I suspect, is the point. From Tennyson to Austin. What a fall was there. All the great ones were now dead. Browning had gone in 1889, Tennyson in 1892, Morris in 1896. In addition Barnes had died in 1880, Dante Gabriel Rossetti followed him four years later, and his greater sister had died in 1894. Swinburne alone remained, and Swinburne had been annexed by Watts Dunton, his genius snuffed out under his guardian's anxious cossetting. That left Meredith, whose earlier poetry Hardy had admired. But the publication in 1898 of *Odes in Contribution to the Song of French History* added nothing to Meredith's poetic status. There was in short a gap to be filled.

And so Hardy the poet sidles into public view. He comes as the last upholder of virtues he associated with the great poets of his youth and early manhood. *Wessex Poems* is in this sense both an act of homage – 'An Ancient to Ancients' – and an affirmation. The great craft of poetry is to be kept in good shape. Hence the sapphics with which the volume opens. But *Wessex Poems* is also very much of its moment. The numerous illustrations which are scattered throughout the volume – over 30 of them – have attracted little discussion, and what there has been typically strikes a note of embarrassment. Millgate speaks for most commentators when he says that 'The impression of idiosyncracy given by the volume was heightened by the inclusion of the drawings, some hauntingly effective, others relatively crude in both conception and execution'. But in a decade where the total art book had become almost a norm, and where the verbal and visual were regularly intermixed, as in *The Yellow Book* and the *Savoy*, Hardy's decision to publish his sketches is an almost defiantly whimsical gesture. It is at once conventional – for his artwork has nothing to do with the Beardsley-dominated art-nouveau style of the 1890s, might even be said to hark back to the illustrated book of earlier decades, to the Pre-Raphaelite *Germ* or Moxon's *Tennyson*, for example – while on the other hand it nods in the direction of contemporary fashion.

Not that anybody could sensibly argue that *Wessex Poems* is intended to be a fashionable collection. It is however, all appearances to the contrary, an intensely ambitious one. To understand why and how, we need to take the measure of that famous passage in *The Life* where Hardy talks about the reception of his poetry and remarks sardonically that critics imputed to his formal inventiveness 'ignorance of what was really choice after full knowledge'. Although the passage is often referred to I am not sure that its implications have been fully understood. It deserves to be quoted in full. 'That the author loved the art of concealing art was undiscerned,' Hardy remarks, and then he goes on:

> For instance, as to rhythm. Years earlier, he had decided that too regular a beat was bad art. He had fortified himself in his opinion by thinking of the analogy of architecture, between which art and that of poetry he had discovered, to use his own words, that there existed a close and curious parallel, both arts, unlike some others, having to carry a rational content inside their artistic form. He knew that in architecture cunning irregularity is of enormous worth, and it is obvious that he carried on into his verse, perhaps in part unconsciously, the Gothic art-principle in which he had been trained – the principle of spontaneity, found in mouldings, tracery, and such like – resulting in the "unforeseen" (as it has been called) character of his metres and stanzas, that of stress rather than syllable, poetic texture rather than poetic veneer; the latter kind of thing, under the name of "constructed ornament", being what he, in common with every Gothic student, had been taught to evade like the plague. He shaped his poetry accordingly, introduced metrical pauses, and reversed beats; and found for his trouble that some particular line of a poem exemplifying this principle was greeted with a would-be jocular remark that such a line "did not make for immortality".

Hardy was not of course the first English poet to measure the line by stress rather than syllable. Coleridge had famously experimented with a four-stress syllabically various line in 'Christabel', and there are the sprung rhythms of Hardy's contemporary, Hopkins, although Hardy could not have known about them. I assume that Coleridge's experiment came about because of his interest in the ballad, whose lines are shaped for song as much as if not more than for spoken utterance. And the ballad tradition is one with which Hardy was intimately familiar. Ballads are inevitably more metrically supple than verse intended for the printed page. They can also mix metres in a manner which few poets in the print tradition would allow themselves the licence to do, and certainly not in a poem whose subject matter is other than 'light'. That would have been regarded as an inexcusable metrical licentiousness. Yet this is precisely what Hardy does. Moreover he does it in one of the very few of the *Wessex Poems* that everyone agrees is a great poem.

'Neutral Tones' shifts from iambic to anapaestic in a way that recalls and revisits the true ballad tradition; its alliterations and internal vowel sounds similarly come out of song conventions; and the very stanza form, the quatrain of three four-stress lines followed by a three-stress line, is derived from and pays homage to traditional ballads:

> We stood by a pond that winter day
> And the sun was white, as though chidden of God,
> And a few leaves lay on the starving sod,
>   – They had fallen from an ash, and were gray.

This very plainly isn't a ballad. No ballad would rhyme the second and third lines as Hardy chooses to do. But that astonishing last line, in which three stresses are distributed across no fewer than ten syllables, tells of Hardy's unwillingness to submit to a formulaic stress-syllable metre. It shows how far he is prepared to go with an art that will conceal art. As Robert Gittings says in his study of *Young Thomas Hardy*, 'the shorter and more varied lines, which seem to flicker and play over the scene like the motions of the unhappy pair, have the effect of speech, and the air of an actual happening'. This seems to me true; and I will add that in the last stanza Hardy deepens the sense of emotional impact, of loss, betrayal, pain, by the line's broken rhythms, their heavy medial pauses, as though the speaker or ruminative voice is forced to register the full measure of the cost of that day, most powerfully in the enjambement between lines two to three, where the sense of pain, of what wrings with wrong, is given shocking immediacy by the words 'your face'.

In his account of the poem Gittings usefully invokes Meredith's *Modern Love*, a complex sequence of sixteen-line sonnets which had been published in 1862 and some details of which are close to details in 'Neutral Tones'. Hardy's own sixteen-line poem even echoes the rhyme scheme of Meredith's sonnets. But Gittings then remarks that although Hardy may have used Meredith as a literary model for his own poem, he 'remains true to the terse and moving sincerity that owes nothing to any model'. In saying this, Gittings is doing no more than repeat a commonplace. Hardy's sincerity is not to be questioned. I can see why. Who, reading 'Neutral Tones', *could* doubt the speaker's emotional fidelity to the painful truth, his uncovering of an experience which has become permanent vision. Nevertheless, there is something odd and indeed unsatisfactory about this reading of the poem, for it takes less than full account of what Hardy is up to. We need to note that he dates the poem 1867 and then recall that whenever he gives the date for a poem it can be regarded as part of the poem's meaning. (Hence, the crucial dating of 'Channel Firing' to 'April, 1914': the poem isn't a war poem but about war readiness.) In 1867 Hardy was himself 27, and in 1898, when 'Neutral Tones' appeared as one of the *Wessex Poems*, he could have confidently expected most of his readers to know his birth date. He was, after all, a famous author.

Now, consider the second stanza. 'Your eyes on me were as eyes that rove / Over tedious riddles of years ago'. Consider the ending of the third stanza with its row of four dots, the effect of which is to suggest that an episode of the distant past has been brought to a close. Consider how this is reinforced by the opening of the fourth stanza: 'Since then, keen lessons that love deceives'. Since when? Oh, since that terrible day in the backward and abysm of time. Surely the man who speaks these words can't be thought of as 27 years old? He's much more likely to be middle-aged, even elderly. By giving the date of the poem's composition Hardy is therefore warning his readers that they shouldn't take it as a personal poem. 'Sincere' it may be, but that is because it convinces us that the person who speaks does so out of a grief Hardy has fully imagined, a visionary experience which, we can say, has taken hold of his mind. Put the matter that way and we shall be less likely to think of Meredith than of Wordsworth, which is exactly what Tom Paulin does in *Thomas Hardy: The Poetry of Perception.* There, Paulin remarks on the congruence of Hardy's vision with a passage in *The Prelude* where Wordsworth 'describes a particular scene – a wall, a single sheep, a hawthorn – which he saw a few days before his father's death'. Wordsworth, Paulin adds, charges the details of his description 'powerfully with the significance of what he is saying'. This is just what Hardy does in 'Neutral Tones', although to say as much doesn't mean that we have to read 'Neutral Tones' as autobiography, whereas we can hardly avoid so reading *The Prelude.*

I have taken what may seem an inordinate amount of time over a small point. And after all, it may be asked, does it much matter whether Hardy is writing 'sincere' 'personal' poems or testifying to the truest poetry being the most feigning? Well, yes, I think it does. Not only because Hardy is so clearly trying out different styles and manners in his early work – to Meredith and Wordsworth we can add Shakespeare, who is almost parodied in the four sonnets dated 1864, 'She, To Him' ('When you shall see me in the toils of Time,/ My lauded beauties carried off from me' the first of them begins) – not only because of these and other debts to which I shall later allude, but also because the volume is called *Wessex Poems.*

The title puzzled even Hardy's friendliest critics and it has continued to puzzle others, often less friendly. Millgate quotes Lionel Johnson as saying that the title seemed 'somewhat cruel to Wessex, which is not an wholly Leopardian land'. Johnson has sensed one of Hardy's debts. Hardy had, so Millgate says, recently been reading the great melancholic Italian poet and he 'acknowledged that there was some justification for Johnson's criticism of the title'. Yes, but *Wessex Poems* is far more various than either Johnson or Millgate implies. It is thronged with dialect voices out of Wessex, with old tales of the Napoleonic days which so preoccupied Hardy, of old customs, as for instance in the dances lovingly named in the unique and entirely wonderful 'Dance at the Phoenix', with its celebration of

> The favourite Quick-step 'Speed the Plough'
>   (Cross hands, cast off, and wheel)
> 'The Triumph', 'Sylph', 'The Row-dow-dow'
>   Famed "Major Malley's Reel",
> 'The Duke of Yorke's', 'The Fairy Dance',
> 'The Bridge of Lodi' (brought from France),
>   She beat out, toe and heel.

'She' is Jenny, a former 'favourite' of the soldiers who, ageing and respectable wife though she may now be, leaves her sleeping husband to go to the dance staged by the King's Own Cavalry as they pass through Casterbridge. (I will note in passing that Hardy's list-making here is picked up by later poets, especially Louis MacNeice and Philip Larkin.) As Edward Thomas remarked in his essay on 'Three Wessex Poets' – the others are Duck and Barnes – Hardy has written songs and narratives which prove his descent from some ancient ballad-maker, perhaps the one who wrote 'A Pleasant ballad of the merry miller's wooing of the baker's daughter of Manchester', or 'Ane ballade, showing the cruel robberies and lewd life of Philip Collins, *alias* Osburne, commonly called Philip of the West, who was pressed to death at Newgate in London the third of December last past, 1597', to be sung to the tune of 'Pagginton's round'. Some of the lyrics to which Hardy fits a narrative originated probably in some such tune.

If this reminds us that Thomas is the author of 'Lob', that great poem which is also an *omnium gatherum* of country names, legend, folklore and song, it also reminds us that by 1914, when he published *In Pursuit of Spring*, which includes his essay on the Wessex Poets, the English Folk Song Society had been in existence for sixteen years. It was in fact founded in the very year that Hardy published *Wessex Poems*. 'Within a year', Dave Harker writes in *Fakesong: The Manufacture of British "Folksong" 1700 to the Present Day*, 'this thoroughly bourgeois Mayfair-based institution numbered amongst its members composers like Elgar, Dvorak and Edward Greig'. Moreover, before Cecil Sharp began his labours of collecting and, according to some, bowdlerising folksong, the task of collecting and transcribing had been borne by, among others, Sabine Baring Gould, whose *Songs and Ballads of the West* appeared in 1890 (five years later came his *A Garland of Country Songs*), William Barrett, with *English Folk-Songs* of 1891, Frank Kidson, whose *Traditional Tunes* was published the same year, and Lucy Broadwood and J. A. Fuller Maitland, who published *English County Songs* in 1893. (Four years earlier Broadwood had brought out his *Sussex Songs*.) In the following years this steady stream would turn into a flood of publications, fed in particular by the work of Sharp and Vaughan Williams.

As far as I know, Hardy was never a member of the English Folk Lore Society. Harker is severe on them all. They were bourgeois to a man and woman, we are told, and incapable of transcending class relationships. More significantly for Hardy, I suspect, they had to learn what he knew intimately. The title *Wessex Poems* is therefore a declaration of Hardy's understanding of and commitment to the kind of cultural history which, with the rise of anthropology and of course, anxiety about 'Englishness', was becoming a newly fashionable study. *Wessex Poems* is in this context an important intervention in a contemporary debate about English culture.

We might expect Hardy to reveal his understanding of this debate not in a sentimental endorsement of 'country values' but by giving Wessex men and women voices through which to exhibit an altogether tougher, disenchanted awareness of what they can expect from life. And so it proves. In 'The Dance at the Phoenix' we are allowed to infer that the woman who goes to the dance – and the significance of her name wouldn't have escaped those of Hardy's readers who knew Rossetti's poem about prostitute Jenny – doesn't at all behave in accordance with good bourgeois expectations of the faithful wife. And what of 'Friends Beyond', the poem which allows a 'group of local hearts and heads' to speak their own words from the grave with a laconic disdain for sentimental presuppositions about the 'loss' of a culture? They simply don't care. True, the poem begins with the poet imagining himself in consoling dialogue with those who have gone before and who whisper to him 'In the muted, measured note/ Of a ripple under archways, or a lone cave's stillicide'. But what they say is hardly calculated to gladden the heart of Baring-Gould or of Cecil Sharp. William Dewy tells the poet that 'Ye mid burn the wold bass viol that I set such vallie by'. In 1895 Baring-Gould had claimed that in the very near future there was bound to be 'A revolt against musical vacuity . . . Then the demand will come – Sing us in future some of the songs of our own dear English Zion. There is something even in music to be learned from our healthy English peasantry … the finest people the world has ever seen …'. In 1898 Hardy's Friends Beyond tell him that 'Curious not the least are we if our intents you make or mar, / If you quire to our old tune'. And it is this resolute, even contented lack of interest in the continuity of a way of life which brings the poet comfort:

> William Dewy, Tranter Reuben, Farmer Ledlow late at plough,
>   Robert's kin, and John's, and Ned's,
> And the Squire, and Lady Susan, murmur mildly to me now.

In a sense 'Friends Beyond' can and I would say has to be read as Hardy's comic rejoinder to those who throughout the 1890s were busying themselves in preserving 'rural' England. But it has to be read in another sense. In its sly way the poem is a formal tour-de-force, for the group of local hearts and heads who murmur familiarly to Hardy do so in trochaic octameters. They, or perhaps it is more accurate to say their author, hint to the readers that the poet can take on the two great poets of the nineteenth century and do as well if not better than they in handling this very odd line. Tennyson had been the first to use the measure for the couplets of 'Locksley Hall', Browning had gone at least one better with the three-line stanzas of his great poem, 'A Toccata of Galuppi's', and from then on trochaic octameters seem to have held a fascination for nineteenth century poets, including some very minor ones indeed (Prowse and O'Donnell). It is of course typical of Hardy that he should adapt and conceal the form by making it a kind of *terza-rima*. (The short middle line establishes the rhyme of each succeeding stanza's first and third lines):

> Gone I call them, gone for good, that group of local hearts and heads;
> Yet at mothy curfew-tide,
> And at midnight when the noon-heat breathes it back from walls and leads
>
> They've a way of whispering to me – fellow-wight who yet abide –
> In the muted, measured tone
> Of a ripple under archways, or a lone cave's stillicide … .

In *Thomas Hardy and British Poetry* Donald Davie accuses Hardy of being responsible for most of the ills which have afflicted 20th century English poetry, above all its disabling modesty and willingness to put up with the second rate. Yet Davie acknowledges that Hardy shames our ignorance because 'as a prosodist … he was immensely learned, with a learning that seems lost beyond recovery'. It is certainly the case that in none of the discussions of 'Friends Beyond' that I have come across have I found any mention of its suave formal brilliance. No doubt the 'good little Hardy' isn't thought to be possessed of what *Wessex Poems* everywhere shows, if only we know how to look or, better, listen for it: that formidable prosodic learning to which Davie pays homage.

One reason for commentators' typical lack of awareness of the volume's formal variety undoubtedly lies with what Davie calls Hardy's 'engaging modesty', which then turns out to be a vice or, in Davie's words, a 'crucial selling short of the poetic vocation'. It is no such thing. The voices that speak through *Wessex Poems* have the kind of authority which, if it isn't always the 'authority of sadness' Larkin claimed for Hardy, at the very least reminds us that one of Hardy's masters was Browning and that the Browning of 'Dramatic Lyrics' would have understood Hardy's close attentiveness to the psychological depths hinted at, betrayed or revealed through his poems' speakers, whether in inner or outer speech. Take, for example, the lyric 'In A Eweleaze Near Weatherbury'. Who speaks it? Why, Hardy, of course. Or so it seems natural to conclude. Yet the manner of speech, which often verges on the whimsically pedantic, especially in the middle stanza and perhaps even in the title – none of my dictionaries carries 'Eweleaze' – might suggest that the poem is spoken by an old bachelor, a schoolmaster even, that the poem is as much a fiction as the name Weatherbury (Hardy's name for Puddletown.)

Tom Paulin remarks of the poem that Hardy's 'rather tame wish to throw over conventional morality and "go the world with Beauty" is futile because she would not "balm the breeze". By superimposing a pair of wire-framed spectacles on a sketch of the eweleaze, Hardy represents himself in the illustration as an elderly man peering at the meadow where he once danced with a girl he loved. Metaphorically, he is also looking at his past and realising that the moment has gone and only exists in his mind now'.

It is true that the sketch gives an eerie feeling of emptiness to a scene that was once redeemed by human presence, and in particular by that voice that would 'balm the breeze', a phrase whose wistful beauty takes my breath away. But the man recalling that moment doesn't have to be Hardy – who as far as I am aware didn't then wear spectacles. We need know of the speaker only that he's someone attuned to ballad measure and to its alliterative devices, which are everywhere in the poem as they are in "Neutral Tones". And we have then to note that where the poem is most personal it also succeeds in being most general, again like Neutral Tones: 'But despite the term as teacher,/ I remain what I was then/ In each essential feature/ Of the fantasies of men'. We don't need to read the word 'teacher' literally – this doesn't have to be either William Barnes or Phillotson – to feel that the speaker wryly acknowledges that his own keen ache for lost youth is not at all unique.

But then again it is. For the ending of the poem exemplifies one of those moments of 'reversed beats' about which Hardy wrote in the *Life*.

> But she'd scorn my brave endeavour,
> She would not balm the breeze
> By murmuring thine for ever!
> As she did upon this leaze.

It is entirely typical of Hardy, it occurs in poem after poem, that as memory becomes vocal so iambic gives way to, modulates into, the ripple of anapaest that here gives the penultimate line its song-like lift. And this then leads to the discreetly urgent affirmation of the last line: As she did upon this leaze. The stresses on 'did' and 'this leaze' give an emphasis to the line which, I would say, allows the speaker both to acknowledge the pastness of the past and its present vitality. *This* leaze and no other.

In his review of *Time's Laughingstocks*, which is one of the very best pieces of writing about Hardy's poetry, Edward Thomas remarks of one poem that 'there is a changing burden which is full if not of magic yet of a deep and strong suggestion which the intellect alone cannot handle'. That was written in 1909, some years before Thomas would find how to acknowledge that he himself was capable of such changing burdens, was in fact a true poet. 'Burden' is the key word. For if it means 'something that is carried: a load', as in the weight of responsibility or of course experience, of the years that gather grayly, it also means 'a line of words recurring at the end of each verse of a ballad or similar song; chorus or refrain'. And at the end of 'In A Eweleaze Near Weatherbury' the changing burden can be felt and heard in the shift from regular iambic to the closing spondee. *This leaze*. I might even suggest that Hardy, the immensely learned prosodist, would have known that the Greek 'sponde' means libation and that in Greek verse the spondee was characteristic of melodies accompanying libations. The last line breathes a blessing as surely as it mourns a loss. There is at the end of the poem, if we have ears to hear, a changing burden full 'of a deep and strong suggestion which the intellect alone cannot handle'. And this directs us to the strongly particular life of the Wessex man, whoever he is, who utters this poem. Far more than the poets who come after him at the turn of century and who hope to make a poetry of social realism which will reconnect poetry to 'ordinary life' – I'm thinking of Masefield, of Wilfred Gibson, of several of those gathered into Edward Marsh's anthologies – far more than any of them, Hardy, as we ought to expect of the author of *Jude the Obscure*, is alert to the claims of the mere uncounted folk, to borrow Kipling's phrase for those who stand outside orthodoxy's agreed census.

And so, even when Hardy is writing in a more self-confessedly autobiographical mode, we need to register a certain ironic quizzicality, a recognition that this could be so for all and that art's joy is precisely to make a song and dance about it. Here lies the importance of the strategically placed concluding verses to *Wessex Poems*, 'I Look Into My Glass'. I once had to endure this being discussed by an earnest academic critic who read the poem in a way that seemed like nothing so much as a concrete mixer trying to sing madrigals. He wanted to prove that the poem was part of Hardy's abiding pessimism. Perhaps, but what I wish to note is that it is written in what became called in the eighteenth century 'short measure' and that short measure is an adaptation of poulter's measure. And poulter's measure came out of attempts by sixteenth century poets in England to find a long line that would somehow answer to Latin hexameters. It was a variation on fourteeners and even less successful than they proved to be because, as later literary historians never tired of pointing out, the alternate six and seven stress lines inevitably made for a forced caesura: a kind of pot hole you stumbled into when traversing the line. By breaking the two lines into four – of 3, 3, 4 and 3 stresses – eighteenth century hymn writers gave the measure a new lease of life. And of course the regular thump of metrical stress works perfectly well as a means for getting across church doctrine:

There is beyond the Sky
A Heaven of Joy and Love,
And holy children, when they die,
Go to that World above.

There is a dreadful Hell,
And everlasting Pains,
There sinners must with Devils dwell
In Darkness, Fire, and Chains.

These stanzas come from 'Song XI: Heaven and Hell', one of Isaac Watts' *Divine Songs for Children, 1715*, and much reprinted throughout the eighteenth century. It shows what Blake was up against when he wrote *Songs of Innocence*. Blake's lyrics are as far removed as may be from the strident metre Watts uses to hammer home his message. Yet Hardy's handling of this recalcitrant metre is so assured, so able to adapt it to the musing, sombre yet wry voice of the speaker, that I defy anyone not to acknowledge how extraordinary is the art that here conceals art. This is song at its most deftly cadenced. And in the closing burden – is it? – we again encounter that shift from regular iambic to spondee which testifies not merely to Hardy's mastery of the reversed beat but, more profoundly, to a pulse of energy which establishes that energy's keen particularity. What is so for him is so for us all.

Yet Time, to make me grieve,
Part steals, lets part abide;
And shakes this fragile frame at eve
With throbbings of noontide

We can all sing that verse, can testify to 'throbbings of a lost noontide'. Faced with 'I Looked Into My Glass' and of many if not most of the poems that make up *Wessex Poems*, we can understand afresh the propriety of the rebuke Hardy delivers against Matthew Arnold's criticism of provincialism. 'A certain provincialism of feeling is invaluable. It is of the essence of individuality'. That Notebook jotting of 1880 is amplified into imaginative utterance in poem after poem of the collection I have been considering. *Wessex Poems* marks a new beginning for English poetry. It provides for ways of considering the local that disturb, as they must, the confident tone of the centre which Arnold assumed, just as they will prove enabling for such very different poets as Edward Thomas, Ivor Gurney, Auden, Larkin and Heaney (and I could name others), all of whom recognise in Hardy the authority not so much of sadness as of redemptive particularity expressed through the seemingly endless and adroit use of forms of which he was the great, the learned master.

1998

D.H. LAWRENCE AS POET

Writing to a friend in February 1914, Lawrence characteristically grumbled that 'In England people have got that loathsome superior knack of refusing to consider me a poet at all: "Your prose is so good," say the kind fools, "that we are obliged to forgive you your poetry." How I hate them'.[1] Lawrence is exaggerating. He knew perfectly well that his *Love Poems and Others* had been favourably received. Edward Thomas called it 'the book of the moment', and for Ezra Pound it was 'the most important book of poems of the season'.[2] Yet it is probably true to say that now, over seventy years after his death, Lawrence is best known for his prose fiction. This is not to be wondered at. He is, after all, a great novelist and short-story writer. But the fiction looms so massively that it seems to have dimmed, if it hasn't obscured, his other achievements: as playwright, social and literary critic, and poet. It is as though so complete a man of letters cannot be allowed to succeed in everything he sets his hand to. And it is of course true that although major novelists have often tried to write in a different literary mode they have seldom succeeded. I think, for example, of Henry James's plays, or of George Eliot's poetry. Yet the rule is by no means absolute. There are Chekhov's stories, Emily Bronte's poems. There are, too, the poems of D.H. Lawrence.

Lawrence's career as a poet divides naturally into four quite distinct phases. The first occupies the years up to 1912, and comes to an end with the publication of *Love Poems and Others* in February 1913. When he put together the body of his poems for a collected edition, Lawrence recalled this early period with wry detachment. 'A young man is afraid of his demon,' he noted, 'and puts his hand over the demon's mouth sometimes and speaks for him. And the things the young man says are very rarely poetry'. Lawrence offers this as a reason for rewriting many of the early poems. 'I have tried to let the demon say his say'.[3] Whether the rewritten poems effectively whip away the restraining hand is not a matter I want to pursue here, although it is at least arguable that this talk of fear of the demon is misleading. The early poems are muffled less by fear than by technical inadequacies.

Inadequacy may not seem to be the right word. Lawrence's early poems are not noticeably inferior to much verse that was appearing in England during the opening decade of the twentieth century. But that is the point. In this early work, Lawrence can look to be little different from a dozen or so of the poets whose reputations, then high, have now sunk below the horizon. This is perhaps inevitable. Any young writer will begin by trying on the styles that seem most available. It takes time to discover, or to have the courage to recognize, that what is available isn't necessarily what is best or, more to the point, appropriate. Auden put the matter succinctly when he remarked of Lawrence's early poems that 'one is continually struck by the originality of the sensibility and the conventionality of the expressive means ... . [Lawrence] learned quite soon to let his demon speak, but it took him a long time to find the appropriate style for him to speak in'.[4] Lawrence is at his most conventional – and awkward – when he works within the bonds of rhyme and regular metre. This is so obvious that there is no point in spending time on it. Nor is there much to be gained by complaining that he chafed against these bonds, and then reproving him for his rashness and impatience in breaking free of them. As Auden brilliantly observes:

> The difference between formal and free verse may be likened to the difference between carving and modelling; the formal poet, that is to say, thinks of the poem he is writing as something already latent in the language which he has to reveal, while the free verse poet thinks of language as a plastic passive medium upon which he imposes his artistic conception. One might also say that, in their attitude towards

> art, the formal verse writer is a catholic, the free verse writer a protestant. And Lawrence was, in every respect, very protestant indeed.[5]

The rashness and impatience, ignorantly and obtusely deplored by such poet critics as R.P. Blackmur and C.H. Sisson, are precisely those qualities that make it possible for Lawrence to snap what for him were the improper constraints of formal verse. Graham Hough's remark on Blackmur's essay is definitive. 'From its own point of view it leaves nothing to be said. Yet at the end the essence of Lawrence's poetry is no more discernible than it was at the beginning'. Sisson claims that 'Lawrence was temperamentally well suited to breaking away from the shackles of post Victorian poetics, but he lacked the reticence, and the ear, for achieving a satisfactory new form'.[6] To say of the author of 'Sorrow' that he lacked reticence, and that the man who wrote 'Gloire de Dijon' lacked an ear, is so wide of the mark as to be heroic in its perversity. The fact is that Lawrence was dissatisfied with formal properties because they could not help him to produce the poems he sensed were struggling for expression. This is only to be expected of the writer who famously instructed J.B. Pinker to 'tell Arnold Bennett that all rules of construction hold good only for novels which are copies of other novels. A book which is not a copy of other books has its own construction'.[7]

And yet, constrained as many of the poems of Lawrence's first volume undoubtedly are, we have already seen that the more discerning reviewers of Love Poems and Others were quick to recognize its strengths. Both Pound and Thomas saluted Lawrence's use of dialect. This is undoubtedly important, in the first place because dialect is a means of redeeming the language from the deadening effects of orthodox or standard English, in the second because it gives utterance and therefore visibility to English people whose manner of speaking is held by orthodoxy not to be 'English' and hence not serious. It is of course true that dialect poetry can be or be made to seem 'quaint'. And it is no accident that 'quaint' became a vogue word of the period. Initially applied to the eclectic manner of contemporary architecture which, in its pastiches of earlier styles – Tudor, Queen Anne – offered to reinstate a vanished past, it then became attached to any cultural artefact that could be regarded as somehow free from the taint of contemporaneity.

Lawrence's dialect poetry is not quaint. It is vivid, eloquent, and it takes its speakers with due seriousness. On the other hand, there is not much of it, and the explanation for *this* can be traced to Lawrence's deep need to break away from home. Here, he is very much part of a wide movement that may be said to have existed on an almost universal scale at the end of the nineteenth century: of the revolt of the sons (and occasionally daughters) against the fathers. In Lawrence's case, however, this is additionally complicated by his complex feelings towards the mother. This is the subject of *Sons and Lovers.* It is also the subject of several of the best poems of *Love Poems and Others.* In his invaluable essay on Lawrence in *The Shaping Spirit*, A. Alvarez singles out 'End of Another Home-Holiday' as perhaps the best of the early poems. As he says, 'the difficulty is in the state of mind: the pull between love and guilt, the tension between man and child'.[8] This is memorably stated in the following lines:

> Love is the great Asker,
> The sun and the rain do not ask the secret
> Of the time when the grain struggles down in the dark.
> The moon walks her lonely way without anguish,
> Because no loved one grieves over her departure.

Vegetative growth is different from human development, and yet the tug towards light is as powerful in the human as in the vegetative. For Lawrence to feel impelled towards such an image indicates that, for all its nourishing warmth, home is an experience which has to be outgrown. So that when, immediately after these lines, he says: 'Forever, ever by my shoulder pitiful Love will linger,/Crouching as little houses crouch under the mist when I turn', it is as though we are to read Love as having rightful claims on him and at the same time expecting rejection, even violent rejection ('linger,/ Crouching' – the effect of those two words is to suggest that love is determined to hang on, even though it may be spurned by a blow, rather as an animal is, or, of course, a beaten woman). The 'little houses' implies a further complex of feelings: affection and irritation, loving familiarity and condescension. They have outgrown their usefulness or their capacity to sustain him. This all feels powerfully authentic and imaginatively intelligent.

The image of the moon is, however, a good deal more conventional. In the act of denying a pathetic fallacy – 'With how sad steps, O Moon' – it virtually reinstates it. As soon as you talk of the moon walking 'her lonely way', with or without anguish, you invite consideration of the plight of the poet himself, and this is surely self-pitying? If so, it is the price we have to pay for what is most original about these early poems, which, as Edward Thomas noted, has to do with 'matters which cannot be subdued to conventional rhythm and rhyme – chiefly the intense thoughts, emotions, or gropings of self-conscious men or women set on edge by love or fatigue or solitude'. And Thomas adds, with memorable exactness, 'If he trusts to make a general appeal, it is by faithful concentration on the particular'.[9]

Still, the general appeal doesn't often make its appearance in these early poems. In sharp contrast, the concentration on the particular is so often and so remarkably evident as to make it obvious that, whatever their flaws, the poems are the work of a great writer. Hence, the springily playful rhythms of 'A Baby Running Barefoot': 'When the bare feet of the baby beat across the grass/ The little white feet nod like white flowers in the wind', which is as far from saccharine coyness as may be, especially in the rippling humour of the stressed assonances, and the tactile alertness of 'her little bare feet in my hands,/ Cool like syringa buds,/ Firm and silken like pink young peony flowers'. Reading this, you realize why the imagists were so keen to claim Lawrence as one of their own, just as the Georgian poets had been. Whatever their differences, both groups saw themselves as breaking out of the bad habits of much Edwardian poetry: the Georgians in their desire to find their subject-matter in what might be called the dailiness of things, the imagists in their determination to cut away the fat of poetic language and to produce for contemplation the bare-bone thing in itself, whatever that thing happened to be.

The title 'Georgian Poetry' was dreamed up in 1912 by Edward Marsh, at that time secretary to Winston Churchill at the Admiralty. Marsh was a connoisseur of the arts and a friend of Rupert Brooke. Together, they 'conceived the idea of issuing a collection of modern poems aimed at disturbing modern lethargy and bringing to general attention the existence of a body of unrecognised talent'.[10] The first volume, *Georgian Poetry, 1911-1912*, appeared at the end of the latter year, and included one poem by Lawrence, 'Snap-Dragon'. A brief prefatory note famously claimed that the anthology was issued 'in the belief that English poetry is once again putting on new strength and beauty'. Lawrence apart, the volume included poems by W. H. Davies, of whom Lawrence at first approved, James Elroy Flecker, of whom he didn't, Wilfrid Gibson, Ralph Hodgson, and others with whom he had little enough in common. A letter to Edward Marsh, written in October 1913, makes clear that Lawrence has already moved well beyond the limits of Georgian poetry, even though he allowed Marsh to put more of his work into *Georgian Poetry, 1913-1915*. Davies, he tells Marsh, now makes him furious.

> It isn't as if he were a passionate writer, writing his 'agon'. Oh my God, he's like teaching a bull-finch to talk. I think one ought to be downright cruel to him, and drive him back: say to him "Davies, your work is getting like Birmingham tinware; Davies, you drop your h's, and everybody is tempering the wind to you, because you are a shorn lamb; Davies, your accent is intolerable in a carpeted room; Davies, you hang on like the mud on a lady's silk petticoat." Then he might leave his Sevenoaks room, where he is rigged up as rural poet, proud of the gilt mirror and his romantic past: and he might grow his wings again, and chirrup a little sadder song.[11]

For Lawrence, in other words, the Georgians were woefully short of ambition. They were tame linnets.[12]

Like the Georgians, with whom they had precious little else in common, the imagists promoted themselves through a number of anthologies. In a period of anthologies and manifestos, of statements that announced new movements, and where the idea of the manifesto had come to be associated with revolt against the status quo, the imagist anthologies have to be seen as far more radical than those put together by Brooke and Marsh. The term 'imagist' or 'imagiste' seems to have been coined by Ezra Pound in the spring of 1912. Of H.D.'s (Hilda Doolittle's) poems he remarks that they are 'Objective – no slither; direct – no excessive use of adjectives, no metaphors that won't permit exaggeration'. As for her then husband Richard Aldington's poems, they provide 'interesting experiments in *vers libre*'. Pound defined an image as 'that which presents an intellectual and emotional complex in an instant of time'. For F.S. Flint, an English poet who worked closely with Pound at this period, imagism was based on three rules:

1 direct treatment of the 'thing', whether subjective or objective
2 to use absolutely no word that did not contribute to presentation
3 as regarding rhythm: to compose in sequence of the musical phrase not in sequence of a metronome.

And Pound, with typically forceful didacticism, laid down some dos and don'ts for his fellow-imagists. 'Use no superfluous word ... . Go in fear of abstraction ... . Use no ornament ... . Don't chop your stuff into separate iambs'.[13]

Both Georgianism and Imagism were conceived of as necessary attempts to 'make it new'. Both gave some encouragement to Lawrence. In the first place, they published him.[14] In the second, they helped confirm him in his conviction as to the rightness of the way he wanted to go.

But it is not necessary to make too much of this. Thomas recognized that Lawrence's subject-matter is far more radical than anything to be found in the work of even the best Georgian poets. None of them explores with such troubling precision the kinds of emotion attendant on those relationships between mother and son which form the natural sequence that runs from 'End of Another Home-Holiday' by way of 'The Bride' and 'Sorrow' through to 'Piano'. And the best of the poems about school are unmatched by anything outside *The Rainbow*. As for the imagists, with the exception of Pound none of them has Lawrence's sense of rhythm or the sureness of his ear. Poems, as Mallarmé told Degas, are made with words not ideas, and at his best Lawrence knows this, too. At his worst, which is in many of the *Pansies*, he forgets what he knows and the result is slapdash and cacophonous. *The Pansies* often lack, Auden rightly noted, the conciseness of prose and the jollity of rhymed verse.[15]

We come back, then, to Lawrence's need to break away from the constraints of formal verse, and in doing so notice that it coincides with that other break – from home and its limitations. The two almost come together in 'The North Country'.

> Out of the sleep, from the gloom of motion, soundlessly, somnambule,
> Moans and booms the soul of a people imprisoned, asleep in the rule
> Of the strong machine that runs mesmeric, booming the spell of its word
> Upon them and moving them helpless, mechanic, their will to its will deferred.

The break isn't complete, as the ineptly managed syntax for the sake of rhyme here makes all too plain. And the large, unfocused claim about people in the North Country is accompanied by a Whitmanesque rhetoric that is almost parodic in effect if not in intention. It would be precisely this insistently vatic side of Whitman that Lawrence would later speak out against. But there is no doubt that Whitman meant more to him than any other poet. Whitman helped him in his breaking away. 'I sound my barbaric yawp over the roofs of the world'. This is Whitman near the end of 'Song of Myself', but it might almost be Lawrence speaking. Lawrence's song of the self involved him in the kinds of exploration, discovery, and assertion out of which much of his best poetry comes. As with other young English writers at the end of the nineteenth century and the beginning of the twentieth, so with Lawrence: Whitman mattered supremely to them all, because it was Whitman who seemed most hearteningly to embody Blake's motto: 'Damn braces. Bless relaxes'. Homoerotic, democratic, always making for the open road, Whitman exemplified, positively and redeemingly, the revolt of the sons against the fathers. All this becomes very evident in the poems that Lawrence begins to write after the publication of *Love Poems and Others.*

II

The second phase of Lawrence's career as a poet covers roughly the period 1913-19 and includes the publication in December 1917 of *Look! We Have Come Through!* Bertrand Russell's remark about that volume is well known. 'They may have come through, but why should I look?' A possible answer might be that the poems explore and record with a rare fullness those 'intense thoughts, emotions, or gropings of self-conscious men or women' which Thomas had identified as so radically new in the subject-matter of Lawrence's earlier work. Yet to say this does not dispose of a problem. The poems of *Look! We Have Come Through!* are, as the insistent and slightly hysterical title makes plain, candidly autobiographical. As a result, they often feel more like fragments of life than poems. This is presumably at the back of Auden's confession that 'I find Lawrence's love poems embarrassing because of their lack of reticence; they make me feel like a Peeping Tom'.16 Besides, there is about the sequence as a whole a lack of balance, a feeling that because these things happened to Lawrence they must be important. Of course, it was important to him that he was able to set up a relationship with Frieda Weekley, the German-born wife of Ernest Weekley, Professor of German at Nottingham's University College. Lawrence and she met for the first time in April 1912, in Nottingham. The following month they went to Germany. As we shall see, partly at least through her introducing him to liberationist ethics, Lawrence could proclaim his discovery of values beyond the prudential and, as he now saw it, life-denying greyness of England and the English. But with that comes a strident, unlovely insistence that people acknowledge what he has achieved. The title of the volume does not merely solicit our attention, it demands our admiration.

It is significant, then, that in a letter to Henry Savage, Lawrence should say that

> There is something wrong with Whitman, when he addresses American women as his Stalwart brides in whom he is to pour the seed for Stalwart Sons. One doesn't think like that. Imagine yourself addressing English women like that, in the mass ... Whitman is like a human document, or a wonderful treatise in human self revelation. It is neither art nor religion nor truth: just a self revelation of a man who could not live, and so had to write himself. But writing should come from a strong root of life: like a battle song after a battle. – And Whitman did this, more or less. But his battle was not a real battle: he never gave his individual self into the fight. ... He never fought with another person.[17]

Lawrence is right to object to Whitman's abstractions, the unfocused generalizations of his worst writing. But it seems clear that the main inference Savage is to draw from the letter is that Lawrence has given 'his individual self into the fight'. *His* self-revelation, *his* human document will, therefore, be of a man who *has* lived. And we have then to note that Lawrence is writing from Italy. The tone of his letter owes much to this. Like many English people before him, and like various of his contemporaries, Lawrence found in Italy a liberation from 'cold Albion'. I think of Byron and Shelley in Venice, of the Brownings in Florence, of Dorothea and Ladislaw in Rome. And in *A Room with a View*, E. M. Forster had allowed his young lovers in Florence to 'come through' to a celebration of the fact that 'love is of the body'. It is not that Lawrence is dependent on this tradition, rather that like other northern discoverers of the Mediterranean he is released into the warmth and light of the south and so discovers a new self. The tradition is well documented by John Pemble, in his *The Mediterranean Passion: Victorians and Edwardians in the South* (Oxford, 1987).

Lawrence's initial breakthrough had, though, occurred in Germany – the Germany to which Frieda had introduced him. It was a particular Germany: of free love, the cult of erotic emancipation, the dream of perfect candour made flesh. From that Germany Lawrence had written to his schoolteacher friend, Arthur McLeod: 'I am in love – and, my God, it's the greatest thing that can happen to a man. I tell you, find a woman you can fall in love with. *Do* it. *Let* yourself fall in love, if you haven't already. You are wasting your life ... . Nowadays, men haven't the courage and the strength to love'. And then, as if this weren't enough, he continues: 'Do you know, I don't think you were fond enough of me. I was very fond of you. But you don't trust yourself, and you don't trust other people. You won't let yourself be really fond, even of a man friend, for fear he will find out your weaknesses'.[18] As with the letter to Savage, this has an unpleasant note of bragging about it. *He* has the courage and strength to love, *he's* unafraid of revealing his weaknesses. In its apparent throwing off of puritan restraint this is very puritan. The stress on individual consciousness, on the authenticity of experience, is also nakedly egotistical. 'Look!'

Yet against this it has to be said that some of the poems in the sequence have about them a rapt attentiveness that isn't at all egotistical. 'Gloire de Dijon' may at first seem merely pictorial, a verbal transcription of a Bonnard painting, for example; but its apparently casual notation is deceptive, its rejoicing in the flesh unashamedly candid, replete with gratified desire.

> In the window full of sunlight
> Concentrates her golden shadow
> Fold on fold, until it glows as
> Mellow as the glory roses.

The unusual use of 'concentrates' as an intransitive verb beautifully suggests how the woman's golden shadow draws all light and energy into itself. (As though it *is* a concentrate: a dense, pure solution.) This sets up the deepening, enriching sounds that echo on from 'golden shadow': 'f*o*ld on f*o*ld, until it gl*o*ws as/ Mell*o*w as the glory r*o*ses'. And the near rhyme of 'glows as/ … roses' delicately brushes the ear so as to prolong the lovely aural effect of the reversed rhyme 'shadow/ glows as'. 'River Roses' is also most delicately composed, a rare example of Lawrence using full rhyme to good effect – in this case, to vivify a sensed wholeness, an emotional amplitude which defies prose analysis but which is undoubtedly there, in the poem.

There is a further point. 'Song of a Man Who Has Come Through' begins: 'Not I, not I, but the wind that blows through me!/ A fine wind is blowing the new direction of Time'. There is more than a hint that this is an apocalyptic wind. Lawrence claims for himself a representative achievement. His breakthrough is both keenly registered as that of an individual and at the same time as part of something larger. What that something was can be inferred less from poems of the period than from the letters and prose fiction, and it is not to be pinned down by any formulaic statement. It does, however, have much to do with the entry into new worlds, both inner and outer; and it was undoubtedly prompted by Lawrence's discovery of life beyond the English bounds in which he had previously been confined. But then there is a sense in which his life is ceaselessly one of discoveries, of breaking beyond bounds, of transgressing limits. In a beautiful, chirpy late letter, he told the young David Chambers: 'Whatever I forget, I shall never forget the Haggs – I loved it so. I loved to come to you all, it really was a new life began in me there'.[19] What some have condemned as rashness or imprudence is better seen as the evidence of Lawrence's eager desire for testing 'new life'.

In this he was by no means alone. The searching for 'new life' is very much a part of modernism. That is to say, it belongs to that prolonged moment across Europe when impatience with an ageing and perhaps decadent civilization led to a number of very differently expressed desires to overthrow it or at all events to liberate energies which under it had been lost or repressed. *Avant-garde: the vanguard:* these terms indicate the storm-troopers of an advancing army. The vanguard originally meant 'the leading division or units of an army'. Avant-garde came to mean 'those artists, writers, musicians, etc., whose techniques and ideas are markedly experimental or in advance of those generally accepted'. In the late years of the nineteenth century and the early years of the twentieth century the avant-garde included in its ranks cubists, expressionists, psychiatrists and anti-psychiatrists, anarchists, socialists, futurists, exponents of erotic emancipation. For all their differences, they had one thing in common: they were sons in revolt against their fathers. In Lawrence's case much of this revolt centres on his relationship with Frieda. The nature of the revolt rooted in Lawrence's life and work is essentially protestant in spirit. As no serious commentator on him has failed to point out, he was preoccupied with the idea of Apocalypse from the days of his childhood attendance at the Eastwood Congregationalist bethel. Millenarian thought is deep within all types of nonconformity, but it is often tempered to fit the social experiences of suffering and rejection. Nonconformist hymns are remarkable for their imagery of blood and wounds, and these are seen as badges borne in Christian witness. Suffer now and store up future rewards: this is the message implicit in such imagery. It can also, of course, be seen as a crucial aspect of that labourist defeatism which socialist historians argue affects the English working class after 1848. The cultural expression of this defeatism is one of consolation, of making do.

Lawrence was passionately opposed to such a culture. He hated the religion of humility, of willy wet-legs, of people conspiring in their own degradation. It is notable that in his essay 'Hymns in a Man's Life' he looks back with gratitude to his Congregational upbringing and especially to those hymns he calls 'healthy'. They are 'martial hymns': 'Fight the Good Fight', for example, and 'Sound the Battle-Cry'. The fight is to build a new world, not in heaven, but on earth: its name is variously Canaan, Moab, Jerusalem, and it shines with the promise of the unfamiliar. At the end of his essay he recalls that 'Thirty-six years ago men, even Sunday School teachers, still believed in the fight for life and the fun of it'. At the time he wrote that sentence he was working on his essay, 'Apocalypse'. There, he remarks that 'We ought to dance with rapture that we should be alive and in the flesh, and part of the living, incarnate cosmos'. Lawrence's revolt is always a great kick at misery, a passionate refusal to submit to the way things are. Submission denies the authenticity of individual experience, of how and what a man *feels*. Lawrence's insistence on the authenticity of experience is also very protestant, which is why Auden is right to say that he was 'in every respect, very protestant indeed'. And it is why Frieda was so crucial in his life.

This needs some explanation. I do not mean to imply that she alone liberated him. It is rather that in committing himself to her, Lawrence eagerly accepted exogamy as a means of journeying beyond the familiar. This marks a deep break with 'little houses'. Frieda necessarily opened him up to a new life. It is this that so deeply engages him in the relationship between Tom Brangwen and Lydia Lensky, which he explores in the first section of *The Rainbow*. 'He seemed to live thus in contact with her, in contact with the unknown, the unaccountable and incalculable' (Chapter 2). Herself part of the avant-garde, Frieda was a powerful liberating force. Both before her marriage to Ernest Weekley and after it, she had been involved in a number of passionate love affairs. The most important of these was with Otto Gross, for whom she nearly left her husband. Gross was a political and social radical whose detestation of the Austria-Hungary in which he had grown up was total. He had chosen the life of anarchist for himself. He scorned the possession of private property, whether animate or inanimate. His cult of eroticism took for granted the outlawing of possessive jealousy. He set up a kind of anti-psychiatry, in which 'psychoanalysis was called upon to make men capable of freedom, to create a ferment of revolution within the psyche, against the dominant ego'. According to Martin Green, 'Frieda wrote Otto, *Du Bist Erotik*, and it was an ideological statement, with behind it a belief in eroticism as a philosophical and metaphysical value, as, above all, a life-creating value'. Green also notes that Frieda, the favourite among Gross's followers, 'found in D.H. Lawrence the man she was ready to commit herself to, as artist and husband. She told him he was of the same kind as Otto and Frick, and she had plans for Lawrence and Frick to collaborate together'. 'Frick' is Ernest Frick, an anarchist and associate of Gross's, who in 1912 went on trial for a bomb outrage in Zurich,[20] and with whom Frieda had also been erotically involved.

The physical and spiritual centre for this group of utopian anarchists was Ascona, a small Swiss-lake village. Lawrence visited it in September 1913, when he was walking from Bavaria over the Alps to Italy. In the course of that journey he came upon a group of Italian anarchists. Recalling the episode in *Twilight in Italy*, he admits to feeling in their leader 'a new spirit … something strange and pure and slightly frightening'.[21] We shall see later that Lawrence tries to confront this complex feeling in 'Hibiscus and Salvia Flowers'. Here, we need to note only that his intense individualism made him distrust the anarchists as conceivably linked together by an abstract programme which denied the very freedom they claimed to champion. Lawrence was with the anarchists in their contempt of prudential values, private ownership, greyness. But: '*noli me tangere*'. For all that Lawrence was occasionally attracted to the dream of an ideal community, he instinctively drew back from the idea of the group, of *any* group, and, beyond this, of those larger communities that made up the old world from which he wanted to escape. As matters turned out, however, he was soon to become inescapably thrown back on the old world. In August 1914, the Great War began. Lawrence, by now once again in England, suddenly found himself immured in a country whose war mania he would not share, but which took away his freedom and treated his wife and himself as dangerous persons. (Frieda's German name was enough to convince more than one of their neighbours that they must be enemy spies.) The war was a denial of individuality. Lawrence wrote to Lady Cynthia Asquith in November 1915, that 'The spirit of war is, that I am a unit … . If I love, then, I am in direct opposition to the principle of war. If war prevails, I do not love'.[22] The war was to prevail for a further three years, years that have been called Lawrence's 'Nightmare'.[23] During them he wrote comparatively little poetry, and the poems he did manage to write are not among his best work.

Then came the armistice. The Lawrences were free to leave England. In Chapter 12 of *Kangaroo*, written in 1922, but the first part of which is about the war years, Lawrence has his protagonist, Somers, look back at the south coast as he and his wife sail away.

> It was a cold day. There was snow on the Downs like a shroud. And as he looked back from the boat, when they had left Folkestone behind and only England was there, England looked like a grey, a dreary-grey coffin sinking in the sea behind, with her dead grey cliffs and the white, worn-out cloth of snow above.

That this was Lawrence's own feeling, there can be no doubt. In his autobiography, *The Flowers of the Forest*, David Garnett recalls Lawrence haranguing a group of friends who had gathered to celebrate the signing of the armistice. 'Europe is done for: England most of all the countries. This war isn't over. Even if the fighting should stop, the evil will be worse because the hate will be dammed up in men's hearts and will show itself in all sorts of ways which will be worse than war'.[24] Lawrence's detestation was certainly intensified by his deep loathing for those who had treated his wife and himself so badly during the war years. But he had developed an almost crazed hatred of modern society. This was often expressed in a Nietzschean rhetoric of snarling contempt for littleness, for which he may well have been indebted to the Asconans, though it was fuelled by what he called 'perfect androphobia'. He uses the phrase in a letter to his friend S. S. Koteliansky, and proceeds to explain its meaning:

> When I see people in the distance, walking along the path through the fields to Zennor, I want to crouch in the bushes and shoot them silently with invisible arrows of death. I think truly the only righteousness is the destruction of mankind, as in Sodom. Fire and

brimstone should fall down.

But I don't want even to hate them. I only want to be in another world than they. Here, it is almost as if one lived on a star, there is a great space of sky and sea in front, in spirit one can circle in space and have the joy of pure motion. But they creep in, the obstructions, the people, like bugs they creep invidiously in, and they are too many to crush. I see them – fat men in white-flannel trousers – pères de famille – and the familles – passing along the field-path and looking at the scenery. Oh, if one could but have a great box of insect powder, and shake it over them, in the heavens, and exterminate them. Only to clear and cleanse and purify the beautiful earth, and give room for some truth and pure living.[25]

Coming on such letters, and there are plenty of them, it is impossible not to feel appalled by the energy of their hatred. It is, or it seems to be, the quintessence of anti-democratic rage; and as such it can be aligned with that distinctively modernist posture which, however different its modes of expression, is also to be found in the arrogant hauteur of Yeats and Eliot's slinky distaste for ordinariness.

And yet at this point it is vital to recall that Lawrence always thought of *Leaves of Grass* as one of his 'great books'. How could he do so, we might ask, in view of that letter? But then Whitman, the poet of democratic America, was by no means a simple, unified being. 'Do I contradict myself?/ Very well then … I contradict myself./ I am large … I contain multitudes'. Whitman does not contain in the sense of holding it in. On the contrary, he lets it out.

I think I could turn and live awhile with the animals … they are so
placid and self-contained,
I stand and look at them sometimes half the day long.

They do not sweat and whine about their condition,
They do not lie awake in the dark and weep for their sins,
They do not make me sick discussing their duty to God,

Not one is dissatisfied . . . not one is demented with the mania of
owning things,
Not one kneels to another nor to his kind that lived thousands of
years ago,
Not one is respectable or industrious over the whole earth.[26]

Again, it might almost be Lawrence himself. What Lawrence took from Whitman is sufficiently fully set out in his great essay on Whitman to need no amplification here.[27] It is, however, important to note that the essay was written at the time when Lawrence felt most cornered by the war. It is as though the very act of working on the essay helped to draw the poison from his system and at the same time allowed him to focus on why Whitman meant so much to him. Above all, it helped to prepare him for the writing of his finest poems. For while these could have been written by nobody but Lawrence, their kinship with the Whitman who thought he could turn awhile and live with the animals is hardly to be denied.

III

The Lawrences finally left England in 1919. They went first to Italy and then on to Taormina, in Sicily. There, Lawrence began to produce some of the poems that would eventually be collected together as *Birds, Beasts and Flowers.* Other of these poems come from his and Frieda's stay in Australia and their time in Mexico and New Mexico. But Sicily reawoke Lawrence's desire to write poetry. Among the poems to have come from that brief period is 'Hibiscus and Salvia Flowers', a characteristically Whitman-like poem in its contemptuous hostility towards the Sicilian socialists and in its contradictory, urgent pull towards their primitive force. As Tom Paulin has remarked in an important essay on the poem, 'The socialists with their salvia and hibiscus flowers are outside hotels, outside European civilisation by their association through the flowers with an ancient Polynesian aristocracy'. Paulin goes on to point out that the alignment of prelapsarian Eve with a Polynesian princess 'forces Lawrence to confront the argument deep in his own imagination between the radical idea of human rights and a conservative idea of tradition, duty, hierarchy, art'.[28] While this may be true we should also remember that at more or less this same moment Yeats and Eliot were confronting very similar arguments in their own imaginations, and that these confrontations would produce such poems as 'The Second Coming', 'Meditations in Time of Civil War', and 'The Waste Land'. But whatever the differences between these works, and they are very considerable, they are still more different from Lawrence's. For although 'Hibiscus and Salvia Flowers' may confront an argument it doesn't do more than announce apocalypse in purely personal terms.

> I long to be a bolshevist
> And set the stinking rubbish-heap of this foul world
> Afire at a myriad scarlet points,
> A bolshevist, a salvia-face
> To lick the world with flame that licks it clean.
> I long to see its chock-full crowdedness
> And glutted squirming populousness on fire
> Like a field of filthy weeds
> Burnt back to ash,
> And then to see the new, real souls sprout up.

If this recalls the androphobia of letters which Lawrence was writing in the later years of the war, it also recalls his remarks about the American consciousness and under-consciousness, made in the course of his essay on Hawthorne.

> The deliberate consciousness of Americans so fair and smooth-spoken, and the under-consciousness so devilish. *Destroy! destroy! destroy!* hums the under-consciousness. *Love and produce! Love and produce!* cackles the upper consciousness. And the world hears only the Love-and produce cackle. Refuses to hear the hum of destruction underneath. Until such

> time as it will *have* to hear.
>
> The American has got to destroy. It is his destiny. It is his destiny to destroy the whole corpus of the white psyche, the white consciousness.[29]

'Hibiscus and Salvia Flowers' makes clear that Lawrence feels it to be his destiny to destroy the white consciousness, where 'white' means everything to do with littleness, meanness, rationality: the world of bungalow culture. It does not, however, amount to anything so portentous as a claim for 'saving civilization', even though his great modernist contemporaries have been seen as committing their poetry to that grand aim.[30] Lawrence's poetry is one of moods, it is not 'philosophical' in the sense that it is possible to call Eliot's poetry 'philosophical', or even Yeats's. Lawrence, it is true, would see this as an essentially meaningless distinction. In one of his most famous 'Pansies' he insists that he loves thought:

> But not the juggling and twisting of already existent ideas
> I despise that self-important game.
> Thought is the welling up of unknown life into consciousness,
> Thought is the testing of statements on the touchstone of the
> conscience,
> Thought is gazing on to the face of life, and reading what can be read,
> Thought is pondering over experience, and coming to a conclusion.
> Thought is not a trick, or an exercise, or a set of dodges,
> Thought is a man in his wholeness wholly attending.

Apply this test to 'Hibiscus and Salvia Flowers' and it is, perhaps, a thinking poem, at least in the sense that there is in it a welling up of unknown life into consciousness. I'm not sure, though, that it can be said to test statements on the touchstone of conscience. Too much of it seems journalese, that quarrel with others out of which, Yeats said, we make rhetoric, rather than the quarrel with ourselves out of which we make poetry. It is not that I expect Lawrence to come to a conclusion. It is rather that, as often the case with his later prose, the enemy is so abstract, so unfocused, that it is difficult to feel that what we have here is a man in his wholeness wholly attending. 'I long to see its chock-full crowdedness/ And glutted squirming populousness on fire/ Like a field of filthy weeds/ Burnt back to ash'. This is slovenly language and I would expect Lawrence in a different mood to realize as much.

The different mood, or moods, is what we find in *Birds, Beasts and Flowers*. These really do reveal a man in his wholeness wholly attending and I can therefore understand why Auden should say that in them 'Lawrence's writing is so transparent that one forgets him entirely and simply sees what he saw'.[31] Certainly no later poet makes us see so intensely the lords and lesser beings of life which Lawrence writes about in these magical poems. I do not think, however, that we can ever forget his presence. He is so palpably involved in the seeing, or, as we should more properly say, in the attending. Alvarez is nearer the mark than Auden when he says of these poems that they are

> quite as personal as any of his others. In them he doesn't merely describe, nor does he go at his subjects with a preconceived idea and try to twist them into meanings they would not naturally take. They are neither all subject nor all poet. It is a matter of a vital and complex relationship between the two, difficult, fluent, inward and wholly unabstract. He even avoids the final abstraction of formal perfection. For that gives to experience a kind of ghostly Platonic idealness: in the end, everything is so perfectly accounted for that the poetic world is complete and isolated. In the relationship Lawrence tries to catch, every thing is in flux; it is a flow between two creatures, with nothing fixed. The artist has constantly to improvise at the full pitch of his intelligence.[32]

That is excellently said and it serves to indicate a difference between Lawrence and poets who have been much indebted to him, such as Theodore Roethke and Ted Hughes. For both of these, no matter how hard they try wholly to attend, there is always the risk of designed meanings, the procrustean tug that distorts the recognition of true otherness. Their birds, plants, and fish, that is, threaten to turn into metaphor. Not the thing in itself, but the thing as something else. With Lawrence this never happens. The result is that when he says to the mosquito, 'How you sail like a heron, or a dull clot of air', the words are visually unimprovable while carrying no hidden or freighted significance. Such language is *absolutely* about what it sees, is wholly attentive. John Clare apart, there is no English poet who can match Lawrence's entire responsiveness to, his complete absorption in, the otherness of life to which he attends in these poems. This is emphatically not the poetry of 'nature'. As Lawrence himself said, 'we must always beware of romance: of people who love nature, or flowers, or dogs, or babies, or pure adventure. It means they are getting into a love-swing where everything is easy and nothing opposes their egoism'.[33] The man who wrote that is recognizably the same man who complained at the manner of Keats's writing about the nightingale. '"Adieu! adieu! thy plaintive anthem fades ...'. It never was a plaintive anthem – it was Caruso at his jauntiest'.[34]

Birds, Beasts and Flowers takes opposition not so much for granted as the grounds of being. That is why Alvarez is right to remark on the 'flow between two creatures, with nothing fixed', and why the poems cannot allow themselves any formal perfection. Although it is impossible to see how they could be improved on, they are in no sense 'closed' forms, they come to no conclusions. Their apparent informality is the sign of Lawrence's resistance to thought as 'a trick, or an exercise, or a set of dodges'. It is also an expression of the shifts in contingence that necessarily occur between perceiver and perceived. You can break off such shifts. You cannot bring them to a conclusion.

There is, however, some evidence that in the poems written in New Mexico Lawrence was moving towards conclusion. I think in particular of 'Mountain Lion' and the much more disturbing 'Eagle in New Mexico'. The closing lines of this poem have about them what he himself might have called 'the blood drowse'. They are heavy with the drugged, dangerous excitement of forbidden thoughts: blood sacrifice, ritual slaughter. It is as though the move from Sicily to the new-old world of Australia and then the Americas urged on Lawrence a commitment to the pre-modern, anti-rational, which he had already confronted and which would find ultimate expression in the doctrinal and terrible *Plumed Serpent*, for which 'Eagle in New Mexico' is in some sense a preparation. Despite its intense, vivid perception, the poem is by no means as open as most in the sequence. The current of feeling that sustains it flows, slowly and thickly, in one direction only, towards the closing lines:

> Even the sun in heaven can be curbed and chastened at last
> By the life in the hearts of men.
> And you, great bird, sun-starer, heavy black beak
> Can be put out of office as sacrifice bringer.

The life Lawrence has in mind presumably fits men to be sacrifice bringers. Not so much lords of life as lords of death.

IV

To praise the best poems of *Birds, Beasts and Flowers* for their openness is not to mistake them for bits of life. They are art, right enough. That much becomes clear when we come across Lawrence's odd and unsatisfactory explanation for the poems – if that is the word for them – of his last years.

> I offer a bunch of pansies, not a wreath of immortelles. I don't want everlasting flowers and I don't want to offer them to anybody else. A flower passes, and that perhaps is the best of it. ... Don't nail the pansy down. You won't keep it any better if you do.

Of this, Auden rightly remarks that 'Lawrence draws a false analogy between the process of artistic creation and the organic growth of living creatures'. Lawrence may hope to produce 'something which will seem as natural as a flower, but the qualities of the natural are exactly what his product will lack'.[35] Many of the *Pansies* are marred by crude rhetoric and by what D.J. Enright has called a 'rasping sterility'. As Enright notes, Lawrence didn't inevitably, as he hoped, 'exclude a "repellent, slightly bullying" effect by putting his thoughts into verse'.[36] Whether you can call *Pansies* and *More Pansies* verse is, I would think, very doubtful. Yet neither are they particularly satisfactory as prose epigrams. More often they are neither one thing nor the other. But then it should be noted that by the time Lawrence came to write them he was very ill, frail, and all but exhausted. And for all that many of them are at best trivial, at worst nasty, there are some *Pansies* which I wouldn't be without.

There are also, from this last period, some more considerable poems, among them 'Bavarian Gentians' and 'The Ship of Death', both of which exist in different versions. This suggests that Lawrence set some store by them. It is understandable. They were composed under the shadow of death and they are a way of coming to terms with oblivion. They seek to find a language of acceptance, of lapsing out. 'Bavarian Gentians' in particular has an incantatory depth which hints at a meaning, an understanding of 'the dark', that is beyond rational comprehension yet not to be written off as delusion. Having said this, however, I have to add that with the exception of 'Bavarian Gentians' none of the last poems seems to me to be among Lawrence's best. And I do not think that anything in them can compare with the ending of Wallace Stevens's great poem 'Sunday Morning', which had already been written, and which images the lapsing out into oblivion more memorably than any of Lawrence's late poems.

> And, in the isolation of the sky,
> At evening, casual flocks of pigeons make
> Ambiguous undulations as they sink
> Downward to darkness, on extended wings.

Other commentators feel more enthusiastic about the late poems than

I can. It is to the Lawrence of *Birds, Beasts and Flowers* that I want to return, again and again.

A NOTE ON THE TEXT

For the poems I have gone to the relevant first editions. They are:

Love Poems and Others, London: Duckworth, 1913
Amores, London: Duckworth, 1916
Look! We Have Come Through!, London: Chatto & Windus, 1917
New Poems, London: Secker, 1918
Birds, Beasts and Flowers, London: Secker, 1923
Collected Poems, London: Secker, 1928
Last Poems, London: Secker, 1933.

For prose I have also gone to the relevant first editions:

Twilight in Italy, London: Duckworth, 1916
Fantasia of the Unconscious, New York: Seltzer, 1922
Sea and Sardinia, London, Secker: 1923
Studies in Classic American Literature, New York: Seltzer, 1923
Mornings in Mexico, London, Secker: 1927.

For the letters I have used *The Letters of D H Lawrence*, edited, with an introduction, by Aldous Huxley, London: Heinemann, 1932. However, the letter to Henry Savage, of 22 December 1913, is quoted by kind permission of Cambridge University Press.

1990

Notes

1 *The Cambridge Edition of The Letters of D H Lawrence*, Volume 11, 1913-16, ed. George J. Zytaruk and James T. Boulton, Cambridge: Cambridge University Press, 1981, 146.

2 Thomas's review is reprinted in A Language Not To Be Betrayed: *Selected Prose of Edward Thomas*, ed. Edna Longley, Manchester: Carcanet, 1981, 106-7. For Pound's review see H. Coombes *D. H. Lawrence: Penguin Critical Anthology*, Harmondsworth: Penguin, 1973, 78.

3 D. H. Lawrence, *The Complete Poems of D H Lawrence,* 'The Phoenix Edition', ed. Vivian de Sola Pinto and Warren Roberts, 3 vols, London: Heinemann, 1957, Volume I, xxxvi.

4 W.H. Auden, 'D.H. Lawrence', in *The Dyer's Hand*, New York: Vintage Books, 1968, 285.

5 Ibid., 287.

6 Sisson's ill-natured and obtuse account of Lawrence may be found in his *English Poetry 1900-1950*, London: Methuen, 1971. Blackmur's essay is included in his *Language as Gesture*, London: Allen & Unwin, 1954. For Hough's remark, see *The Dark Sun: A Study of D.H. Lawrence*, Harmondsworth, Penguin, 1961, 224.

7 Quoted by F. R. Leavis in *D.H. Lawrence, Novelist*, Harmondsworth: Penguin, 1964, 315.

8 A. Alvarez, *The Shaping Spirit: Studies in Modern English and American Poets*, London: Grey Arrow Books, 1963, 147.

9 Thomas, op. cit., 107.

10 *Georgian Poetry*, edited and introduced by James Reeves, Harmondsworth: Penguin, 1962, xiii.

11 *Letters*, Volume II, 92.

12 For a more sympathetic and illuminating account of the Georgian movement, see C.K. Stead, *The New Poetic*, London: Hutchinson, 1964, passim.

13 See *Imagist Poetry*, ed. Peter Jones, Harmondsworth: Penguin, 1972, esp. 17-19.

14 Lawrence appeared in the imagist anthologies for 1915 and 1916.

15 Auden, op. cit., 288.

16 Ibid.

17 *Letters*, Volume II, 130.

18 *The Cambridge Edition of the Letters of D.H. Lawrence*, Volume I, 1901-13, ed. James T. Boulton, Cambridge: Cambridge University Press, 1979, 148.

19 *D. H. Lawrence: Selected Letters*, Harmondsworth: Penguin, 1950, 172.

20 For all this and more see Martin Green, Mountain of Truth: *The Counter Culture Begins, Ascona 1900-1920*, New Jersey: University Press of New England, 1986. Green provides a very full account of Frieda's involvement with Ascona and of Lawrence's more tangential relationship with some of its luminaries.

21 D.H. Lawrence, *Twilight in Italy*, Harmondsworth: Penguin, 1960, 144.

22 *Letters*, Volume II, 424.

23 See Paul Delany, *D. H. Lawrence's Nightmare: The Writer and His Circle in the Years of the Great War*, Hassocks: Harvester Press, 1979.

24 Ibid., 385.

25 Letters, Volume II, 650.

26 *Walt Whitman: Leaves of Grass. The Original Edition*, ed. Malcolm Cowley, London: Secker & Warburg, 1959, 55-6.

27 In *D. H. Lawrence and Edward Carpenter: A Study in Edwardian Transition*, London, Heinemann, 1971, Emile Delavenay is able to show that Lawrence's attachment to Whitman was typical of its period. Those whom Delavenay calls the 'Midlands Intelligentsia' were particularly sympathetic to both *Leaves of Grass and Democratic Vistas*. But it needs to be said that Lawrence was far less interested in Whitman's political vision than he was in 'The Song of Myself' and all which that offered.

28 *In D.H. Lawrence in the Modern World*, ed. Peter Preston and Peter Hoare, London, Macmillan, 1988, 186.

29 The essay on Hawthorne, also written during the Nightmare years, was published in *Studies in Classic American Literature*, 1924. I am here quoting it from *D. H. Lawrence: Selected Literary Criticism*, ed.

Anthony Beal, London: Mercury Books, 1961, 347-8.

30 Lawrence is absent from Lucy MacDiarmid's study, *Saving Civilisation: Yeats, Eliot and Auden Between the Wars*, Cambridge: Cambridge University Press, 1984.

31 Auden, op. cit., 292.

32 Alvarez, op. cit., 150.

33 Quoted by Charles Davey in *D.H. Lawrence: A Living Poet*, London: Brentham Press, 1985, 31. Davey's enthusiastic pamphlet concentrates on Pansies, which he feels to be far more successful than I can bring myself to do.

34 Beal, op. cit., 101.

35 Auden, op. cit., 283-4.

36 Enright's remark occurs in the course of his review of the *Collected Poems* and is to be found in Coombes's *Critical Anthology*, op. cit., 447.

THE OCCUPATION OF THE LAND

Edward Thomas, *A Language Not To Be Betrayed*. Selected prose with an introduction by Edna Longley. 290pp. Carcanet, 1981.

In his study of *Walter Pater*, Edward Thomas wrote that 'Only when a word has become necessary to him can a man use it safely; if he try to impress words by force on a sudden occasion, they will either perish of his violence or betray him'. And in the course of a particularly powerful passage, where he identifies what it is in Pater's prose style that most displeases him, Thomas remarks that 'it retained no sign of an original impulse in it. If there had been a strong impulse the after elaboration had worn it completely away. This detachment made language seem to be as hard and inhuman a material as marble, and like marble to have had no original connection with the artist's idea'. To read through this selection of Thomas's prose is to become aware of something which his poems also declare and everywhere embody: that a writer's language must be personal to him, but that it must also speak for a deep attachment to those realities from which the language derives and which it identifies.

This essential conviction of Thomas's has been best expressed, I think, by Stan Smith, in an essay of outstanding merit, the title of which is identical with the book under present review, and which appeared in the journal *Literature and History* (No. 4, Autumn, 1976). Referring to the poem 'I never saw that land before', from which comes the line 'A language not to be betrayed', Smith notes how in the central stanza 'a man establishes some actual, tangible relations with the landscape, marking it with his presence'. And he adds that the revelation implied in the poem's concluding lines – 'And what was hid should still be hid/ Excepting from those like me made / Who answer when such whispers bid' – is only available 'when a language is shared, when there is bidding and response'. Or as Thomas himself put it in 'Words', when asking 'Choose me, / You English words':

> Make me content
> With some sweetness
> From Wales
> Whose nightingales
> Have no wings –
> From Wiltshire and Kent
> And Herefordshire,
> And the villages there, –
> From the names, and the things
> No less.

I think it a matter of real regret that Edna Longley does not seem to know of Smith's essay, for her own very fine Introduction is a major critical essay on Thomas (as is her edition of his *Poems and Last Poems*); and her subtle understanding of Thomas would have been valuably complemented by Smith's. Like Smith, she recognizes just how central a poem 'Lob' is; and she unerringly identifies the importance of Thomas's remark that poetry 'springs apparently from an occupation of the land, from long, busy, and quiet tracts of time, wherein a man or a nation may find its own soul. To have a future, it must have had a past'. A perception such as this makes clear why Thomas felt that he had no option but to fight in the Great War; and it also helps to explain why in a sense all his poems are war poems. For they are deep voicings of an apprehension of England which more truly testifies to an occupation of the land than all the thin and thick volumes of patriotic verse that tumbled from the presses during the years of that war.

There is a further point. For this sense of occupation of the land must be what lies behind Thomas's otherwise surely inexplicable praise for Doughty's 'The Dawn of Britain', a would-be epic which I once tried to read but which defeated me before I had gone thirty pages, and yet about which Thomas can say that

> I had no worthy sense of the great rich age of this home of my race till I found it here; it is not a little matter that (some day) children will grow up with the emotion of this book in their breasts, with such an harmonious view of early history and folklore and ancient monuments and the physical beauty of Britain as we can only grope for.

Wherever you turn in Thomas you find this concern with occupation of the land. How else account for the way in which, in *The South Country*, he lists as though he is savouring them the names of southern counties and their rivers; and speaks with such familiar affection of the names on sign-boards at cross-roads? And how else account for those quite magical poems to his children ('If I should ever by chance grow rich / I'll buy Codham, Cockridden, and Childerditch, / Roses, Pyrgo, and Lapwater, / And let them all to my eldest daughter')? You name the names, the names are inseparable from the places, and they choose you as much as you choose them.

It is this that enables us to understand why Thomas should write with such devastating contempt of Maeterlinck and Swinburne. The essay on Maeterlinck's 'Serres Chauds' attacks the poem because it

> ignores the fact that no word, outside works of information, has any value beyond its surface value except what it receives from its neighbours and its position among them. Each man makes his own language in the main unconsciously and inexplicably, unless he is still at an age when he is an admiring but purely aesthetic collector of words; certain words – he knows not why – he will never use; and there are a hundred peculiarities in his rhythms and groupings to be discovered. In the mainly instinctive use of his language the words

> will all support one another, and if the writing is good, the result of this support is that each word is living its intensest life.

This is as near as one can come to Thomas's poetic credo. The relationship between a poet and his language is, or ought to be, an intensely personal one from which the positivist sense of user and used has been utterly banished. So Thomas can even discover what is personal in Pater's style: 'When he has to say that Leonardo was illegitimate, he uses eight words: 'The dishonour of illegitimacy hangs over his birth'. He at once makes the 'dishonour' a distinction with some grandeur: he almost makes it a visible ornament. ... Nearly every one of the essays in *The Renaissance* opens abruptly. Pater cannot wind into our confidence. He is a shy man, full of "it may be" and "we may think", and he has the awkward abruptness of a shy man'.

In his review of *Selected Poems of Francis Thompson*, Thomas remarks that Thompson 'never seems to have got on terms, as it were, of married familiarity with words, so that they remain in his verse as a permanent memorial of this nympholepsy'. Alter the figure slightly so that you may take account of a different talent, and you arrive at Thomas's judgement on Swinburne. Swinburne has 'almost no magic felicity of words'; it therefore follows that a poem such as 'A Channel Passage' is 'an inhuman perversion of language and metre'. Much more important, however, is the fact that 'Since the adjective is most ready when words are wanted, he used a greater number, yet without equally great variety. He kept as it were a harem of words, to which he was constant and faithful'. There then follows an attack on Swinburne's characteristic use of those adjectives which is quite simply one of the best examples of close reading that I have come across, and which makes us realize what a wonderful critic Thomas was. (Interestingly, in the course of dismissing Swinburne's view of England with 'The sea-coast round her like a mantle', and 'The sea-cloud like a crown', Thomas remarks that this would be 'a grave weakness in a poet who encouraged reading closely with eye and ear'.) The demolition of Swinburne is not merely exactly witty ('Rhyme certainly acted upon

Swinburne as a pill to purge ordinary responsibilities'); it is also criticism that could only be produced by a considerable poet. For its understanding of what is wrong with Swinburne takes for granted an intimate awareness of what poetry should be. True, Thomas called reviewing an unskilled labour, and noted that most reviewers were content with 'important-looking abstractions and generalities'. But this is emphatically not the case with his own reviewing, which is confident, precise, and just plain right.

Quite why Thomas hadn't committed himself to writing poetry by 1912, when the Swinburne book appeared, can't of course be known. But the usual explanation seems as far as we are likely to get. Thomas remarks of Swinburne that 'Other poets tend towards a grace and glory of words as of human speech perfected and made divine, Swinburne towards a musical jargon that includes human snatches, but is not and never could be speech'. Where, then, could such speech be found? The answer of course is in the poetry of Robert Frost. 'This is one of the most revolutionary books of modern times, but one of the quietest and least aggressive'. The opening sentence of one of Thomas's reviews of *North of Boston* (he wrote several) makes clear how much Frost meant to him. The language of Frost's poems, he goes on, 'is free from the poetical words and forms that are the chief material of secondary poets. The metre avoids not only the old-fashioned pomp and sweetness, but the later fashion of discord and fuss. In fact, the medium is common speech and common decasyllables .... The more dramatic pieces have ... the beauty of life seen by one in whom mystery and tenderness together just outstrip humour and curiosity'. (Mere curiosity is no doubt dangerous because in its implied aggressiveness it excludes bidding and response).

Nearly all of Thomas's concerns with and for poetry come together in what he says of Frost; and reading through this marvellous selection of his prose we are bound to share the excitement of his discovery. I suppose that it is a matter of being wise after the event, and yet it is impossible to avoid the feeling that all the time Thomas is on the look-out for the poet who can release his own poetry. He writes with acute, loving perception of Hardy, but Hardy won't quite do: 'He cannot escape from his own muffled cadences, which at their liveliest suggest old people dancing an old dance, his reluctances and pauses; or from his sombre intellectual vocabulary'. Even so, Hardy comes near to what is wanted; in one poem 'there is a changing burden which is full if not of magic yet of a deep and strong suggestion of something which the intellect alone cannot handle'. Thomas sees how good – and bad – W.H. Davies could be; is just and generous to de la Mare (the review of *Peacock Pie* is a perfect example of the delicate adjustment of tone to the subject so that Thomas can find exactly the right way to praise the book); and he writes with lucid understanding about Yeats, Lawrence and Pound. I am not sure whether isolated quotation will demonstrate this, but here he is, for example, on Yeats: '"Speech delighted with its own music" is the best definition of Mr Yeats' verse'. On Lawrence: 'he writes of matters which cannot be subdued to conventional rhythm and rhyme – chiefly the intense thoughts, emotions, or gropings of self-conscious men and women set on edge by love or fatigue or solitude. If he trusts to make a general appeal, it is by faithful concentration on the particular ...'. And, an uncannily prescient remark on Pound: 'He is so possessed by his strong conceptions, that he not only cannot think of wrapping them up in conventional form, but he must ever show his disdain for it a little'.

But it is when he comes to Frost that you know Thomas has arrived at the poetry he wants, from others and from himself. It comes out, above all, perhaps, in the following statement: 'There are moments when the plain language and lack of violence make the unaffected verses look like prose, except that the sentences, if spoken aloud, are most felicitously true in rhythm to the emotion'. No doubt Thomas knew of Frost's concern with how the rhythms of a poem must be intimately expressive of sentence sound, and of the revelations which such voiced rhythms contain; yet it was what he himself had been saying, as this volume makes clear. And making it clear is Edna Longley's overriding concern. I do not see how the work she has done could have been done any better.

1981

DISCOVERING ENGLAND: THE VIEW FROM THE TRAIN

In the first years of the twentieth century cars began to invade the English countryside. They also began to invade the pages of English novels just as, some half-century before, the railway had entered nineteenth-century fiction, most memorably in *Dombey and Son*. But whereas Dickens had given a cautious welcome to the age of the train, the age of the car received a far more hostile press. There are two reasons for this. Cars were from the first associated with leisure rather than use. Secondly, they were the playthings of the idle rich, especially the new rich, and their very appearance emphasised how wide was the gap between those who went without the meat and those who ostentatiously drove or, more frequently, were driven about England. (The age of the car was not of course restricted to England, but this essay is.) 'It is only since the coming of the automobile that I have known what it is to be poor,' someone remarked in 1902.[1] Toad owned a car, in which he went a gallivanting gaily down the road.[2] And Toad, though he came from an ancient family, had allowed himself to be seduced by the new, the flashy. Hence his readiness to exchange a dream of exculpatory vagabondage, the gypsy caravan, for the life of aggressive selfishness defined by car ownership. In Kenneth Grahame's ultra-conservative fable, the Wild Wooders, those ill-bred stoats and weasels, operate as stand-ins for a newly threatening working-class, ready to infest and overrun the settled calm of rural England. Toad's joy in his car provides woeful evidence of how far the rot has extended. The Wild Wooders are eventually forced from Toad Hall by a combination of country gentlemen – Badger, Ratty and Mole – armed with antiquated weapons (cudgels and the like). Theirs is a square which does not break. Toad Hall is made safe for the shires. But it is a near thing.

The Wind in the Willows, published in 1908, is deeply instructive about pre-1914 attitudes to the car. So is *Howards End*.[3] The male Wilcoxes, those men of business and military life, travel about England by car; and as they go they leave behind them a trail of damage. Early in the novel Mrs Wilcox tells Margaret Schlegel that her husband and daughter have been on a tour of Yorkshire, but

> "they must cut short their tour, the weather is so bad, and the police traps have been so bad – nearly as bad as in Surrey. Ours is such a careful chauffeur, and my husband feels it particularly hard that they should be treated as road-hogs."
>
> "Why?"
>
> "Well, naturally he – isn't a road-hog."
>
> "He was exceeding the speed-limit, I conclude. He must expect to suffer with the lower animals." (Chapter X)

Given that the speed limit was only twenty miles per hour (The Motor Car Act of 1903 had raised it from the previous fourteen miles per hour, which had been set in 1896) 'road-hogs' – the use of the phrase in England dates from 1898 – might not have seemed much of a menace. But in his splendid *England 1868-1914*, Donald Read remarks that, soon after the 1903 Act came into being, the police

> had recourse to speed traps, disregarding complaints that they were 'un-English'. The immediate occasion for the establishment of the Automobile Association in 1905 was the ardour of the Sussex police in trying to curb speeding. The Association's scouts warned approaching members by not giving them the customary salute. In 1900 only 2,548 persons had been found guilty of traffic offences in England and Wales; by 1910 [the year of publication of *Howards End*] the total had reached 55,633. This amounted to over 9 per cent of all offences. For the first time, large numbers of the upper and middle classes were finding themselves on the wrong side of the law.[4]

Later in the novel there is an incident in which the Wilcox car, speeding through the Shropshire countryside, carelessly runs over a small girl's cat. Margaret attempts to make reparations, reflecting as she does so that she and her smart friends 'had no part with the earth and its emotions. They were dust, and a stink, and cosmopolitan chatter, and the girl whose cat had been killed had lived more deeply than they'.(Chapter XXV)

The sentimental ruralism in *Howards End* requires Forster to use the car as a symbol of intrusive, unsettling power. Car owners are not 'rooted', have no sense of England: they are merely in motion. Forster remarks of a drive Margaret is made to take through Hertfordshire, and by which she is unimpressed, that

> perhaps Hertfordshire is scarcely intended for motorists. Did not a gentleman once motor so quickly through Westmoreland that he missed it? And if Westmoreland can be missed, it will fare ill with a county whose delicate structure particularly needs the attentive eye. Hertfordshire is England at its quietest, with little emphasis of river and hill; it is England meditative. (Chapter XXIII)

The house named Howards End stands in Hertfordshire and is a very obvious symbol of a heart of England.[5]

This phrase is much associated with Edward Thomas and it is therefore of some significance that Thomas should also speak out against the motor car. In *The South Country*, published a year before *Howards End,* he mourns the loss of

> those lone wayside greens, no man's gardens, measuring a few feet wide but many miles in length – why should they be used as receptacles for the dust of motor cars or as additions to the property of the landowner who happens to be renewing his fence? They used to be as beautiful and cool and fresh as rivers, these green sisters of the white roads – illuminated borders of many a weary tale. But now, lest there should be no room for dust, they are turning away from them the gypsies who used to camp there for a night.

Thomas's progressive ruralism (I take the phrase from Alun Howkins) is such that he inevitably opposes the rights of gypsies to those of the landowners he calls 'the pheasant lords'. Propose giving gypsies a pitch for the night, he says, and these lords will regard you as 'an enemy of the community or even a Socialist'.[6] Such lords not only owned vast tracts of land, they also owned motor cars.

By the time war came to Europe, in August 1914, many more people owned cars. According to Read, a total of 32,451 cars were registered in the UK in 1907. Seven years later this number had grown to 132,015, 'within a total of 388,860 motor vehicles of all kinds – private cars, motor cycles, buses, coaches, taxis, and goods vehicles'.[7] It would not be long before motorized transport as a mode of travel became proof against the arguments of those who had initially objected to it as an indicator of class difference. In the inter-war period the motor car for some and for others the motor bus (especially the Green Line Service) were accepted as legitimate ways of discovering rural England, of claiming some sort of kinship with it, and even of being strengthened by the rude health with which it was associated. (The 1930s was a decade much preoccupied with the state of the nation's physical health.) Hence the advertisements for Hovis Teas, showing an average two plus two middle-class family walking expectantly towards a small tearoom set somewhere in the English countryside, while behind them their parked car, a family saloon, stands silhouetted against hedgerow beyond which can be glimpsed cornfields and a spread of elms.

The apotheosis of the car came with the post-war Shell Guides to Britain and that company's commissioning of artists – among them Paul Nash, John Piper and Edward Bawden – to produce rural scenes that could be used in poster campaigns for Shell petrol.[8] By then, it almost goes without saying, car ownership was the ambition of most, and although different models were aimed at different classes and aspirations, the car was well on its way to becoming the commonest form of transport as well as an obvious means to and end of leisure. Yet for all this, the car has not for the most part been the means by which writers choose to report their 'discoveries' of England. And it most certainly was not the preferred mode of travel for those who set out to discover 'England' in that crucial period before the First World War when the idea of England was becoming increasingly problematic. (Hence my use of quotation marks.) True, not long after the outbreak of war, Lawrence told Lady Cynthia Asquith that 'when I drive across this country, with the autumn rustling and falling to pieces, I am so sad, for my country. ... So much beauty and pathos of old things passing away and no new things coming ... the winter stretches ahead, where all vision is lost and all memory dies out'.[9] But this apocalyptic reading of England is less acceptably re-visited by Connie Chatterley when, in her chauffeur-driven car, she looks out at the slag heaps of Tevershall:

> It was as if dismalness had soaked through and through everything. The utter negation of natural beauty, the utter negation of the gladness of life, the utter absence of the instinct for shapely beauty which every bird and beast has, the utter death of the intuitive human faculty was appalling. 'What could possibly become of such a people, a people in whom the living intuitive faculty was dead as nails ... ?[10]

In the first and greatly superior version of the novel, called *John Thomas and Lady Jane*, Lawrence distances himself from Connie's response to Tevershall's industrial landscape. She has no sooner done with her reflections on this place of deadness than she realizes that Tevershall is where her lover – Parkin in that version – comes from. Her view of Tevershall is in other words that of the outsider, whose class assumptions prevent a true understanding of what it is she sees. Unfortunately, in the third and final version of *Lady Chatterley's Lover* Lawrence chooses to omit Connie's discomforting recognition that her lover's birthplace cannot be as dead as she thinks it.[11] Where Lawrence's wartime vision unironically endorsed or at all events appealed to a widely shared sense of breakdown, Connie must be seen as insulated from a more complex reality by the contained, motorized box in which she is free, as passive spectator, to rehearse her prejudiced misunderstandings. And it is worth noting that at the very end of the 1920s Evelyn Waugh uses the car in his dystopian vision of a future England as a means to ensure the destruction of various vile bodies.

In the previous century's fiction, vile and not so vile bodies had sometimes been disposed of by the steam-engine. (The most famous example is of course Anna Karenina but in English fiction there are Carker the Manager and Lopez, whose suicide at the Tenways Junction so conveniently clears the way for a satisfactory ending to Trollope's *The Prime Minister*.) Yet for the most part writers seem more at ease with the train than with the car. Wordsworth had famously opposed the coming of the railway to the Lake District, but his reasons for doing so help to explain why other writers would be unlikely to take his side, especially as he himself admitted in 1839 that 'I like railway travelling much'.[12] What he did *not* like was the prospect of 'loads of visitors' overrunning the lakes, especially as such visitors were certain to be working people from industrial Lancashire.

> Instead of tempting artisans and labourers … and the humbler classes of shopkeepers, to ramble to a distance, let us rather look with lively sympathy upon persons in that condition, when, upon a holiday, or on a Sunday, after having attended divine worship, they make little excursions with their wives and children among neighbouring fields, whither the whole of each family might stroll, or be conveyed at much less cost than would be required to take a single individual of the number to the shores of Windermere by the cheapest conveyance.[13]

In his sonnet 'On The Projected Kendal and Windermere Railway' (1844), Wordsworth asks, 'Is then no nook of English ground secure/From rash assault?' The question was bound to seem prompted by selfish privilege. One reason for writers to feel at ease with train travel was precisely that it was not the preserve of the privileged. Yes, the carriages were divided between first-, second-, and third-class, with marked differences in standard of comfort and degrees of attention paid by railway staff to the travelling public, and yes, first-class travellers were protected from having to know much if anything of those who travelled third. (At some places, Malvern for instance, third-class passengers were not even allowed to alight at the station proper but had to get off further along the line.) Nevertheless, train travel was not exclusive to one class.

Nor could train travellers be held to account for crashes and accidents. By contrast, car drivers were – and are – responsible for the safety of themselves and others. They can be held accountable for death and injury. But there is no such thing as a rail-hog. In addition, a decision to make use of the train was, as it remains, very different from a decision to make use of a car. The vast majority of those who travel by car own a car. But the person who travelled by train didn't own the train. (And I am not forgetting the days of British Rail.) Train travel has never of itself been ostentatious, and, though ostentation can be brought to it, for most passengers train travel makes for anonymity. It also – or perhaps therefore – leaves you free to look about, to observe what goes on in the carriage and beyond the window. The man who drove through Westmoreland and missed it might well have remarked that he couldn't afford to take his eyes off the road. The train traveller experiences no such need, has no such excuse.

On the other hand, train journeys provide the opportunity for social occasions. There used to be works' outings, there are still day excursions and football specials, and about such occasions there was and is a carnival atmosphere. People meet on trains, whether by design or happenstance. You can of course reserve a seat for yourself. In the past you could reserve an entire compartment. But train travel inevitably brings the majority of passengers into contact with other passengers. When you go by train you do not choose your fellow travellers. You may know a few, but the majority will be strangers with whom you form a 'frail/ Travelling coincidence'.

Lastly, the steely direction of rail lines symbolizes an insistence on departure and arrival. There is a pathos about the railway station that has to do with the sensed rupture of lives: of individuals or families carried away from those they love. Hence the power of Auden's 'Dear, though the night is gone', a dream poem about the ending of a love affair whose setting is a room 'Cavernous, lofty as/ A railway terminus'. And hence Hardy's 'On the Departure Platform', where the male speaker recalls that 'We kissed at the barrier; and passing through/ She left me...// And she who was more than my life to me/ Had vanished quite'. It should come as no surprise that Hardy wrote several poems set on trains or at stations. (They include 'Midnight on the Great Western' and 'In A Waiting Room'.) These develop in different ways, but all take departure as their starting point. 'Joining and parting lines' define what lies beyond the station, and for Hardy parting is compelling because it focusses the irrecoverable uniqueness of a moment. The same may be said for joining, although I know of far fewer poems which celebrate that particular uniqueness. There is, though, John Montague's fine love poem, 'All Legendary Obstacles', whose last two stanzas run:

> At midnight you came, pale
> Above the negro porter's lamp.
> I was too blind with rain
> And doubt to speak, but
> Reached from the platform
> Until our chilled hands met.
>
> You had been travelling for days
> With an old lady, who marked
> A neat circle on the glass
> With her glove, to watch us
> Move into the wet darkness
> Kissing, still unable to speak.

Whereas in Hardy's poem the lover is cut off from the vision of 'she who was more than my life to me', the conclusion of Montague's poem brings the lovers together in a visionary moment intensified by the exclusion of the old lady from their circle of grace. In both cases, it is the presence of a watcher that gives the moment its significance. And it is altogether typical, or so I think, that the old lady on the train should at this moment become a kind of voyeur. This is a condition of travel. What you see from the window is invariably a life from which you are excluded but to which you may nevertheless feel in some way drawn. The old lady had, after all, been a travelling companion to the loved person now enclosed in silent communion with, from that old lady's point of view, a complete stranger.

The above remarks may have laboured the obvious. If so, my excuse is that they have a bearing on poems I want now to consider in some detail. Each of these poems offers a view of England at a crucial moment in twentieth-century history and it is essential to the meaning of each that the view should be a view from the train. Edward Thomas's 'Adlestrop' is so well known as perhaps to seem in need of no further comment than it has already attracted. Yet none of the discussions known to me focusses on what I think most important about this magical poem.

Yes. I remember Adlestrop –
The name, because one afternoon
Of heat the express-train drew up there
Unwontedly. It was late June.

The steam hissed. Someone cleared his throat.
No one left and no one came
On the bare platform. What I saw
Was Adlestrop – only the name

And willows, willow-herb, and grass,
And meadowsweet, and haycocks dry,
No whit less still and lonely fair
Than the high cloudlets in the sky.

And for that moment a blackbird sang
Close by, and round him, mistier,
Further and further, all the birds
Of Oxfordshire and Gloucestershire.

It feels at first difficult to know what prompts the apparently inconsequential memory with which the poem begins. 'Yes'. The affirmation of that single word, of the voice starting out of silence, seems immediately denied by the full stop that follows it, although a reason for memory doing its unprompted work emerges as the syntax struggles to discover significance in the place name and then, more securely, focusses on the run-over word, 'Unwontedly'. Express trains do not usually stop at wayside halts. Besides, there was no apparent reason for the unwonted stop: no one left and no one came on the bare platform. But this odd event, or rather seeming non-event, nagging at some corner of Thomas's consciousness, reminds him that the time was 'late June'. Still, it's a puzzle. Why *should* he remember this moment? Why *this* moment? What can have triggered the memory? The answer to these questions does not come through rational explanation but by the sudden release of further memory. The apparently dismissive 'only the name' at the end of the second stanza is followed not by a full stop but by the rhythmic surge that takes us into the third stanza, and now the poem moves in a way entirely different from the sluggish waywardness of the first two stanzas. It is as though a blockage has been cleared from the mind's conduit to the past, and the lines now pulse with an ebullience that brims over the closing stanza's last line: 'Of Oxfordshire and Gloucestershire'. The feminine rhyme on 'mistier/Gloucestershire' signals a radical departure from the monosyllabic masculine rhymes with which the poem had previously made do. (There is a stress on the syllable 'shire' but it is not especially heavy and the word can easily be pronounced as a dactyl, as can – I would say should – 'mistier'.)

The second half of 'Adlestrop' provides an evocation of what Thomas himself called a 'heart of England'. There is no space here to enquire into the reasons for his compulsive searching for what proved endlessly elusive both as place and name.[14] I want merely to note that the phrase 'late June' is subtly resonant not merely of a time of month but of time on a larger scale. Thomas wrote 'Adlestrop' early in 1915, when he was beginning to ask himself whether he should enlist for military service. (He joined the Artists' Rifles in July of the same year.) 'Late June' must then look back to the month of immediate pre-war England. That this is so can be verified by an entry in one of Thomas's Manuscript Field Note Books in the Berg Collection of the New York Public Library. It reads:

> 23 June 1914. A glorious day from 4.20 a.m. and at 10 tiers of white cloud with dirtiest grey bars above the sea of slate and dull brick by Battersea Park. Then at Oxford tiers of pure white with loose longer masses above and gaps of dark clear blue above hay-making and elms. Then we stopped at Adlestrop, through the willows could be heard a chain of blackbirds' songs at 12.45 and one thrush and no man seen, only a hiss of engine letting off steam.
>
> Stopping outside Campden by banks of long grass, willowherb and meadowsweet, extraordinary silence between two periods of travel – looking out on grey dry stones between metals and over it all the elms willows and long grass – one man clears his throat – a greater than rustic silence. No house in view. Stop only for a minute till signal is up.[15]

It is clear that when Thomas came to write his poem he amalgamated details from the Note Book in such a way as to convert several 'minutes' into the one. He also, more significantly, imbues that key minute with an implication it did not have for him on June 23, 1914, and which it could not have had before the events of August of that year. Then, and only then, 'late June' took on the meaning of a last moment of prelapsarian England. There is even a hint that the remorseless modernity represented by the express train, that emblem of a world of machinery of which the Great War was to prove the confirmation, grants Thomas a minute's stay against the irresistible force with which he is being carried into the future. And it is notable that the English shires through which birdsong travels are empty of people. 'No man seen ... . No house in view', the prose entry records. The poem allows us to infer that a heart of England has been emptied of human presence or is so ancient as to be as yet untroubled by such presence. Either way, it is 'late June'. The visionary minute has gone.

'Adlestrop' can therefore properly be called a war poem, not in the obvious sense that it is about battlefield and carnage, but because of its deep apprehension of an England changed forever, a lost England.[16] Moreover, Thomas feels himself to be very much the isolated observer: 'I remember', 'I saw'. This condition of being a kind of travelling flâneur may be contrasted with an earlier prose piece where Thomas had delightedly recorded the talk of two men with whom he and others travelled in a crowded third-class carriage. One was a sailor, 'a tall, ponderous, kind-faced man made in three distinct stories, who supported his enormous red hands upon knees each fit to have been the mould of a hero's helmet'. The other, who belatedly joins them, Thomas guesses to be 'a printer, perhaps – with a twisted face and simple and puzzled expression that probably earned him many a laugh from street-corner boys'. Both, in other words, are somehow behind the times. Their talk is soon filled with bawdy reminiscence to which the other occupants of the compartment listen: a small boy stares 'open-mouthed and wide-eyed', a trim shop assistant cannot 'conceal his cold contempt for men so sunken as to give themselves away like this', and a 'dark, thin, genial, pale-faced puritan clerk' looks pitifully 'at these *children*, for such he regarded them and would not wholly condemn'. Nor does Thomas condemn the other onlookers. On the other hand he does reflect that 'All were botanists who had heard and spoken words but had no sense of the beauty and life of the flower because fate had refused, or education destroyed, the gift of liberty and joy'.[17] The key words here, liberty and joy, point to Thomas's own emotional and political commitments. Liberty and joy are the properties of sailor and printer. Printers are always embodiments of liberty for socialists and Thomas was a socialist.

These properties or values are attributed to the elusive, never-to-be-tracked-down man whom Thomas meets for one minute at the beginning of his great poem, 'Lob'. That man, with a face 'by life and weather cut/ And coloured, – rough, brown, sweet as any nut,/ A land-face, sea-blue eyed', tells the wandering poet: "Nobody can't stop 'ee. It's/ A footpath, right enough."' Wiltshire speech goes with the inherited and assumed right of common ownership of the land. When, later in the poem, Thomas seeks some information about who the man might have been, someone tells him that it sounds like a man 'I saw when I was a child./I could almost swear to him. The man was wild/ And wandered. His home was where he was free'. Wandering is a testament to freedom, to liberty. It is the inherent claim both to untrammelled possession of the earth held in common and to untrammelled thought and speech.[18] The old Wiltshireman is a revisiting of the emblematic printer and sailor (he combines both land-face and sea-blue eyes) but is more elusive than the two men in whose salty speech Thomas so rejoices.

It seems that 'Lob' was written sometime between March and April, 1915, a few months after 'Adlestrop'. And it may be important that in both poems Thomas's imagination is triggered by an unlooked-for event whose significance is slow to reveal itself.[19] But at least in 'Lob' Thomas is able to talk to others. In 'Adlestrop' he is quite cut off from the scene the express train so unexpectedly and momentarily intrudes upon. 'Someone clears his throat', but not to talk to Thomas.

And yet, isolated as he may be, he is not *really* the travelling flâneur. For there is an unmistakably strong sense of emotional commitment to, a deep recognition of, a place that is at once legendary – the primal garden – and geographically placeable: Adlestrop, Oxfordshire, Gloucestershire. And it is this complex of feelings which the poem uncovers or perhaps recovers and as a result of which Adlestrop itself becomes far more than a remembered name.

In a letter to T. S. Eliot, his editor at Faber, Louis MacNeice explained that his new, long poem, *Autumn Journal*, which he had written between August and December 1938, was 'Not strictly a journal but giving the tenor of my intellectual and emotional experiences during that period ... It contains reportage, metaphysics, ethics, lyrical emotion, autobiography, nightmare'.[20] Eliot himself called the poem 'both a panorama and a confession of faith' and the opening lines are nothing if not panoramic.

> Close and slow, summer is ending in Hampshire,
>   Ebbing away down ramps of shaven lawn where close-clipped yew
> Insulates the lives of retired generals and admirals
>   And the spyglass hung in the hall and the prayer-books ready in the pew
> And August going out to the tin trumpets of nasturtiums
>   And the sunflowers' Salvation Army blare of brass
> And the spinster sitting in a deck-chair picking up stitches
>   Not raising her eyes to the noise of the 'planes that pass
> Northward from Lee-on-Solent. Macrocarpa and cypress
>   And roses on a rustic trellis and mulberry trees
> And bacon and eggs in a silver dish for breakfast
>   And all the inherited assets of bodily ease
> And all the inherited worries ... .

'Panorama', the OED says: 'A picture of a landscape or other scene, either arranged on the inside of a cylindrical surface with the spectator in the centre (a cyclorama) or unrolled and unfolded and made to pass before the spectator so as to show the various parts in succession'. That root meaning comes from the late eighteenth century, when panoramic views of cities were all the rage and attracted sizeable audiences to showrooms across London. Later, the term comes to mean 'A complete and comprehensive survey or presentation of a subject'. MacNeice's panorama does not, though, offer a mere survey of a scene. The observing eye moves like a tracking camera from the outer scene of lawn and yew into an interior shot – the hall; and it allows the poet to guess at the lives of retired generals and admirals as well as 'the spinster sitting in a deck-chair'.

How does MacNeice *know* she is a spinster, we may wonder? The probable answer is that he thinks of her as one of those many women who, after the Great War had killed their husbands, lovers and fiancés, were left alone to pick up their lives as the woman in the deck-chair picks up stitches. (In 1911 the ratio of females to males was 1068 to 1000; in 1921 this had become 1096 to 1000. The difference may not seem all that great but we need to remember that it was concentrated in the age group 20 to 35.) And the image of the spinster carries a further *frisson.* This knitter in the sun can, after all, hint at a classical Fate, the sign of epoch's end. 'Summer is ending'. The Great War had begun in August, 1914. In the summer of 1938 many people felt that the next war was imminent. On 28 May Hitler had given orders that the Sudeten-German question must be settled once and for all. In mid-August German troop manoeuvres suggested that the Nazis were about to invade Czechoslovakia. 'War seemed to be coming nearer as August ended', C. L. Mowat remarks in *Britain Between the Wars*, and the opening lines of Autumn Journal bear testimony to this.[21] The retired generals and admirals may be insulated from reality but the spyglass and prayer-books 'ready in the pew' tell of premonitional fears, as perhaps does the 'noise of planes'. (A Cabinet-approved programme of 1936 to build 8000 aeroplanes for the Royal Air Force in three years was upgraded in April, 1938, to a programme for 12,000 new aeroplanes in two years.) But in that case why does the spinster not look up? Probably because the noise of these planes is reassuringly familiar. Lee-on-Solent was where BOAC kept its fleet of flying boats, and at a guess the aeroplanes that 'pass/ Northward' are on urgent, voluntary errands to the still free world.

Imminent destiny as against the dailiness of life. The tension is caught in the playful, vivid images of nasturtiums' tin trumpets and sunflowers' 'blare of brass – of children's and Salvation Army's playing at war – and the same may be said for the upper-class alfresco breakfast scene. It is just possible that MacNeice knew Elizabeth Daryush's great sonnet, 'Still Life', written a little earlier, with its evocation of

the polished breakfast-table, laid
round a bowl of crimson roses, for one –
a service of Worcester porcelain, arrayed
near it a melon, peaches, figs, small hot
rolls in a napkin, fairy rack of toast,
butter in ice, high silver coffee pot,
and, heaped on a salver, the morning's post.

The heiress who comes in to breakfast feeling that 'even the unopened future lies / like a love-letter, full of sweet surprise', is, so the concluding couplet hints, about to experience a dark awakening from her life of unquestioning privilege.[22]

But where Daryush focusses on a single scene, MacNeice's panoramic survey allows the alfresco breakfast no more importance than any other view that passes before his and our eyes. All are equably brought to our attention as the leisurely sentences unspool over the verse paragraphs. (The first sentence alone runs for nine-and-a-half lines.) The poet is after all on a train, and so has time to look about him at the changing scene. And what he observes prompts reflective consideration. In this opening entry of *Autumn Journal* MacNeice thinks of the young who will not stay where it is 'All quiet on the Family Front' but who have 'taken the train to town or the two-seater / Unravelling rails or road, / Losing the thread deliberately behind them – / Autumnal palinode'.

The image of the unravelled, lost thread is teasingly complex. I assume MacNeice to mean that the young, knowing there is no escape route from the labyrinthine ways of fate, have chosen to abandon the hopeless search for a solution to Europe's ills and instead head for the momentary pleasures that beckon from London. Their autumnal palinode expresses a rejection of earlier dreams (or hopes) for a purposive, ameliorative account of history. As he had already written, in the poem which provides the title for his collection of 1938, *The Earth Compels*, 'Our freedom as free lances/ Advances towards its end ... And soon, my friend,/ We shall have no time for dances'. It is no coincidence that E. M. Forster, the writer who meant so much to the MacSpaunday group, was at this time announcing in his credo, 'What I Believe', that the unquenchable lights of his aristocracy – the plucky, the considerate and the sensitive – signal to each other under the encroaching darkness, '"Come along – anyway, let's have a good time while we can"'.[23]

Yet the promise of a good time, however brief, may be no more than illusion.

> And I am in the train too now and summer is going
> South as I go north
> Bound for the dead leaves falling, the burning bonfire,
> The dying that brings forth
> The harder life, revealing the trees' girders,
> The frost that kills the germs of laissez-faire;
> West Meon, Tixted, Farnham, Woking, Weybridge,
> Then London's packed and stale and pregnant air.

This is not merely an account of autumn weather. It blends literal and metaphoric in a forecast of the imminent and perhaps to be welcomed death of economic liberalism. The burning bonfire does not have to presage the blitz (although fears of aerial bombardment were by 1938 understandably real); nor need it be read as that everlasting bonfire of hell evoked with such drunken relish by the porter of Dunsinane. But as the train journey moves inexorably into London, first through named north Hampshire towns and then those of Surrey, so actual places are brought within the scope of a threatening, inescapable future. London's air is dense with lack-lustre frowstiness, of exhausted lives, yet at the same time it throbs with expectancy. The hard time coming promises a new beginning as much as it threatens an end. Hence the appropriateness of a train journey, of the panoramic implications of the unfolding view. For this links the lives of retired generals and admirals to the young who are abandoning the insulated country life for London's ambiguous pleasures. Or rather, the line from privileged southern retreat to metropolis establishes connections that the former may wish to deny but which history will enforce. And unlike Thomas, who remembers a momentarily glimpsed and irrecoverably lost vision of prelapsarian England (lost that is to all but imaginative recall), who is outside the event memory summons up and which seals off past from present ('And for that minute a blackbird *sang*), MacNeice uses only present tense and present participle. Moreover, while he may at the very opening of the poem see himself as a detached observer, noting with a kind of novelistic exactness the details that make up lives unlike his own, the shared train journey, that takes him into London's 'packed and stale and pregnant air', delivers him into a present and, beyond it, future which will be held in common. 'And I am in the train too now'.[24]

'The Whitsun Weddings', which was written in the autumn of 1958, is undoubtedly the most famous post-war English poem of train travel. Although it does not lack for praise it has come under attack from two very different directions. The first is that most eloquently voiced by Donald Davie. Davie thought of Larkin as the nation's unofficial poet laureate, although he did not mean this to stand as unqualified praise. 'We recognise in Larkin's poems the seasons of present-day England, but we recognise also the seasons of an English soul'. And these seasons run together to produce a level uniformity of response to England and its landscapes that Davie, with 'The Whitsun Weddings' in mind, describes as 'scrupulously neutral'.

> There is no meaning, no 'placing', in the way in which preindustrial things like farms, cattle, hedges, and grass are interspersed with industrial things like chemical froth and dismantled cars. And for Larkin indeed this seems to be one of the rules of the game; there is to be no historical perspective, no measuring of present against past ... . Larkin, as regards landscape and architecture and indeed literature also, agrees to tolerate the intolerable for the sake of human solidarity with those who don't find it intolerable at all ... [This is a] poetry of lowered insights and patently diminished expectations.[25]

Although Davie struggles to set out what he might have called a 'scrupulously neutral' account of Larkin, his strong dislike for what he takes to be Larkin's non-judgemental level gaze comes through loud and clear.

Merle E. Brown, on the other hand, is far from granting Larkin the democratic tolerance of which Davie as good as convicts him. In *Double Lyric: Divisiveness and Communal Creativity in Recent English Poetry*, Brown takes Larkin to task for his snobbish condescension towards the wedding parties he describes. No neutrality here, Brown says, not in the implied distaste with which Larkin talks of

> The fathers with broad belts under their suits
> And seamy foreheads; mothers loud and fat;
> An uncle shouting smut; and then the perms,
> The nylon gloves and jewellery-substitutes,
> The lemons, mauves, and olive-ochres

And who is Larkin to be certain that of all the wedding parties on board his train 'none/ Thought of others they would never meet/ Or how their lives would all contain this hour', while the privileged poet, more sensitive, more reflective, 'thought of London spread out in the sun'?[26]

Although we may at first think it impossible to sustain both objections – Larkin can hardly be accused of too much tolerance *and* of too much disdain – it could be argued that whereas he is distressingly little bothered about the degrading of the English countryside – and by extension its cultural history – he *does* see the wedding parties in terms that are familiar to us from Ealing Comedies and TV sit-coms: of working-class stereotypes presented as amiably comic butts of a more refined humour, in this case the poet's, and with which we as readers 'of good sense' are invited to identify. In a footnote to a characteristically knotty piece he contributed to a special number of *Agenda* devoted to his own work, Geoffrey Hill protests that such good sense, claimed for Larkin by Christopher Ricks, represents 'an assumption, a narrow English possessiveness ... 'Good sense', so propertied, so keen to admit others, at a price, to its properties, strikes me as a deplorable kind of *bienseance*'.[27] What, we may ask, with Hill's protest in mind, would the fathers, the uncles and above all the girls make of Larkin's poem? Would they see the good sense of Larkin's view of them as almost comic postcard caricatures?

To ask these questions is inevitably to draw attention to what may seem fatally limiting in Larkin's position as poet-voyeur. His stance as man of lonely, cosseted sensibility can look perilously close to self-congratulation. And it is precisely this of which Merle Brown convicts him and which Hill echoes in his attack on narrowly propertied good sense. But is it fair? 'At first I didn't notice what a noise/ The weddings made', Larkin reports. Then they begin to invade his consciousness. 'Struck, I leant / More promptly out next time, more curiously, / And saw it all again in different terms: / The fathers with broad belts ...'. 'Different terms' may well suggest, indeed I think it does suggest, that Larkin now decides to accommodate the wedding parties to the available clichés of Donald Magill or Ealing Comedies. Hence the colon after the key word 'terms': what follows is a catalogue of available images. He does not, that is, claim that he is able to see the truth about these parties, but that the images which seem appropriate to the middle-class intellectual/writer are quite likely to reveal more about class separateness than those whom they pretend to define. The uncle may not really be shouting smut although to the middle-class watcher from the window it seems appropriate that he should be doing so. In which case Larkin is not so much condescending to those about whom he writes as admitting to the probable inadequacies of the terms available to him. That he is far from certain he has properly accounted for what he registers is surely apparent when he remarks that 'each face *seemed* to define/ Just what it saw departing: children frowned / At something dull; fathers had never known // Success so huge and wholly farcical ...' (my italics). And then he adds, 'Free at last, / And loaded with the sum of all they saw, / We hurried towards London ...'. They see, but what they see remains a mystery he can only guess at.

But why does he then think of himself as the one who is reflectively attuned to 'how their lives would all contain this hour', while none of them 'Thought of the others they would never meet'? To repeat Brown's question, how does he *know*? Isn't this to identify himself as a man apart, a special case: a poet? The questions necessarily point a criticism of Larkin. But the most satisfactory answer to them is one that releases him from the criticism. It is that he imagines the couples happily wrapped up in each other for this hour at least, whereas he really is on his own. Larkin's assumption of the enclosed contentment of the couples is far more acceptable than Brown's stern belief that even in the hour after marriage the newly-weds would or ought to be thinking about the others they would never meet. Can't they have even one hour to themselves? Especially as the future awaits them, 'with all the power/ That being changed can give'. In the poem's last stanza Larkin, who at the outset had certainly been the self-absorbed poet, now repeatedly identifies himself with the couples: 'There *we* were aimed … *we* raced across/ Bright knots of rail ... *we* slowed again' (my italics). What he calls 'this frail/ Travelling coincidence' has momentarily at least brought him into some sort of imaginative symbiosis with lives very different from his own. Hence, the great, irreducibly ambiguous ending:

> And as the tightened brakes took hold, there swelled
> A sense of falling, like an arrow-shower
> Sent out of sight, somewhere becoming rain.

This is both orgasmic and detumescent, holding out the hopes of fertility and fears of loss. The excitement of arrival is also the sadness of parting. What after all can be predicted for the frail travelling coincidence when it has ended in London? Class will probably divide from class as couple from couple, and couples may themselves divide. Yet the effect of 'being changed' may be a true transformation to set against frail coincidence. Perhaps the rain will water and so make fertile London, 'its postal districts packed like squares of wheat'.

And to say this brings me back to Donald Davie and his scarcelyconcealed contempt for Larkin's tolerant acceptance of the second-rate, of industrialized landscapes. Not even Davie would deny the almost luminous quality of Larkin's evocation of this landscape, which begins where

> The river's level drifting breadth began,
> Where sky and Lincolnshire and water meet.
>
> All afternoon, through the tall heat that slept
>   For miles inland
> A slow and stopping curve southwards we kept.
> Wide farms went by, short-shadowed cattle, and
> Canals with floatings of industrial froth;
> A hothouse flashed uniquely: hedges dipped
> And rose: and now and then a smell of grass
> Displaced the reek of buttoned carriage-cloth
> Until the next town, new and nondescript,
> Approached with acres of dismantled cars.

Thomas's express train was headed across the English shires, MacNeice had journeyed north to London from the 'home counties', but Larkin's train curves *south* to the capital. It is Larkin alone who registers something of the England of burgeoning town and depleted countryside, of the nation's mixture of industry and rural circumstance. Here, then, it is surely significant that 'industrial froth' is almost magically transformed by the playful/pastoral cloudiness of 'floatings'. (And it is equally significant that Davie converts Larkin's phrase into 'chemical froth' and so ignores the fact to which Larkin pays attention: that the spoiled canals are at any rate evidence that people work here.) Larkin also of course registers Lincolnshire's wide spaces in a manner Tennyson himself might have envied: the leisurely connectives of 'sky and Lincolnshire and water' dawdling from the languorous ease of that previous line: 'The river's level drifting breadth began'. I know we are supposed to shun 'practical criticism' on the grounds that it colludes with the very text it is our duty to resist. Resist if you will; I would rather rejoice that someone can write as wonderfully as this. And I would also note that in writing as he does here and later in the poem, where he notes how 'An Odeon went past, a cooling tower,/ And someone running up to bowl', Larkin absorbs and converts a changing landscape into a panoramic vision that is akin to MacNeice's and yet which accepts all its signs as collective evidence of the place where the wedding parties come from. This is middle England. Write *it* off and you write *them* off.

To say this brings me back to Connie Chatterley's musings over a spot of middle England. 'What could possibly become of such a people, a people in whom the living intuitive faculty was dead as nails'. F. R. Leavis used to quote that approvingly to show how Lawrence was able truly to diagnose the ills of England. (Ills which clearly had not reached Downing College, Cambridge.) Davie is aligned with such diagnosis. The Leavisian tone, especially in its contempt for ordinary lives, was, in the late 1950s – the time when Larkin wrote 'The Whitsun Weddings' – the predominant tone of English letters, especially in the academy. Jibes against such ordinariness were routinely delivered *ex cathedra* and *ad hominem*. Not long after 'The Whitsun Weddings' had first seen the light of day I was in the audience when Leavis assured his listeners that there could never be another Dickens because 'this is the age of telly and Tottenham Hotspur'. His admirers nodded and laughed approvingly.

Larkin's train journey is one of discovery. As he acknowledges, his terms for the people about whom he is made curious may well mark him out unreally from the rest. But then this is a fact of class to which the journey's travelling coincidence momentarily at least both testifies and by an effort of imaginative sympathy overcomes. He gets beyond 'terms' so to say. What is seen and heard first beyond the window and then in the carriage is not so narrowly propertied that it cannot be accepted in a spirit of generous good sense.

1997

Notes

1 Donald Read, *England 1868-1914*, London, 1979, 417. Read takes the remark from an article by Joseph Pennell on 'Motors and Cycles: The Transitional Stage', *Contemporary Review*, 1 February 1902. Pennell argues that because only the wealthy can afford them, cars powerfully emphasize class divisions.

2 Kenneth Grahame, *The Wind in the Willows*, London, 1908.

3 E. M. Forster, *Howards End*, London, 1910.

4 Read, *England, 1868-1914*, 417.

5 For more on this see my essay 'The Sunlight on the Garden' in Carola M. Kaplan and Anne B. Simpson (eds), *Seeing Doub1e: Revisioning Edwardian and Modernist Literature*, New York, 1996.

6 Edward Thomas, *The South Country*, 1909; rpt. London, 1993), 196. As to dust, Read notes that 'the condition of many country roads at the end of the nineteenth century was poor. Clouds of dust were thrown up by the speeding pneumatic tyres of bicycles and cars'. *England 1868-1914*, 416. For both Forster and Thomas, such dust is a metaphor for the dust of death.

7 Read, *England, 1868-1914*, 417.

8 In a lecture given at Loughborough University in 1991, the historical geographer Peter Bishop noted that by a remarkable coincidence Constable's 'Cornfield' was sold to the National Gallery in 1837, the year of the discovery of protein. From then on the painting became iconographically identified with promoting bread as staple diet. Hence the fact it is so often incorporated into advertisements for flour and bread. Hovis adverts were especially adept in making use of it. As to Shell, its *Guide to Britain* – first published in 1964 – is offered both as a summation of earlier and more local guides and also as a *vade-mecum* for the traveller by car anxious to discover odd corners of Britain. It should be noted that Shell-Mex house plays host to a significant collection of mid-twentieth-century British artists, all of whom were at one time or another employed by the company.

9 *Letters of D. H. Lawrence*, Cambridge, 1982, vol. II, 431-32.

10 D. H. Lawrence, *Lady Chatterley's Lover*, London, 1928, chapter 11.

11 Lawrence was revising his novel after the defeat of the general strike in 1926, when authority was increasingly exercising triumphalist repressive power. Connie Chatterley's diatribes against England therefore tend to be uttered with authorial approval.

12 Quoted by Mary Moorman, *William Wordsworth: A Biography*, 2 vols, Oxford, 1968, vol. II, 561.

13 For a fuller account see Moorman, vol. II, 561-65.

14 For Thomas's search for a heart of England see my pages on him in *Modern English Poetry*: Hardy to Hughes, London, 1985, esp. 84-92.

15 Quoted by R. George Thomas, *The Collected Poems of Edward Thomas*, Oxford, 1981, 135-36.

16 Perhaps the most eloquent expression of this sense of loss is to be found in the title essay of Henry James's *Within The Rim*, London, 1915.

17 This forms an episode from a chapter called 'A Railway Carriage', *The South Country*, 73-75. The railway carriage would be third-class. Such carriages made possible a social mix, where 'real life' could be encountered. The carriage in which MacNeice travels in the opening section of *Autumn Journal* must, given the nature of some of its occupants, also be third-class. For more on this see Note 24, below.

18 For more on 'wandering' see my *English and Englishness: Poetry and Ideas of Nationhood* 1688-1900, London, 1990, esp. 71-74 and 135-60.

19 I have read that Thomas may have thought the name Adlestrop was derived from 'Apple Orchard' and thus signified a kind of primal, Edenic garden. I cannot find the evidence for this (false) etymology. He was however fascinated by place names as was Ivor Gurney; both poets belong to a moment when the recovery of a multi-layered English history was being attempted, or disinterred (as can be seen from their and others' interest in folk-ballad and tale); and Thomas was an assiduous collector and, implicitly,

historian of place names as of much else beside.

20 Quoted by Edna Longley in *Louis MacNeice:* A Study, London, 1988, 56.

21 For a good account of the events of the latter half of 1938 see C. L. Mowat, *Britain Between the Wars*, 1918-1940, London, 1956, 605-25.

22 Daryush's poem was first published in *The Lost Man and Other Verses*, Oxford, 1936. As she was the daughter of Robert Bridges and to that extent an 'Oxford' poet it is entirely possible that MacNeice knew her work.

23 'What I Believe' was published as a Hogarth pamphlet in 1939 and re-printed in *Two Cheers For Democracy*, London, 1951. My quotation comes from *Two Cheers*, 84. However, the essay was first published earlier. At the beginning of 1938 The Nation (New York) invited Forster to contribute to its series 'On Beliefs'. His essay, then called 'Two Cheers for Democracy', was published later that year, in time for MacNeice to have read it. For this, see P. N. Furbank, *E. M. Forster: A Life*, 2 vols, London, 1977-78.

24 In a longer account I would wish to discuss some other moments in *Autumn Journal* where train travel is all-important as a way of 'seeing' contemporary history. And in these instances, too, MacNeice goes third-class or its foreign equivalent. Here, I will note that Eric Ravilious's famous and haunting water-colour of 1940, 'Train Landscape', features a view of what I assume to be the white horse of Uffington as seen from the window of a third-class carriage, or, more strictly, compartment. (The figure 3 is prominent on the door placed in the middle of the picture.) Ravilious must have been working on the painting at the time of or in the aftermath of the blitz and the painting is intended to suggest that England will be forever England, that the English will collectively resist foreign invasion. The white horse was for long thought to have been carved by King Alfred to celebrate his victory over the Danes in 878. William Morris had referred to that belief in his essay, 'Thoughts Under an Elm tree', an impassioned plea for the worthwhileness of a socialist vision of England, 'an England worth fighting for'. Ravilious was a member of the AIA and had donated works to be

sold to raise money for the International Brigade fighting in the Spanish Civil War.

25 Donald Davie, *Thomas Hardy and British Poetry*, London, 1974, 65-71.

26 Merle E. Brown, *Double Lyric: Divisiveness and Communal Creativity in Recent English Poetry*, London, 1980.

27 See footnote 69 to 'Four 'Psalms of Assizen', in *Agenda*, 34.2 (1996): 27.

FROM SEVERN TO SOMME

Ivor Gurney and the poetry of pain and protest

Ivor Gurney, *Collected Letters*. Edited by R.K.R. Thornton. Ashington: Mid-Northumberland Arts Group/ Manchester: Carcanet, 1991. 579pp.

Since the publication in 1982 of P.J. Kavanagh's edition of the *Collected Poems*, Ivor Gurney's reputation has been on the up. Before then, he was typically dismissed as a minor Georgian poet whose survival depended on a few, regularly anthologized poems. Now he is coming to be regarded as a poet of the utmost importance. Yet as his letters reveal, had it not been for the First World War, it is unlikely that he would have taken poetry at all seriously. From 1911-14, Gurney was a student at the Royal College of Music, and music was both his first love and the art which he then intended to practice. True, he had begun to scribble verses during his time at the College, but there is no evidence that he saw this writing, which is, after all, common enough among students, as constituting any kind of commitment. It certainly didn't draw out of him the kind of excitement that pours through an early letter to his friend, the Gloucestershire poet, F.W. Harvey, about a compositional success:

> Willy, Willy, I have done 5 of the most delightful and beautiful songs you ever cast your beaming eyes upon. They are all Elizabethan – the words – and blister my kidneys, bisurate my magnesia if the music is not as English, as joyful, as tender as any lyric of all that noble host. Technique all right, and as to word setting – models ... How did such an undigested clod as I make them? That, Willy, I cannot say. But there they are ... .

That was written in the Spring of 1914. Not much more than a year later, Gurney tells Marion Scott that he is writing a ballad on the Cotswolds and that 'Someday maybe I'll write music with not less facility. *I* call this hefty good verse. Yet it flows (as R.L.S. said) like buttermilk from a jug'. There then follows a fairly unremarkable ballad, together with the comment that it 'strikes me as being a damgood piece of verse, and yet when I feel like it, it means the simple trouble of sitting down, opening my poetical pores and exuding as fast as pen will write – almost'. Two months later, in November 1915, he tells another female friend, Mrs Voynich, that 'though I have had more training in music than verse, yet a sonnet comes far easier to me than a prelude or any other small form in music. Perhaps it is because I am compelled to think of and have more to do with books than music, but it is certainly true that arrangement of words comes with far less effort than the other'. The point is only partly that soldiers, of whom Gurney was by then one, could pack books but not pianos in their kitbags; there is no doubt that poetry released in him a facility that he lacked as a musician.

And yet, while he was right to say that sonnets came to him far more easily than preludes, it has to be added that they came far too easily. Had Gurney been killed after writing his letter to Mrs Voynich, it is unlikely that he would now be more footnote to the tragic history of the War. The poetry he had begun to produce with such ease was amateurish, often embarrassingly so. It is to be doubted whether he fully understood this, at least in the first flush of enthusiasm at discovering he could write. He could, after all, see, on every side, work that was no better than his and yet which was regularly published and praised. More important, perhaps, he had no one with whom he could intelligently discuss his work. His fellow-students at the Royal College of Music were training to be professional musicians, and from the evidence we have it seems that their interest in literature was at best conventional. Marion Scott, the recipient of the bulk of the letters published in the volume under review, had been a student musician from 1896-1904, and when Gurney made her acquaintance, she was committed to working for the College. She probably knew a good deal about music, but it seems clear that she had precious little understanding of poetry. Her devotion to Gurney is deeply touching, her determination to help him get his poems published wholly honourable. But it would be difficult to argue that she was able to provide him with the tough, reliable criticism it seems reasonable to suppose he needed if he was to climb away from the cosy Georgianism in which his early work is effortlessly bedded.

Here, we are bound to register the contrast with Edward Thomas. Unlike Gurney, Thomas took a very long time to come to believe that he could write poetry, but in Robert Frost he had what Gurney lacked – a good friend who was also a serious poet and shrewd judge of literary worth and who recognized that in his prose writings Thomas had in fact served a hard apprenticeship to the craft of poetry. Besides, as a professional man of letters, Thomas knew most of the poets of the day and was required to write about a good deal of contemporary poetry, and Edna Longley's edition of his critical writings (*A Language Not to be Betrayed*) reveals just how fine a critic he was. By comparison, Gurney must appear to have been at a double disadvantage: he wasn't a trained writer, and with the exception of Harvey, a very minor poet, he didn't include writers among his friends.

To these disadvantages we must add a third – Gurney's recurrent mental illness, references to which thread their way through his letters. Quite what the illness was, is difficult to determine. The first reference to it comes in a letter to Marion Scott, sent some time during the summer of 1913. 'Thus it turns out – My brain, heart, nerves and physique are certified sound, but that I am overworked and quite run down'. Two years later, when the illness returns, it is given a name. Writing to Mrs Voynich in August, 1915, Gurney assures her that 'my health goes on improving, but slowly. Still, now I know what neurasthenia is; I realise and fight it – a great step'. In discussing the illness of 1913, Gurney's biographer, Michael Hurd, falls into line with Gurney's own account, which itself is clearly a rehash of what his doctor had told him. It was, Hurd says, 'a type of nervous breakdown brought on by the sustained effort of creative work'. Was this what was meant by neurasthenia? The term dates from the mid-nineteenth century and according to Eric Leed was mostly applied to 'a generalised anxiety syndrome that had been found primarily in private hospital rooms and exclusive sanatoria'. Before the outbreak of the war, that is. But from then on, neurasthenia became very much the illness associated with experience of war.

So at least Leed argues in his book *No Man's Land: Combat and Identity in World War I*. He quotes a Dr Hunt, medical officer at Gallipoli, as remarking that 'every man coming out of the Peninsula was neurasthenic, whether he was supposed to be fit or not ... all were in a condition of profound neurasthenia'. And Robert Graves is on record as saying that three months of trench warfare was enough to make any soldier neurasthenic. This may well be so, but it needs then to be said that at the time when Gurney was diagnosed as neurasthenic he was still in England. He didn't in fact get to France until May, 1916. And anyway, Gurney's illness seems rather to be linked with hypermania than with the 'functional nervous weakness, nervous debility', which were identified as the classic symptoms of neurasthenia. As he was emerging from the illness of 1915, he told Mrs Voynich that 'it is hard to control the mind. I only hope it will be as quick in the right direction one day'.

Two points emerge from all this. One, that while his experiences of war undoubtedly exacerbated Gurney's mental condition, they certainly didn't cause it. Two, that applying the medical definition of this condition, neurasthenia, at least in any sense in which the term was customarily used, seems to be a long way wide of the mark. These letters show that Gurney had far more insight into the nature of his illness than the doctors, even if he had to use their name for it. At its heart is all that can be unpacked from the word 'quick'. 'How the leaves must be flying on Cranham, and up and down and round in swirls on Portway!' he wrote to Marion Scott in October 1916, when he was in France. 'Painswick Beacon will stand as high and immovable as ever, and Birdlip too; I can do without them. But O for the wild woods and the leaves flying!' Like so much in the letters, this is on the verge of turning into lines of the urgently-stressed, bounding verse that would come to characterize the work of his great period. And it may explain why in a letter of February, 1917, he told Scott that 'there is no time to revise here, and if the first impulse will not carry the thing through, then what is written gets destroyed. One virtue I know little of – that is, patience; and my mind is Hamlet's, a wavering self-distrustful one, though quick and powerful at times'.

There is a further point. Once he had begun to write poetry, Gurney stuck at it, even when officially neurasthenic. In the letter to Marion Scott, already quoted, in which he speaks of verse flowing like buttermilk from a jug, and which was written at that time in 1915 when he was undoubtedly ill, he tells her that 'I find ballad making very grateful and comforting to the mind, and to praise one's own county makes it not the less joyous'. It is a crucial remark. 'Painswick Beacon ... and Birdlip too. I can do without them'. But he couldn't. In his introduction to the *Collected Poems*, P.J. Kavanagh rightly rejects the claim that Gurney can be stuck with the 'limiting tag of "local poet"'. Nevertheless, his deep commitment to place, his unsentimental, historically-informed understanding of his specific part of England, is absolute, and provides the material out of which most of his finest work is fashioned. He was never in any doubt about this. 'It is to be torn up by the roots for me to live flatly in a flat marsh like Essex, where the air is stagnant and unalive', he told Mrs Voynich. A month later, in October 1915, he writes to Marion Scott: 'As my health and spirits improve, so within me I find a store of poetry, an accumulation of pictures – dead leaves, Minsterworth Orchards, Cranham, Crickley and Framilode each. They do not merely mean intensely to me; they are me ...'. Another two months, and he is telling Mrs Matilda Chapman (the 'Comtesse' as he delighted to call her), 'as for Winter Trees – I believe, never are they so beautiful as now. Never are afterglows so far beyond words to describe as in Winter. And never is Teatime so lovely a thing to be looked forward to – or regretted most in the Army'. This finds an echo in a much later, tenderly solicitous letter he sent to F.W. Harvey, who was by then a prisoner of war, recalling with and for him the sunsets of their Gloucestershire, 'and Autumn afterglows'. And these finally find their way into one of his great poems, 'Felling a Tree'. Again, prose is on the way to becoming poetry, is quick with that 'football rush of him' – to appropriate the phrase he used to characterize George Chapman's prosodic energy.

But that was in the future. Even at the time of the letter to Harvey, Gurney was still caught in the restraints of Georgianism. Yet what these letters reveal is how far his reading was opening him up to poetry, and how astonishingly sure his judgment seems always to have been. He may have lacked the specific strengths Thomas took from his friendship with Frost and from his work as professional man of letters, but he got a long way on his own. It is pretty remarkable that in August 1915 he should tell Marion Scott that 'The sonnet of R.B. you sent me, I do not like. It seems to me that Rupert Brooke would not have improved with age, would not have broadened, his manner has become mannerism, both in rhythm and diction'. And in his voracious reading, recorded in letter after letter, he came unfailingly to recognize the poets who mattered, who could be of use to him. He discovers Wordsworth, Browning, Yeats ('"Suddenly I saw the cold and rook-delighting heaven" absolutely electrified me') and Edward Thomas. Above all, there is Whitman. 'Whitman is my latest discovery', he tells Mrs Voynich in September 1915, 'and he has taken me like a flood'; and the following year, begging Marion Scott to send books to him in France, he bursts out: 'Walt Whitman. I want him badly, worse than all the rest'. Later, he would discover Chapman, Jonson, and other sixteenth- and seventeenth-century writers, and between them they would help to set him free to write the poems of his great period. But Whitman meant the most, as of course he did to Lawrence. Lawrence and Gurney discovered Whitman at virtually the same moment, and Whitman offered both men a way to break free of poetic forms in which they could write with fatal ease but which allowed neither to develop what they really wanted to say.

Yet Gurney's passionate admiration is not limited to a liberation from Georgian constraints that Whitman offered him. Or rather, such constraints should not be thought in purely formal terms. Although his expressions of enthusiasm are for the most part very vague, on one occasion, at least, he is clear enough about why Whitman matters so much. 'Whitman, lover of common men', he calls him, in a long letter to Marion Scott, dated August 1, 1916. Some will perhaps see in this a hint of the homoeroticism which had undoubtedly brought Whitman other English admirers, such as Swinburne and Edward Carpenter. Gurney's letters, however, give very little away about his sexual preferences. The relationship with Marion Scott was friendly but no more than that, on his side at least; and although there seems to have been a brief fling with a V.A.D. nurse, Annie Drummond, whom he met while he was being treated in an Edinburgh hospital in the autumn of 1917 for the effects of gas, mention of her in letter soon dries up. On the other hand, there is nothing in them to suggest that he was drawn to Whitman because of the American poet's homosexuality. No, 'Lover of common men' refers to Whitman the democrat.

This is a key issue. Gurney may not be a socialist, although the letters certainly reveal a radical streak in him. We do, however, need to recognise that his view of war is very different from those officer poets whose voices are still often taken to be not merely an authentic response to its experiences but are held to be definitive. Here is Gurney writing to Mrs Voynich in June 1916. 'Our battalion [*sic*] gradually goes down in numbers and up in honour. We have been praised by the Corps Commander, singled out of the whole division for notice. Which is good, and I am indeed proud of my steady quiet comrades. Who vanish one by one notwithstanding, while the rest of us wait our turn'. The laconic wit of this is recognizably the same as that of 'The Silent One', a poem written in 1919: 'a finicking accent said/ "Do you think you might crawl through there: there's a hole."/ Darkness, shot at: I smiled, as politely replied – / "I'm afraid not, Sir."' It's a sobering thought that the 'finicking accent' might have belonged to Siegfried Sassoon or Wilfred Owen. It certainly didn't belong to the Silent One himself, whom Gurney recalls as someone who 'had chattered through/ Infinite lovely chatter of Bucks accent'. Here, therefore, it is important to note his joyful reports of the remarks of a man in his Company, Pte Tim Godding. 'A sergeant was going round collecting birthdays, (not for generous purposes) and one man hesitated to answer. Said T.G. "He don't know his birthday, he don't know his name. The sun hatched it"'. And to the same correspondent, Mrs Voynich, he writes, 'Someone was poking fun at him, and Tim, patient for a time, got all his own back with "Ah, mate, I was born too near a wood to be frightened with owls"'. 'These men,' he tells Herbert Howells, his friend from College days, 'are rough as a rule who swear frightfully, but are good men inside, and full of things for such as I to imitate'. The uneasy use of the nob's pronoun suggests well enough Gurney's sense that Howells is hardly likely to approve a love of common men.

The war, it seems clear, opened Gurney up to contradictions or confusions out of which much of his best poetry is made. Sending some poems to Marion Scott in March 1918, he told her, 'I hope you will like them, poor things. What is happening is that my real groove lay in Nature and Music, whereas Pain and Protest forced the other book into being'. The 'other book' is a reference to his first published volume, *Severn and Somme*, which had been published in November of the previous year. From now on, he assures Marion Scott, what he writes will be chiefly influenced by Edward Thomas and 'perhaps by Robert Graves – a true poet'. But, in fact, Gurney's true poetry engages with both sets of terms, although Pain and Protest show themselves less in the poems of that first volume than in some of the letters. For example"

> Since men who do so much for England have at last come to see what they love in Her, and what they would have Her be, and what they themselves desire to be – Since these men if they return are to do the work and to shape England anew, will they not have something to say on all the proposals for night-schools that are to make us the Swots of Europe, thereby dethroning Germany from that proud

position, and all the schemes to make them merely the builders of a huge trade? Are we to provide statistics to please the heart of the Times Economic Supplement leader writer! By heaven, I think not.

The rhetoric may feel a bit over-heated, but the anger and contempt for the voices of authority are unmistakable. They come out again in the poem 'Poor Folk', written in January 1917, no doubt under the influence of Sassoon's satires, but with a political edge that his poems lack (although it should be recalled that by then Sassoon was turning to the socialism he would publicly embrace in the post-war years). 'As how the poor who fight so well in France/ Die with a smile for England in some ditch,/ Seem never really to get a proper chance – / Their wars and justice made for them by the rich'. And then there is the letter of October 16, 1917, in which he tells Marion Scott that 'It is of more importance that the Duke of Bilgewater should respect and sympathise with Bill Jones than that the sun should never set on the British Empire, whose liberties have been kept alive by revolt against the fathers of the present "Prussians of England"'. He is replying to her protest against a sonnet he had sent her in which he had attacked those who made English people slaves 'under your mastery./ We'll have a word there too, and forge a knife./ Will cut the cancer threatens England's life.

Marion Scott was clearly shaken by the angry promise voiced in those lines, which, she could hardly avoid noticing, were being written at precisely the moment when revolution in Russia was gathering to a head. She saw herself implicated in the Prussians of England whom, in what she must have taken to be an exceptionally violent image, the sonnet vows to cut out. Not so, Gurney tells her, in the course of explaining that he cares 'more for the liberty of Englishmen, than for Liberty of England'. The people he has in mind are 'the foul hellspawn that preach war and escape service. Who will oppose disarmament ... . Who see nothing in the tragedy of Russia but a failure of discipline, and never a hint that slavery may sometimes result from oppression. What is Northcliffe? Winston Churchill? Devonport? Rhondda? And what but geographical accident shows them English?'

With this letter in mind, we can understand why he was so excited by 'Lob' and wanted to learn it by heart. 'Nobody can't stop 'ee. It's/ A footpath right enough'. England ought to be held in common by common men. But Thomas did not survive the war. Gurney did. He therefore knew of the defeats that could be visited on such men. From this comes 'Strange Hells', which juxtaposes the horror of war with what awaited the soldiers who managed to return to England:

> Where are they now, on state-doles, or showing shop-patterns
> Or walking town to town sore in borrowed tatterns
> Or begged. Some civic routine one never learns.
> The heart burns – but has to keep out of face how heart burns.

The near explosive rage of these lines – their burn – suggests what difficulties Gurney would find in keeping under control the 'I' who was required to speak to the owners of finicking accents. This may have something to do with his inability to find post-war work and with the terrible collapse of 1922. Whatever the explanation for this collapse, the letters he wrote out of despair as his mind gave way in the autumn of that year are almost too painful to read. But in the three years between his return to England and his final breakdown – and even in some of the later poems – he produced a body of work whose greatness is inseparably connected to his ability to engage both Pain and Protest and Nature and Music.

The *Collected Letters* will obviously provide invaluable material for any student of Gurney's work. It is therefore a matter of some regret that they should have been less than adequately edited. R.K.R. Thornton is to be praised for having tried to date each and every letter, but his annotation of them is very unsatisfactory. He tells us that when Gurney mentions the Choral Symphony he is referring to Beethoven's Ninth, and he identifies the more obvious quotations from or allusions to Shakespeare with which the letters are studded. But less obvious quotations go wholly unremarked, even though they indicate what

Gurney has been reading and are therefore of considerable importance. Gurney's own mis-quotations are sometimes picked up, sometimes not. And there are a troubling number of straightforward errors. Bennett did not write a novel called *Burned Alive*. Edward Thomas did not write a poem called 'Choose Me Your English Words'. Yeats's 'The Folly of Being Comforted' did not appear in Responsibilities. And so on. Any poet deserves better than this, and so marvellous a poet as Gurney deserves a great deal better.

1991

EDWARD THOMAS, IVOR GURNEY AND ENGLISH SOCIALISM

I don't know whether it was the great socialist historian R. H. Tawney who coined the phrase 'social history', but it seems likely. At all events, he made good use of it in a lecture called 'Social History and Literature', which he gave to the National Book League in 1949. The evidence of such history, Tawney tells his audience, is everywhere. And he offers as example:

> A tump – which the cultured call a tumulus – with neolithic bones which the aged roadman at last consented not to throw away; a precipitate lane beside it, known to the natives, though not to writers of guidebooks, as King Charles' Hill, because, on an early day in August 1643 some enterprising staff officer contrived – Heaven knows how – to get the army down it on its way to the siege of the godly city the unforeseen tenacity of whose obstinate shopkeepers wrecked the year's campaign; twenty minutes one way the room in which, thirty years before, the Catholic Throckmorton of the day had brooded with Catesby over projects for the famous plot; twenty minutes the other the farm called Abbey Farm, seized two generations earlier, by the Defender of the Faith from a local religious house; a mile north the high point known as Wittentree Clump, where the wise men of the district are thought to have assembled in Saxon times and the home guard in our own … .

All these places and more besides, Tawney concludes, can be visited with the aid of 'tolerable boots and a longish afternoon'.[1]

But Tawney is above all interested in discovering what the literature of an historical moment can tell us about the society which produced it and to which it, in a variety of ways, bears testimony. The moment he chooses to discuss at some length is Elizabethan England. And it soon becomes clear that Tawney sees that England as pretty much his ideal. It was, he tells his audience, 'a loosely knit, decentralised society, whose pattern of existence was a round of individual activities in a framework fixed by custom'. Over much of England land resources were so abundant in relation to population that "the wild wood' of the ballads, with its deer, its distinctive crafts, and its opportunities for lawless independence, was not only an economic necessity … but, in case of need, a trusted friend and refuge'. Moreover, in this England, 'Except among the nobility, and often among them, local sentiment was more powerful than class connexions; personal relations than the play of economic mechanism; custom than law; the wisdom of the elders and the lore of the region than stereotyped truths or fallacies standardised for class consumption'. The literature of this England, Tawney claims, draws on a body of experience which is not the monopoly of a single class, but is, in some degree, a general possession. It voices 'the outlook on life, not of an elegant elite, but of the world of common men'. As to music, it mattered to all. Tawney quotes a musical historian as remarking that music of the latter half of the sixteenth century 'proves most eloquently that the ordinary folk, especially the peasantry, were not only not incapable of creative thought, but a very important part of Elizabethan musical life'. This doesn't mean, Tawney adds, that composers such as Dowland and Morley self-consciously borrowed from folk melodies: 'The significant fact is the existence of a public whose spontaneous appetite for musical enjoyment made it alert to welcome and transmit them'.

As I imagine these quotations make clear, Tawney takes Elizabethan England to be the nation's great good time. And so when he comes to characterise the period in social historical terms, he sees it as the child of that happy interlude between two worlds: 'the meaningless ferocity of a feudalism turned senile … and the demure austerities of the first, pious phase of capitalism'.

To repeat, Tawney's lecture was given in 1949. The date is significant.

'Social History and Literature' testifies to Tawney's ardently humanist democratic socialism and ought therefore to be read as offering a corrective vision of the ideal society to the Labour administration then in power, whose philosopher-spokesman Tawney was and remained (Hugh Gaitskill would give the oration at Tawney's funeral in 1962, almost the Labour leader's last public appearance).

But what has this to do with either Edward Thomas or Ivor Gurney? A great deal, as it happens. Tawney is of their generation. He was born in 1880, one year after Thomas and ten years before Gurney. Like them, he fought in the First World War – as an n.c.o. – and like them his understanding of social history had much to do with his readiness to push his feet into a pair of tolerable boots in order to spend longish afternoons tramping the English countryside. I have no reason to suppose that he knew Gurney's 'Cotswold Ways', but had he done so he would have given immediate assent to its opening line: 'One comes across the strangest things in walks' (*Poems*, 95). And Gurney is plainly of a mind with Tawney about Elizabethan England, not only because the late nineteenth-century recovery of English music and composers of that period clearly affect Gurney's own musical preoccupations, but because in poem after poem he testifies to his belief in poetry as a craft rooted in common life. That is why, in 'We Who Praise Poets', he can speak of the task of making a poem as akin to the crafts of carpenter and stone mason:

> The crafted art, the smooth curve, and surety
> Come not of nature till the apprentice free
> Of trouble with his tools, and cobwebbed cuts,
> Spies out a path his own and casts his plots.
> Then looking back on four-square edifices
> And wind-and-weather-standing tall houses
> He stakes a court … .
> (Poems, 110)

And, for Gurney, England's 'Golden Age' coincided with the latter half of the sixteenth century. He says as much in a sonnet whose title is indeed 'The Golden Age'. Its concluding sestet runs:

> O for some force to swing us back there to some
> Natural moving towards life's love, or that glow
> In the word to be glow in the State, that golden age come
> Again, men working freely as nature might show,
> And a people honouring stage-scenes lit bright with fine sound
> On a free soil, England happy, honoured and joy-crowned.
> (*Poems*, 158)

This is almost a versification of Tawney's image of Elizabethan England.

I am not here concerned with the plausibility or otherwise of that image, with its stress on 'freedom' – a word to which I shall return. It hardly needs saying that other historians have produced very different readings of the period. I want merely to ask why Tawney should wish to identify Elizabethan England as an ideal moment. And the answer, obviously enough, is that during this period England somehow escapes being either feudal or capitalist. Tawney, growing up at the end of the nineteenth century, did not much like the dominant forces operating in the England in which he found himself. Nor did either Thomas or Gurney. Among those of the previous generation at odds with the values of nineteenth-century England, there had been a shared tendency to look back to an even earlier moment of England's social history in order to discover the nation's 'golden age'. For William Morris, that age roughly coincided with Chaucer. 'Here is God's plenty,' Dryden famously remarked of Chaucer's work. Morris thought the plenty less God's than the people's. And, taking his cue from Ruskin, Topsy saw in the work of medieval craftsmen a testimony to plenty which alone makes life worth living:

> Wealth is what Nature gives us and what a reasonable man can make out of the gifts of Nature for his reasonable use. The sunlight, the

> fresh air, the unspoiled face of the earth, food, raiment, and housing necessary and decent; the storing up of knowledge of all kinds, and the power of disseminating it; means of free communication between man and man; works of art, the beauty which man creates when he is most a man, most aspiring and thoughtful – all things which serve the pleasure of people, free, manly, and uncorrupted. This is wealth.[2]

These words come from Morris's great essay, 'Useful Work Versus Useless Toil', written in 1885. Like virtually all English socialists who came to maturity in the last years of the nineteenth century, Tawney was much influenced by Morris. As of course was Edward Thomas. In an article on Morris written in 1911, Thomas remarks that Chaucer, as man and poet, was 'social and not isolated', and that he offered 'not an individual but a corporate view of life.[3] In other words, Chaucer is as much immersed in the dailiness of things as the stone-mason or carpenter. And that Thomas thought that this was highly desirable for a poet is spelt out when he says that poetry for Morris

> was not, as it has tended more and more to be in recent times, a matter as exclusive as a caste. Morris was not half-angel or half-bird, but in all that he did a man on close terms with life and toil, with the actual troublous life of every day, with toil of the hands and brain together … .[4]

No wonder, then, that Thomas should have told Gordon Bottomley that 'Except William Morris there is no other man whom I would sometimes like to have been'.[5]

Morris wanted people to be 'free, manly, and uncorrupted'. There may be a dig at contemporary aestheticism in that word 'manly', but more likely Morris intends to recommend lives not warped by long factory hours and what he calls 'the shabby hell' of the late nineteenth-century city. Thomas shared Morris's detestation of the industrial city, just as he shared his belief in the value of free work. Indeed 'freedom' is a – perhaps the – key word for him, as it is for Gurney. (Gurney's appeal to 'Men working freely as nature might show … On a free soil' is cheek-by jowl to Morris's understanding of true wealth as being found in man's co-operative work with nature.) And it is this, I think, which explains what Stan Smith in his excellent monograph on Edward Thomas has called Thomas's 'Tolstoyan poems about digging and sowing and cutting wood'.[6] (These will of course be echoed by Gurney in such poems as 'The Hoe Scrapes Earth', 'Felling a Tree' and 'The Mangel-Bury' (*Poems*, 113, 136, 163).

Tolstoy is a relevant name to introduce here because his view of the dignity of peasant life and of co-operative labour is closely linked to many of the developments of arts-and-crafts communities which came into existence at the end of the nineteenth century, several of them in Gloucestershire itself. One such group settled first at Ewen, near Cirencester, then moved via Lord Bathurst's estate to Daneway. Here, Ernest Gimson, Sidney and Ernest Barnsley, together with assorted wives and children, settled down to make furniture (some of the finest went to Rodmarton Manor), much of it influenced by what Clive Aslet, in his splendid study *The Last Country Houses*, calls 'the traditional country crafts which could still be seen in Gloucestershire at the turn of the century, but which were on the point of extinction'.[7] Aslet instances 'the chamfer motif', and this motif may possibly have been somewhere at the back of Gurney's mind when he spoke of apprentice poets having to learn 'the crafted art, the smooth curve'. This is no more than speculation. And I offer as no more than a hunch the possibility that he could have known of Detmar Blow's 'soviet' at Hilles, the house Blow built for himself and his family in Gloucestershire. Blow, who had begun his apprenticeship to architecture as a disciple of Ruskin – Morris's master also – was deeply committed to the arts-and-crafts movement. And – further speculation – it may well have been this desire not just to escape the city but to find a kind of pre-capitalistic freedom, a communitas, which brought the Dymock poets together.

Such freedom can't always escape the charge of being merely *ersatz*. Aslet points out that the craftsmen employed by Gimson and the

Barnsleys were too skilled for their or the firm's own good: 'It was a paradox of Arts and Crafts furniture design that there was little demand for what were thought of as cottage-style products: Gimson and Barnsley, like Morris, found themselves "ministering to the swinish luxury of the rich"'.[8] As for Blow's democratic belief that there should be no servants' quarters and that servants should eat together with the family, 'at separate tables but sharing the same food and some of the same conversation. … this proved so embarrassing to both parties that the experiment had to be abandoned'.[9]

Blow is a good deal more innocent than Thomas. For while Thomas understands the social and moral propriety of Morris's concern to bring worker and intellectual together, he is also well aware of the gap that exists between the two. Thomas often writes from a position of one who yearns for a life from which he feels himself excluded simply because he belongs within a world of capitalist – and therefore – class separations. But he is passionately aware of another life, out there, back there – from which he is also separated. This becomes plain in a key moment in *The South Country*. Thomas here tells of his sense of the presence of natural beauty and joy restoring us

> not to the Middle Ages, not the days of Mr Doughty's heroic princes and princesses of Britain, not to any dim archaeologist's world of reeking marsh and wood, of mammoth and brutish men, but to a region out of space and out of time in which life and thought and physical health are in harmony with sun and earth … and out of all of it arises a vision of the man who will embody this thought, a man whom human infelicity, discontented with the past, has placed in a golden age still farther back, for the sufficient reason that in every age he has been a dream.[10]

'Free, manly, and uncorrupted' he might almost have called such a man.

In fact he called him 'Lob'.[11] For Lob tells the wandering poet who travelling through Wiltshire, fears he may be trespassing on private ground, 'Nobody can't stop 'ee. It's a footpath right enough', and he then adds:

> You see those bits
> Of mounds – that's where they opened up the barrows
> Sixty years since, while I was scaring sparrows.
> They thought as there was something to find there
> But couldn't find it, by digging, anywhere.

Lob here speaks out of an England not to be recovered by archaeology, nor as enclosed within any historical moment. Is it then a dream? Is Lob himself a dream? If so, he is a dream of that Englishness which Tawney located in his vision of Elizabethan England, where lore, custom, and individual activities made common men free men, liberated from feudal constraints and not yet tied to capitalist demands. Later in the poem another person tells Thomas that Lob is like 'one I saw when I was a child. I could almost swear to him. The man was wild and wandered. His home was where he was free'. 'Free': the word returns like a mantra. Lob is the free-born Englishman.

There is another, glimpsed example of such freedom in *The South Country*. It comes when Thomas takes a train journey and in what must be a third-class carriage (where the common people sit) he listens in on the talk of a printer and old sailor as they reminisce about their lives and loves. Other occupants of the carriage eavesdrop on the men's chatter (a word I use deliberately, for reasons that will emerge in due course).

> A trim shop assistant pretended to read about the cricket, but listened and could not conceal his cold contempt for men so sunken as to give themselves away like this.
>
> A dark, thin, genial, pale-faced puritan clerk looked pitifully – with some wrinkles of superiority that asked for recognition from his fellow-passengers – at these *children*, for as such he regarded them, and would not wholly condemn.
>
> Others occasionally jerked out a glance or rolled a leaderless eye or rustled a newspaper without losing the dense veil over their individuality that made them tombs, monuments, not men.

> One sat gentle, kindly, stupidly envying these two their spirited free talk, their gestures, the hearty draughts of life which they seemed to have taken.
>
> All were botanists who had heard and spoken words but had no sense of the beauty and life of the flowers because fate had refused, or education destroyed, the gift of liberty and joy.[12]

The one who sits envying the men is presumably Thomas himself (how else would he know that the listener felt envy?). He is with the others in that they all belong in a sealed-off world of separate individuals which lacks that 'corporate view of life' to be found in Chaucer – whose poetry is, it goes without saying, saturated with other voices (as is Thomas's). As for the printer and sailor, there is a deft, telling play on words in Thomas's ironic exposure of the shop-assistant's contempt for the fact the man 'give themselves away like this'. The free, unbridled talk of printer and sailor exists outside a world of money, where you sell your labour as dearly as you can and give freely of nothing. Printers are or at least were habitually connected to lawlessness, in that their activities brought them into conflict with rules and laws governing what the state decides is fit for all to know. As for the sailor, he is an obvious example of a wanderer (Lob is 'sea-blue-eyed'). Both men, Thomas says, possess the gift of liberty and joy. Neither lives by what can justifiably be called prudential values.

But both seem somehow marginal, as Lob does. They are fugitives from the forces of respectability that surround them in the railway carriage. Thomas seeks out the marginal because there and perhaps there only are to be found energies which operate as a decisive, overwhelmingly attractive alternative to the timid containments of those for whom fate or education – let's call it capitalism – have denied the possibility of liberty and joy. Hence the fact that Thomas is drawn to tramps, to the songs of people on the margins, like the Lincolnshire poacher, and to the gypsy.

Gypsies have traditionally had a bad time of it in English life as in literature. An early example is the 'Roman' dismissal of Cleopatra's 'gipsy's lust', a sneer at once xenophobic, racist and sexist. There is of course no temptation to identify Shakespeare with that view, but it would be difficult to disentangle Jane Austen (in *Emma*) and George Eliot (in *The Mill on the Floss*) from the panic which gypsies cause their fictional heroines. The unstated though implied dread of sexual licence has something to do with this. Gypsies are unbridled. They are also or perhaps therefore lawless; in the double sense that they don't obey the law and that they are outside it. They have no respect for property, whether such property comes in the shape of children, wives or land. They are not rooted, they are wanderers. They also of course carry with them the tang of forbidden dangers – the evil eye – and of pleasures: they are exotic, not English; they are other. The blood in Heathcliff's veins may be partly black blood, but it may also be gypsy blood. In his great *Dictionary of the English Language* (1755), Samuel Johnson defined gypsy as '1. A vagabond who pretends to foretell futurity; 2. A reproachful name for a dark complexion; 3. a name of slight reproach to a woman'. As for vagabond, it means, Johnson says: '1. without any settled habitation, wanting a home; 2. a vagrant, a wanderer, commonly in the sense of reproach; 3. one that wanders illegally, without a settled habitation'. And 'wandering' for Johnson 'hath always an ill sense'.

As I pointed out in my book *England and Englishness* (1990), Johnson's fear of wandering is an essential element of his settled conservatism, his deep disquiet at any expressed readiness to kick over the traces, whether these had been set up by court, parliament, church, or social propriety. For there were wanderers from the straight and narrow as much in temperament as in politics. And the two could go together. A wandering mind was likely to lead to a readiness to think the unthinkable: it was an expression of freedom which might eventually lead to a refusal to accept the dictates of state authority, a denial of the commonplace so forcefully urged by Dryden, that 'settled quiet is mankind's concern'. On the other hand, an assertion of the right to wander came up against, and was almost certainly prompted by, a recognition that more and more state institutions and laws made such wandering difficult to achieve. As I also pointed out in *England and Englishness*, between 1750 and 1800 over two-and-a-half thousand acts were passed which privatised land and/or forbade access to formerly common land to the common people. To wander was to trespass, to encroach on parcelled-out England. In the eyes of the law, at least, poachers and gypsies were alike in their lack of respect for private property. And as E. P. Thompson and others have remarked, what they did respect were customary rights. Such rights brought them into direct conflict with the newer, legally-enforcible rights of land owners.

It should therefore come as no surprise that the one great poet before Thomas to write sympathetically about gypsies was John Clare. Clare was drawn to gypsies because he saw them as fugitives from a law that was decisively tilted in favour of those who made and so defended property rights and whose lives were circumscribed by the lure of material possessions. Gypsies embodied an altogether freer way of living, one not hooped about by prudential values. Clare also knew all about the horrors of enclosure: the enclosure of the fields round his own village was the single most traumatic experience of his life. Once fences and hedges were thrown up, he was no longer free to wander his native land. 'Accursed wealth o'er bounding human laws/ Of every evil thou remainst the cause', he wrote in his poem 'Helpstone'.[13] When the poem was published in 1820 those lines were cut at the insistence of his patron, Lord Radstock (the direct ancestor of William Waldegrave). They smacked, the noble patron protested, of radical slang.

The same charge – or praise – could with equal justice be levelled at the following:

> And those lone wayside greens, no man's gardens, measuring a few feet wide but many miles in length – why should they be used either as receptacles for the dust of motor-cars or as additions to the property of the landowner who happens to be renewing his fence? They used to be as beautiful and cool and fresh as rivers, those green sisters of the white roads … . But now, lest there should be no room for the

> dust, they are turning away from them the gipsies who used to camp there for a night. The indolent District Council ... will send out its policeman to drive away the weary horses and sleeping children from the acre of common land which had hitherto been sacred – to what ? – to an altar, a statue, a fountain, a seat? – No! to a useless patch passed on easy terms to the pheasant lords. The gipsies have to go. Give them a pitch for the night and you are regarded as an enemy of the community or perhaps even as a Socialist.[14]

Thomas's protest on behalf of gypsy right to common land must be linked to his deep disquiet at an England where property values have driven out what he regards as older, pre-capitalist, customary rights: of the land held in common. That England is glimpsed in 'May 23' where the poet meets Jack Noman 'With a cowslip bunch in his button-hole and one in his cap':

> Fairer flowers were none on the earth
> Than his cowslips wet with the dew of their birth,
> Or fresher leaves than the cress in his basket.
> 'Where did they come from, Jack?' 'Don't ask it,
> And you'll be told no lies.' 'Very well:
> Then I can't buy." "I don't want to sell.
> Take them and these flowers, too, free.
> Perhaps you have something to give me?'[15]

The lovely anapestic ripple of these lines provide a kind of licensed gaiety of conversation, one that plays up the largesse of giving as opposed to selling, and which is reinforced by 'Take them *and* these flowers, too, free'. To honour that line's rhythmic movement you have to stress the surely unimportant word 'and'. In doing so you realise how important it is: Jack Noman takes and gives flowers free because they come from 'no man's gardens', to pick up the phrase from *The South Country*. He can give this and that, much as printer and sailor give themselves.

A similar disregard for prudential value comes through the talk of the woman who addresses Thomas in 'The Gypsy'.[16] She tells him that 'you've got a lucky face':

> 'And you've a luckier,' I thought, 'if such a grace
> And impudence in rags are lucky. Give a penny
> For the poor baby's sake.' 'Indeed I have not any
> Unless you can give change for a sovereign, my dear.'
> 'Then just half a pipeful of tobacco can you spare?'
> I gave it. With that much victory she laughed content.
> I should have given more, but off and away she went
> With her baby and her pink sham flowers to rejoin
> The rest before I could translate to its proper coin
> Gratitude for her grace.

Whatever the proper coin might be, it certainly isn't barren metal. Gratitude for this glimpse of a way of living that encompasses the gypsy's 'grace' (a charged word) can't be quantified. Nor can the poet's delight in her brother when he plays 'a rascally Bacchanal dance "Over the hills and far away"'. The gypsies, Lob, Jack Noman, the printer and sailor – all seem to be visitants from that England which for Thomas is knowable, cherishable, but out of reach: 'a season of bliss unchangeable/ Awakened from farm and church where it had lain/ Safe under tile and thatch for ages since/ This England, Old already, was called Merry' ('The Manor Farm').[17]

When Thomas decided to volunteer for armed service he explained his decision to Eleanor Farjeon by scooping up a handful of soil and holding it out to her. I see nothing vainglorious in the gesture. He was certainly not proclaiming that some corner of a foreign field would be forever England. The handful of soil was the token of his readiness to fight for an England whose values his poetry celebrates as 'Merry', a term much used by utopian socialists at the end of the nineteenth century. Merrie England was the title of a hugely popular pamphlet-book published by Robert Blatchford in 1893. There, Blatchford, a keen follower of William Morris, sets out to remedy what he calls 'The Problem of Life'. The problem is simple enough: it lies in the mixture of social and material inequality in an England which, despite natural abundance, requires the majority of its citizens to labour long and hard for pitiful returns and which condemns others to outright poverty. This is capitalism. The alternative is socialism.

It isn't necessary to examine here the exact nature of Blatchford's socialist thought. I need merely to record the fact that his discontent with the condition of England was widely shared and would lead many of the next generation to ask why they were at war with Germany. Hence the following:

> We ought to realise that the real struggle, in which this war is only an episode, is not merely between our own country and anything so unstable and transitory as modern Germany, but between permanent and irreconcileable claimants for the soul of man, and that what makes the German spirit dangerous is not that it is alien, but that it is horribly congenial, to almost the whole modern world. For the spirit of German Imperialism is too often the spirit of English and American Capitalism, with its cult of power as an end in itself, its coarse material standards, its subordination of personality to mechanism, its worship of an elaborate and soul-destroying organisation; and the materialism, which in Prussia reveals itself in adoration of the power of the State, in England reveals itself in adoration of the power of money. The latter is not more noble, it is more ignoble, because less disinterested, than the former. If it is not so violent, it is more slyly corrupt, and, as far as the mass of mankind are concerned, it is almost as tyrannical.

Tawney again. The words, which come from his essay, 'A National College of All Souls', were written early in 1917 (and re-printed in 1953 in *The Attack and Other Papers*). They anticipate by several months that sonnet, 'To The Prussians of England', which Ivor Gurney sent to his friend, Marion Scott, and which seems by the violence of its language to have terrified her. Addressing those whom he sees as the English

Prussians, Gurney says:

> Our silly dreams of peace you put aside
> And brotherhood of man, for you will see
> An armed mistress, braggart of the tide,
> Her children slaves, under your mastery.
> We'll have a word there too, and forge a knife,
> Will cut the cancer threatens England's life.
> (*Poems*, 52)

I have suggested in *The Radical Twenties* (1997) that this poem may have been written in the full knowledge of the Russian Revolution of October, 1917, and that Gurney's pledge that he and his fellow soldiers 'Will cut the cancer threatens England's life' was bound in the circumstances to seem to Scott a promise of revolution to come.

This being so, we might recall Tawney's words about 'the struggle between permanent and irreconcileable claimants for the soul of man' in order to recognise that soldiers in the later years of the war were all-too likely to feel passionately – even violently – opposed to a system which required them to go on being killed, especially as they knew that the chance of a negotiated peace had been scuppered by the government under pressure from the military. GHQ had insisted that total victory was achievable. As Haig infamously said: 'we have more soldiers than they do'. That was what the planned attack on the Somme was to prove.

It proved no such thing. The disillusionment of line soldiers with the war effort spread rapidly after the tragi-farce of that bloody and appalling failure. Soldiers now saw themselves as fighting 'the bosses' war', as the phrase went. Recognition of this was accompanied by and sharpened class awareness. There was no 'brotherhood of man'. I am not about to claim Gurney as a revolutionary socialist, but I do think it remarkable that in 'The Silent One' (*BP/FM*, 49) he should have given such unmistakable proof of his sardonic refusal to co-operate with 'the bosses' war'. In that poem, you will recall, an officer with

> … the politest voice – a finicking accent, said.
> 'Do you think you might crawl through there: there's a hole.'
> Darkness, shot at: I smiled, as politely replied –
> 'I'm afraid not, Sir.' There was no hole, no way to be seen,
> Nothing but chance of death, after tearing of clothes.

This is not so much dumb as eloquent insolence. The officer conceals an order under the pretence of asking a question. There is no question mark after his words: 'Do you think you might crawl through there: there's a hole'. Gurney, however, pretends that the order *is* a question. He plays the officer's game of finicking politeness: 'I'm afraid not, Sir'. The capitalised form of address stresses the gap between the two of them.

But so does the finicking accent. The poem begins:

> Who died on the wires and hung there, one of two –
> Who for his hours of life had chattered through
> Infinite lovely chatter of Bucks accent:
> Yet faced unbroken wires: stepped over, and went
> A noble fool, faithful to his stripes – and ended.

The complex of feelings here is registered through the shifting syntax and terms used to describe the Silent One. His 'lovely chatter of Bucks accent' has been somehow betrayed by his willingness to face unbroken wires. For how else understand the word 'Yet' – it points the force of a contradiction between how he spoke and what he did, as though, given his accent, he shouldn't have acted the noble fool, faithful to his stripes. Of course, the soldier would have had no choice. Obey orders or get shot for cowardice or desertion. But the lines point a terrible contrast between the man's identity as given through speech and the identity forced on him by circumstance: in the one he is fluent, freely able to 'chatter'. In the other he is a noble fool, his life brutally 'ended'. (For that word is most brutally reductive, quite without either consolation or hint of nobility.)

Gurney's *Collected Letters* make clear his love for the 'chatter' of his fellow soldiers. One, Private Tim Godding, he makes into a kind of Shakespearian folk hero because of his idiomatic speech, thick with countryman's sayings (*Letters*, 74). Godding is a man of chatter. In customary usage the word carries a hint – perhaps more than a hint – of condescension. Women and children chatter. Chatter is inconsequential, light, holiday from the matter of serious speech. But Gurney doesn't so regard it. For him 'chatter' is an expression of freedom, is non-prudential, is a way of giving yourself, unguarded, unconstrained. Thomas's printer and sailor are chatterers. Chatter moreover is an expression of the mind's delight in wandering. It doesn't keep to the straight and narrow. Infinite lovely chatter testifies to a way of life which is the polar opposite of a world of which the war – in which men were fed to machines – is apotheosis.

This may seem extreme. I don't think it is. Whether the war radicalised Gurney or sharpened a radicalism already rooted within him I don't know. We as yet lack the biography that will explain his intellectual development. I do however know that we can understand him best if we acknowledge that much of his poetry comes out of a deeply radical cast of mind. That is one of the reasons he so hugely admired Thomas and in particular 'Lob', which he hoped to learn by heart. Gurney's 'The Lock Keeper' is unimaginable without Thomas's great poem behind it. I can't here say much about 'The Lock Keeper', but I will at least note Gurney's expressed desire to praise 'the man who goes in my dark mind/ With sand and broad waters and general kind/ Of fish-and-fox and-bird lore, and walking lank', who is also a man enjoying, so he says, 'talk with equals', one who is remarkable for 'Cunning of practice, the finding, doing, the getting – Wisdom of every various season or light – / Fish running, tide running, plant learning and bird flight' (*Poems*, 103-106). The lock-keeper, like Lob, carries with him a wealth of countryman's lore, and like Lob he is wild and wanders. He is an emblem of all that it is most desirable to set against 'polite' living: cautious, contained, a life spreading like a deadly stain across England. As Gurney said in 'The Bargain': 'Villas will stand there and look polite; with folk polite … [but] it can never be right' (Poems, 72)

Gurney didn't like the coming of villa or bungalow culture. He was by no means alone in this. At about the same time, Clough Williams Ellis was protesting in *England and the Octopus* (published in 1928) at ribbon development: of strict rows of box-houses reaching out tentacularly into the countryside and bringing with them not merely evidence of uniformity but of the private, constricted spirit, of a rejection of community, above all, perhaps, of indifference to beauty, of what Lawrence, again writing at more or less the same moment in *Lady Chatterley's Lover* (1928), called 'the instinct for shapely beauty which every bird and beast has'. Putting it this way may well suggest that Gurney is not so much radical as deeply reactionary. But no: his detestation of the 'polite', the 'finicking' is prompted by a desire for what I will risk calling a fullness of being which, for all their differences, Morris, Thomas, Tawney and he have in common. This is why he writes those poems about work, such as 'Hedger' and 'Felling a Tree' (*Poems*, 161, 136), which celebrate absorption in a task at once mental and bodily.

These poems concentrate on country tasks. But in case that seems to offer Gurney as a natural ally for the preservers of rural England as green-welly country, we should note that he also writes about city workers. 'North Woolwich' (*80 Poems*, 68) contrasts modern London – seen as a kind of Morrisian 'shabby hell' – with ancient Greece. Naturally the comparison is all in favour of 'Hellene memories'. But Gurney is not content merely to indict 'that ugly, that evil smelling Township' of London (Canning Town, to be precise). He imagines its possible redemption, through the intercession of a 'Christ from Heaven' who comes down 'Pitiful and comradely, with tender signs,/ [to] hot the tea, and shield a chap from fines./ A foreman carpenter not yet full grown'. Awkward though the poem is, Gurney is here imagining a kind of Christian socialism which was one form of developing radicalism in the late years of the nineteenth century and with which he may well have come in contact during and after his student years.

The hope of redemption seems frail enough. But the injustices of the war and its aftermath undoubtedly increased Gurney's radicalism.

We can see how, from the closing lines of 'Strange Hells', where he speaks of the thousands of returned soldiers

> ... on state-doles, or showing shop-patterns
> Or walking town to town in borrowed tatterns
> Or begged. Some civic routine one never learns.
> The heart burns – but has to keep out of face how heart burns.
> (*Poems*, 140-41)

Here, Gurney's failure to learn 'civic routine' provides for a bitter ironic play on the idea that the returned soldiers should agree to be made invisible, put out of mind like a nasty memory. (Badly wounded soldiers weren't allowed to attend the ceremony for the unveiling of the tomb of the unknown soldier: it was argued in official quarters that they would lower the dignity of the occasion.) Gurney is their spokesmen, as he is for the children of West Ham, in 'The Wish' (*Poems*, 160), which combines sound architectural advice with a radical awareness of social deprivation. Like Clough Williams Ellis, who was campaigning against the use of brick for working-class housing on the grounds that brick needlessly increased the cost – brick admitted damp and cold – Gurney makes the case for 'Wooden-frame houses square, with some-sort stuff/ Crammed in to keep the wind away that's rough/ And rain; in summer cool, in cold comfortable enough'. The houses should be

> Not crowded together, but with a plot of land,
> Where one might play and dig, and use spade or the hand
> In managing or shaping earth in such forms
> As please the sunny mind or keep out of harms
> The mind that's always good when let go its way
> (I think) so there's work enough in a happy day.

The poem speaks up for the rights of all to good housing – shades of Morris's belief in 'housing necessary and decent'. It also voices that old idea of land entitlement and fulfillment through work and comradeship which is at the heart of the radical tradition and which can be traced back to – well, to John Ball. 'When Adam delved and Eve span/ Who was then the gentleman?' The famous chant of the Peasants' Revolt was taken up by William Morris and used as an epigraph for A *Dream of John Ball* (1888), his great vision of utopian socialism. It can be heard in Edward Thomas's recognition of the worth of 'the actual, troublous life of every day and toil of the hands and brain together' which, as Stan Smith has pointed out, is very close to the famous Clause 4 of the Labour Party's constitution, 'to secure for the workers by hand and brain the full fruits of their labours', and it runs like a band of gleaming quartz through all of Tawney's writings. For all of them, such work, such being, is diametrically opposed to modes of existence which Gurney sums up in 'A Wish' as

> … the too exact
> Straight streets of modern times, that strait and strict
> And formal keep man's spirit within bounds,
> Where too dull duties keep in monotonous rounds.
> (*Poems*, 160)

Gurney's punning on 'straight' and strait' tell us of his deep revulsion against an England in which wandering and chatter are dismissed as of no consequence. As he himself said, 'only the wanderer knows England's graces'.

1998

Notes

1. R. H. Tawney, *The Radical Tradition*, Harmondsworth: Penguin, 1966, 195.
2. William Morris, *Selected Writings and Designs*, edited by Asa Briggs, Harmondsworth: Penguin, 1962, 120.
3. First published in The Bookman in February 1911, this review of Morris's Collected Works is reprinted in *A Language Not To Be Betrayed: Selected Prose of Edward Thomas*, ed. Edna Longley, Ashington & Manchester: Mid NAG & Carcanet, 1981, 37.
4. Edward Thomas, *The South Country*, London: J. M. Dent, 1909, 117. Hereafter *South*.
5. *Letters from Edward Thomas to Gordon Bottomley*, ed. R. George Thomas, Oxford: Oxford University Press, 1968, 158.
6. Smith, op. cit., 181.
7. Clive Aslet, *The Last Country Houses*, New Haven: Yale University Press, 1982) 227.
8. Ibid., 231.
9. Ibid., 248.
10. *South*, 117-18.
11. Edward Thomas, *Collected Poems*, ed. R. George Thomas, Oxford: Oxford University Press, 1981, 53-57. Hereafter Poems.
12. *South*, 75.
13. John Clare, 'Helpstone' in: *The Oxford Authors: John Clare*, ed. Eric Robinson and David Powell, Oxford: Oxford University Press, 1984, 4.
14. *South*, 196.
15. *Poems*, 36-38.
16. *Poems*, 32-33.
17. *Poems*, 18.

POETRY AND POLITICS IN THE 1920S

There is a widely-accepted view that in the aftermath of the Great War and faced with what seemed to be a wrecked Europe, poets saw themselves as required to take on the task of 'saving civilization'.[1] Given that the poets in question were politically conservative, this in practice meant saving civilization from the barbarians. For Eliot, 'the hooded hordes swarming/ Over endless plains', threaten both the achievements and future of western culture. 'Falling towers/ Jerusalem Athens/ Vienna London'. If we ask who exactly these hordes are, the answer seems to be: those who have brought about and/or who constitute the new mass democracies and, perhaps, newly created democratic nation states, from Communist Russia through, say, the Weimer Republic to Ireland-in-the-making. On 7 April 1921, Eliot wrote a deeply instructive letter to Richard Aldington, in the course of which he confessed that

> Having only contempt for every existing political party, and profound hatred for democracy, I feel the blackest gloom. Whatever happens will be another step towards the destruction of Europe. The whole of contemporary politics oppresses me with a continuous physical horror like the feeling of growing madness in one's brain. It is rather a horror to be sane in the midst of this, it is too dreadful, too huge for one to have the feeling of superiority. It goes too far for rage.[2]

It is not clear what event or events Eliot has especially in mind as advancing 'the destruction of Europe'. The previous year, dockers at Tilbury had refused to load arms which the government had promised Poland and white Russia; but although Eliot would have been dismayed by the dockers' success in forcing Lloyd George to back down from the promise to which Churchill and others had committed him, that was now in the past. So too were the revolutions in the defeated axis powers of Germany and the Austro-Hungarian empire. A free Ireland? But in April 1921 that was still far from certain.[3] These occurrences may have helped form Eliot's 'blackest gloom', but it is more likely that he is thinking specifically of England and its growing industrial unrest, particularly among the miners, the railwaymen and the transport workers.

There were good reasons for this unrest. In 1920 the government had announced plans to hand back to mine and railway owners those essential industries which had been under state control during the war years. The date set for the re-privatisation of both mines and railways was August 1921, but according to Henry Pelling,

> the heavy losses being made by the coal industry led [the government] to advance the date of transfer of the mines by five months. The coal owners for their part could see no alternative to heavy cuts in wages, which of course the Miners refused to accept. The result was that on the day of decontrol, 31 March, the Miners were locked out and the Triple Alliance was again invoked. The Railwaymen and the Transport Workers agreed to begin a sympathetic strike on Saturday, 16 April ... .[4]

In the event the railwaymen backed down and created what in Labour history is known as 'Black Friday'. The General Strike of May 1926 would be an attempt to make good the damage done to the Labour movement by the failings of April 1921. It, too, failed. But I am fairly certain that the strike was instrumental in helping Eliot's decision to take out British citizenship, and to announce that he was a royalist, anglo-catholic and conservative.

Eliot himself acknowledged that 1926 was a key year. When he closed down *The Criterion* with the coming of the Second World War, he wrote an editorial farewell in which he remarked that

> Only from about the year 1926 did the features of the post-war world begin clearly to emerge – and not only in the sphere of politics. From about that date one began slowly to realize that the intellectual and artistic output of the previous seven years had been rather the last effort of the old world, than the struggles of a new.[5]

He would presumably have regarded *The Waste Land* as belonging to a last effort of the old world. 'These fragments I have shored against my ruins'.

Eliot finished his great poem in December 1921. That same year Yeats published *Michael Robartes and the Dancer*, which includes 'Easter, 1916' and 'The Second Coming'. In the former Yeats broods over the 'terrible beauty' of the blood sacrifice and what it foretells about the making of an independent Ireland. 'The Second Coming' is also about the creation of a new society, even a new world order. Here, however, Yeats is far less equivocal. 'Mere anarchy is loosed upon the world'. The perpetrator of anarchy is of course the famous beast out of Revelations. 'And what rough beast, its hour come round at last,/ Slouches towards Bethlehem to be born?' The poem has been the subject of much commentary, most of it concerned with Yeats's 'Vision': that is, his reading of history as consisting of two-thousand year cycles in which one kind of civilization passes into its opposite. Here I want merely to note that the rough beast which 'slouches' must surely be the working class. We know that shortly after the October revolution in Russia Yeats began a (re-)reading of Wordsworth's poetry at the same time as he was re-reading Burke on the French Revolution; and in his copy of *The Prelude* he marked some lines of the 1850 text of Books X and XI which deal with the Revolution. In the first of these Wordsworth speaks of 'The indecision on their part whose aim/ Seemed best, and the straightforward path of those/ Who in attack or in defence were strong/ Through impiety' (ll.130-33); and in the second, very famous passage, he tells of how he himself lost 'all feeling of conviction, and, in fine,/ Sick, wearied out with contraries,/ Yielded up moral questions in despair' (ll.302-305). These two moments find an obvious echo in the lines of 'The Second Coming': 'The best lack all conviction, while the worst/ Are full of passionate intensity'.[6]

But who are the worst? Those who make revolutions? Very probably. Political radicals, then, even communists? Quite likely. For though in 'Easter, 1916' Yeats acknowledges the worth of Pearce and Connolly, he knew that both were communists; and the 'blood-dimmed tide' of 'The Second Coming' may well catch up the events and aftermath of the Easter Rising as well as the Bolshevik rising and, then, assassination of the Czar and his family. Communists and their sympathisers and radical allies are 'Leaders of the Crowd', Helens of 'social-welfare dream', or dreamers of 'some vague utopia'. As such, they let loose 'a roof-levelling wind', which threatens to destroy everything that stands in its way, including, of course, 'monuments of unageing intellect'. In ranging promiscuously among a number of poems which Yeats wrote in the post-war period I mean to do no more than point towards how thorough-going was his commitment to identifying the enemies of civilisation as the champions of mass democracy. This was what history had let loose, and it was from *this* that civilization had to be saved, even if such salvation had to be accomplished within the pages of a book. Here, if nowhere else, there could be the celebration of 'beautiful lofty things'.

II

Eliot was American. Yeats was Irish. What of the English? Older English poets were either finished, no good, or so traumatised by the war that they had nothing to say either to or about the post-war world. This is also a widely-accepted view. Robert Bridges' 'Low Barometer' was the nearest any of them came to confronting or at least trying to negotiate a sense of the post-war world (dis)order. In that poem there is to be found at least some recognition of the horrors that have wrecked the cherished dream of England as the great, good place. Gone, perhaps forever, is the 'record of the long, safe centuries,' to use Henry James's formulation.[7]

Some have seen corpses long interr'd
Escape from harrowing control,
Pale charnel forms – nay, ev'n have heard
The shrilling of a troubled soul,

That wanders till the dawn hath cross'd
The dolorous dark, or Earth hath wound
Closer her storm-spredd cloak, and thrust
The baleful phantoms underground.

Bridges' fear of those baleful phantoms explains his endorsement of closer ties with the defeated nations, for which *The Times* gave him a verbal battering. But the faded diction and strict metres of 'Low Barometer' all too plainly speak from and for an older world. They voice a last, desperate, unavailing effort to keep under control the nightmare vision of a world given over to death.

Bridges apart, the older generation of poets is most importantly represented by Hardy who, when Robert Graves visited him in August 1920, was supposed to have told the younger man that English poets would have to continue 'writing on the old themes in the old styles, but try to do a little better than those who went before'. I have set out elsewhere my reasons for doubting that Hardy said any such thing, but whatever the truth of the matter there can be no doubt that the words have been used against both him and later English poets, including those who were at work in the 1920s and of whom Sidney Bolt remarks that 'the themes of these poets were too new to be accommodated by minor modifications of the style they inherited'.[8]

Bolt does not say which poets he has in mind, but they could include any number of those whom Edward Marsh included in his *Georgian Poetry 1920-1922*. All the usual names are there: Abercrombie, Blunden, W.H. Davies, de la Mare, Graves, Harold Munro, Robert Nichols. Lawrence's 'Snake' has also slipped in, but looks to be very much the intruder in this otherwise pre-lapsarian collection of English poetry in which it is all-but impossible to find any mention of a recent war.

Reading through the anthology is a very odd, disturbing experience; and it must have been even more so in 1922. It is as though Marsh is hoping to persuade his audience that the age-before-last survives intact. Nothing of importance has happened between the first of his anthologies, which he had put together in 1912, and now. Faced with Marsh's anthology and the kind of poetry it champions – which it has to be said went on being produced in large quantities during the post-war years – it is not difficult to see why literary historians have come to regard the 1920s as a blank page in the annals of English poetry. There simply wasn't any.[9]

Or rather, none of it deserved serious consideration. As the decade went on it became possible to see that a trio of poets killed in the war would in all probability have been the major writers of the post-war years. But with Owen, Rosenberg and Edward Thomas all dead, who was left? The answer seemed and has continued to seem to be: Blunden, Graves and Sassoon. I am not going to deal with them here, beyond saying that as officer poets they found the war a deeply disturbing experience: not primarily because of the inevitable horrors of trench warfare but because the experience called into question most of the beliefs and allegiances which they had acquired through their class, education and upbringing, and none of them could bear to follow where the questions led. Blunden wrote a number of poems that looked back on the war as a dystopic experience: a time of wrecked pastoral. Then he went back to writing pastoral poems. Sassoon was for a while a socialist. He contributed to *The Daily Herald*; he spoke on party platforms; and in one poem he diffidently expressed support for striking miners. But the setting for that poem is his Gentleman's Club; and Sassoon honestly admits that, hearing his 'port-flushed friends discuss the Strike' he would almost like/ To see them hawking matches in the gutter'. 'Almost': the wry shame-facedness of that looks towards the characteristic note of his autobiography, *Sherston's Progress*, published in 1936, by which time Sassoon had long abandoned his socialism.

In a poem-review of Sassoon's autobiography, Hugh MacDiarmid asks 'What is *Sherston's Progress* but an exposure/ Of the eternal

Englishman / Incapable of rising above himself, / And traditional values winning out / Over an attempted independence of mind ... It is not that Sherston was either / A weak or cowardly person. / It is rather that his rebelliousness was only / Superimposed on his profoundly English nature'.[10] By 'profoundly English nature', MacDiarmid means, I think, a willing and /or finally unquestioning obedience or conformity to class and national expectations. England expects. Sassoon had once and bravely confronted those expectations. By making his famous protest against the continuation of the war he risked court-martial and execution. He was saved from the consequences of his action by the intervention of his friends.

Pre-eminent among them was Robert Graves. We know that Graves, like Blunden and Sassoon, was severely traumatised by his war experiences. In later years he suffered recurrent nightmares and during the 1920s his mental condition was often precarious. By the end of that decade he had had enough. He wrote *Goodbye To All That* and with Laura Riding left England for Majorca. Once there, he tried his hand at a play called *But It Still Goes On.* This has no merits as drama but forms a kind of apologia in which the hero, Dick, at one point talks of his sense of a catastrophe, of 'the bottom dropping out of things'. This is how he explains it:

> ... perhaps one easy way of describing the catastrophe is to say that it was the moment when the last straw broke the back of reality, when one unnecessary person too many was born, when population finally became unmanageable, when proper people were finally swamped. Once they counted; now they no longer count. So it's impossible for a proper person to feel the world as a necessary world – an intelligible world in which there's any hope or fear for the future – a world worth bothering about – or, if he happens to be a poet, a world worth writing for – a world in which there's any morality left to bother about, but his own personal morality: *that* gets more and more strict, of course.[11]

The Nietzschean contempt for little people and belief that mass democracy takes away function from that 'proper person', the poet, is Graves's own right enough, although Laura Riding's influence is plain to see. (Before coming to England she had been briefly involved with 'Fugitive' poets and shared their Southern scorn for democratic politics.)

In short, the soldier poets who survived the war found themselves unable or unwilling to try to explore its meaning or the contradictory experiences to which it had exposed them. They can hardly be blamed for this. But their decision to seal the war off from their consciousnesses will explain why we continue to look to Eliot and Yeats for deep, authoritative (and authoritarian) readings of the post-war world. There are no other poets to whom we can turn.

III

Except that there are. Both Ivor Gurney and Edgell Rickword fought in the war and both survived it, although at great cost. Gurney, who had a history of mental disturbance which the war exacerbated, was from 1922 until his death in 1937 shut away in asylums, first in his native county of Gloucester, and then at Dartford, Kent. Rickword was wounded and after the war began to suffer from nightmares which lasted until his death in 1979. Both were poets, Gurney a great one. Both were politically radical – although in Rickword's case this has been said to have put an end to his poetry (it didn't), and in Gurney's case it has been largely ignored by the few commentators he has so far attracted. Yet Gurney's radicalism is bound up with his war experiences and is integral to his best poetry. Rickword's came later. His move from post-war discontent to left-wing politics occurs over a long period and *may* be connected to the fact that, like Blunden, Sassoon and Graves, he was an officer. Gurney wasn't. And this is of the greatest possible significance.

To see why we have only to look at one of Gurney's finest war poems, 'The Silent One'.

Who died on the wires, and hung there, one of two –
Who for his hours of life had chattered through
Infinite lovely chatter of Bucks accept:
Yet faced unbroken wires; stepped over, and went
A noble fool, faithful to his stripes – and ended.
But I weak, hungry, and willing only for the chance
Of line – to fight in the line, lay down under unbroken
Wires, and saw the flashes and kept unshaken,
Till the politest voice – a finicking accent, said:
"Do you think you might crawl through there: there's a hole."
Darkness, shot at: I smiled, as politely replied –
'I'm afraid not, Sir.'

There are certain issues in these lines to which I shall return, but for the moment I want to note that the 'finicking accent' clearly belongs to an officer, whose exquisite politeness is such that he disguises a command as a question. No question mark follows 'Do you think you might crawl through there: there's a hole'. But the line-soldier can play the game of pretending to answer a question. Hence, 'I'm afraid not, Sir'. The capitalisation of Sir alerts us to the politeness which Gurney takes good care to retain in this exchange with the officer. Nevertheless, he is rejecting the officer's claim to authority. He has no wish to be a hero, a noble fool. Yet it doesn't seem enough to call Gurney's attitude anti-heroic. A better word might be 'bolshie', not in the sense that Gurney comes across as sullenly unresponsive – he smiles, replies politely – but in the sense that 'bolshie', which entered the language at this time, was used to mean 'left-wing, unco-operative, recalcitrant'. (I quote from the O.E.D. definitions.)

Words come into existence because they are needed. Bolshie defined a new consciousness. And the coupling of left-wing with unco-operative implies that co-operative people are right-wing or at least support the status quo. In war this has to mean obeying the orders of your superiors, no matter how daft or murderous those orders might be. As officers, Owen, Graves and Sassoon had to give orders to their men; and at a shrewd guess all of them possessed what the men would regard as 'finicking accents'. We are told that all three officer-poets were much admired, even loved by the men they led, and there is no reason to doubt the truth of this, nor to question the more general claim that an emotional bonding often developed between line soldiers and their serving officers. They were after all equally exposed to hardship and danger. And yet Gurney's 'bolshie' response to the voice of authority in 'The Silent One' serves to remind us that while officers might well think of the war as one with which they ought to be at ease or to which they should be reconciled – it was what their education had prepared them for – the rankers had far less reason to accept it. For them, the war increasingly became 'the bosses' war.

'The Silent One' was never published in Gurney's lifetime. It seems to have been written in 1919, by which time publishers had turned against his poetry, perhaps because they no longer wanted war poems and very probably because they sensed in Gurney an attitude that did not accord with simple statements of duty and of patriotic pride. They could hardly have missed it. Yet to speak of attitude is to imply that Gurney is merely 'bolshie', and this is far from the truth. It is rather that as a poet-survivor of the war he becomes the spokesman for 'boys who served time overseas', as he says in 'Mist on Meadows', who 'could not guess, alas!/ How England should take as common their vast endurance'. 'Where are they now?' he asks in another poem, and replies

> on state-doles, or showing shop-patterns
> Or walking town to town in borrowed tatterns
> Or begged. Some civic routine one never learns.
> The heart burns – but has to keep out of face how heart burns.
>
> ('Strange Hells')

The masterly use of enjambement between the second and third lines intensifies the terrible indignity of those many returned soldiers who were forced onto the dole or into a vagrant life. And I take it that by the civic routine one never learns Gurney wishes to direct us to the bitter irony of ex-soldiers who had fought to make 'a land fit for heroes' and who now offend against 'decency' by their beggarly appearance. Nor can the 'boys' risk showing their bitterness or anger, not anyway if they hope to gather a crust or a stray penny. They must instead learn 'to keep out of face how heart burns'.

But the heart is also Gurney's, his anger the anger of those with whom he had fought and whom he now sees as cast off by the very nation on whose behalf they had vastly endured suffering. Gurney's anger springs from political consideration. An attentive reading of his letters makes plain that during the war years he had moved towards an increasingly politicised awareness of what he hoped for from post-war society. Letters he wrote during 1917 to his great friend Marion Scott show this beyond any doubt. This is not to suggest that key events of that year were decisive in turning him towards political radicalism. They may have had that effect but, lacking as we do a proper biography, much in Gurney's intellectual development remains a mystery.[12] We do, however, know that shortly after hearing of the Kerensky revolution he wrote to Marion Scott to tell her that 'it is the bloomingest nuisance that a thing so well intentioned as the Russian Revolution can so upset things'. He does not explain what the upset is, but it is reasonable to suppose that he would have had in mind Allied distrust of the democratising of their Eastern ally. Two months later he tells Scott that England suffers under a 'wrong materialistic system'. Again, he does not explain the remark but the context suggests he has in mind the vulgar wealth which had been so dominant a presence in pre-war England, his dislike of which lies behind a remark contained in a letter of the previous year, in which he tells her that 'the people here say that France was very happy and well-governed before the War. Can you imagine an Englishman saying as much of England?'

Then, on October 16, 1917, comes a key letter. Gurney begins by reassuring Marion Scott that he hadn't intended her to take personally a sonnet 'To the Prussians of England' which he had enclosed with his previous letter. This is the sonnet.

When I remember plain heroic strength
And shining virtue shown by Ypres pools,
Then read the blither written by knaves for fools
In praise of English soldiers lying at length,
Who purely dream that England shall be made
Gloriously new, free of the old stains
By us, who pay the price that must be paid,
Will freeze all winter over Ypres plains.
Our silly dreams of peace you put aside
And Brotherhood of Man, for you will see
An armed Mistress, braggart of the tide,
Her children slaves, under your mastery.
We'll have a word there too, and forge a knife,
Will cut the cancer threatens England's life.

Scott, who seems to have been innocently patriotic and a good 'hun-hater', must have been disturbed by Gurney's dream of an international Brotherhood of Man and his rejection of Britannia as a warrior-nation. But I suspect she was most deeply shaken by the promise of violence with which the sonnet ends. And after all, for Gurney to write in *October 1917* of forging 'a knife' to cut England's 'cancer' – when it is plain that by 'cancer' he means the ruling class – could hardly be taken as other than revolutionary.

In trying to justify himself, and at the same time assuage her fears, Gurney explained that he cared 'more for Englishmen, than for liberty of England'. And in order to explain that remark, he adds:

> It is of more importance that the Duke of Bilgewater should respect and sympathise with Bill Jones than that the sun should never set on the British Empire, whose liberties have been kept alive by revolt against the fathers of the present 'Prussians of England.'[13]

Gurney's respect and sympathy for Bill Jones is intimately linked to his relishing of the salty speech of the soldiers with whom he fought, their idiomatic expressions, their various dialects. In several letters he quotes stray remarks he has overheard, of 'infinite lovely chatter'. And the poems rejoice in the speech of line soldiers. Their utterances, both what they say and how they say it, are revelations of wit, warmth, *aliveness*, which makes the class assumption of authority so much malign, ignorant nonsense. To take two examples. In the first of two poems called 'First Time In' Gurney recalls 'roguish words by Welsh pit boys/ ...sung – but never more beautiful than under guns,' and in 'Billet' he tells of the private in the Glosters who

> took on himself a Company's heart to speak,
> 'I wish to bloody hell I was going to Brewery – surely
> To work all day (in Stroud) and be free at tea-time – allowed
> Resting when one wanted, and a joke in season,
> To change clothes and take a girl to Horsepool's turning,
> Or drink a pint at 'Travellers Rest' and find no cloud.'

This savouring of the speech of line soldiers prompts or makes possible that political vision, that intense desire for democratic relations, which partly accounts for Gurney's 'bolshieness', but which, far more importantly, is the source of much of his best work. Here, then, we need to register the importance to Gurney of Edward Thomas.

When Gurney heard of Thomas's death he told Marion Scott 'This is a great loss'.[14] But at the time he seems to have know few if any of Thomas's poems. By autumn, 1917, however – that key period in his life – he is beginning to weigh their significance. And by the early spring of 1918 he is able to provide one correspondent with a long list of Thomas's poems he particularly likes and to tell another that Thomas is a genius. In March 1918 he writes to Marion Scott that his own future poetry is likely to be 'influenced by E.T. chiefly.[15] Thomas did indeed come to be a pervasive influence on Gurney's poetry, although in ways that mostly lie beyond the confines of this essay. Thomas's socialism is, however, a different matter. With the honourable exception of Stan Smith, commentators have chosen to ignore Thomas's politics, even though he himself said that 'Except William Morris there is no other man whom I would sometimes like to have been', and even though he makes plain that his admiration for Morris has to do with the fact that for Morris 'poetry was not, as it has tended more and more to be in recent times, a matter as exclusive as a caste. He was not half-angel or half-bird, but in all that he did a man on terms with life and toil, with the actual troublous life of every day, with toil of the hands and brain together'.[16]

I have no means of knowing whether Gurney had read *The South Country*, from which that quotation comes. I suspect he had, but like so much else to do with Gurney we still lack information about his reading. We do, however, know that in August 1918 he told his friend Haines that he had started to learn 'Lob' by heart, that he wished Thomas 'had written piles of stuff more,' and that 'some day the prose works will (I hope) delight me likewise'.[17] Lob, Thomas's tutelary Englishman, is the embodiment and spokesman for English liberties, uttering the words of the free-born Englishman that carry with them natural authority going with the speech of place, of belonging. P.J. Kavanagh says that 'when there are people in [Gurney's] poems they are seen with rather an abstract, lonely, passion of respect'. This may sometimes be the case, but I have given examples – and they could be multiplied – of Gurney not merely seeing but hearing those people; and their utterances put flesh on the bones of respect, 'prove' it, to use a word Thomas himself favoured. It is therefore worth remarking that Gurney wondered why Thomas 'doesn't break out into divine unliterate clearness more often?' He reported a 'Snatch of Shakespearean wit, from Pte Tim Godding. A sergeant was going round collecting birthdays ... and one man hesitated to answer. Said T.G. 'He don't know his birthday, he don't know his name. The sun hatched it'. And of The Dynasts he said that it was 'quite Shakespearean ... O the country talk, the songs'.[18]

As to Lob. The man was wild / And wandered', the narrator of the poem is told. By the time Gurney came across 'Lob' he had already written his own 'Song': 'Only the wanderer /Knows England's graces,

/ Or can anew see clear/ Familiar faces'. He enclosed this lovely poem in a letter to Marion Scott of January 1917 and it appeared in the first of the two volumes to be published in his lifetime, *Severn and Somme, 1917*. (*War's Embers* followed two years later.) In retrospect he must have come to regard wandering as part of his heritage as a free Englishman; and he would have understood that Thomas is using the word to carry the same political weight that it bears in Blake, Wordsworth and Clare. Wandering is a right because the land is what we have, or ought to have, in common.

After his return to England, Gurney became an inveterate wanderer, even a compulsive one. His wandering is both a Thomas-like eagerness to look, to know, to 'bite the day to the core', and an affirmation of an Englishman's rights. And these are not merely country rights. The poet who wrote 'One comes across the strangest things in walks' ('Cotswold Ways') also wrote 'North Woolwich', which begins with him looking down at the smoky squalor of the dockside Thames, and reflecting on the fall this represents from 'the bright/ Morning of new Time amongst tall derricks/ And floating chimney pots with empty tackle/ Drawn by fierce asp-things slowly out of sight'. The forced image of asp-like tugs is there to underline a contrast between twentieth-century Thames and the pristine beauty of the ancient mediterranean, of 'Hellene memories' and 'Sappho's easy happy mirth'. So far, so inconsiderable, even inept. Poems that contrasted times when the world was new to now, when it has grown old and grey and weary, had been ten-a-penny ever since Wordsworth's sonnet 'The world is too much with us'. And Wordsworth knew rather more about Triton than Gurney does about Sappho.

But Gurney's poem then turns from conventionalities to the quite startlingly original. The last section begins with what looks like another routine contrast between ancient Spartan youth and the present decadent city-bred young who lack 'that smoothly running muscle'. The poor physical condition of the working-class had become a much-canvassed matter of concern in late nineteenth-century England; and it was accompanied and/or prompted by debates about degeneration of the stock.[19] But Gurney is not bothered about that.

> Gaol waits for them would face without a stitch
> Heaven's nakedness, those feet are black as pitch
> Should gleam on gold sands white or in stadium lines.
> Can Aphrodite bless so evil dwelling
> Or Mercury have heed to Canning Town?
> Nay, rather, for that ugly, that evil smelling
> Township, a Christ from Heaven must come down,
> Pitiful and comradely, with tender signs,
> And hot the tea, and shield a chap from fines.
> A foreman carpenter, not yet full-grown.

East End missions were a feature of Christian socialism from the middle years of the nineteenth century. But this is something else. This workingman Christ, 'on close terms with life and toil, with the actual troublous life of every day', is 'comradely'. Gurney's use of the term will owe something to Whitman, whose poetry he knew and deeply admired. It will also owe something to that close bonding between trench soldiers on which I have already commented and which, as Paul Fussell and others have suggested, is often marked by homo-eroticism.[20] But Gurney's use of the word 'comradely' is at once more social and political. The Pagan Gods can do nothing for modern London. Christ, the foreman carpenter, can.

Or can he? If the poetry is in the pity Gurney feels for London's working-class youth, then the politics are seeded in the recognition that comradeship is what will save them, will 'hot the tea, and shield a chap from fines'. Christ the carpenter is an image of such comradeship but only in so far as he is a working man, 'not yet full-grown'. For by that last phrase I take Gurney to mean that those who become more than foreman grow away from comradeship. They become bosses, separated from 'toil of the hands and brain together'. And it is this separation which Gurney opposes. His socialistic convictions have much in common with Morris and for that matter with the Tolstoyan belief in the redemptive power of physical labour, where that is an expression of what Morris's master Ruskin called 'the full man.' And, like both Morris and Tolstoy, Gurney fears the city as a place of degrading labour – 'useless toil' Morris called it – and therefore of degraded men and women. Work here is not so much with the hands as by the 'hands'. That is why London is a place of 'evil dwelling'. And it is why, in a later poem called 'A Wish', he begins: 'I would hope for the children of West Ham/ Wooden-frame houses square, with some sort stuff / Crammed in to keep the wind away that's rough, / And rain; in summer cool, in cold comfortable enough'.[21]

Gurney wrote 'A Wish' sometime after his terrible breakdown in the autumn of 1922. This may explain the lines in which he voices a wish for the children of West Ham to have houses with plots of land where they might

> use spade or the hand
> In managing or shaping earth in such forms
> As please the sunny mind or keep out of harms
> The mind that's always good when let go its way
> (I think) so there's work enough in a happy day.

As he well knew, there was not enough work for millions of men who had fought in the war and who were now reduced to 'state-doles, or showing shop-patterns/ Or walking town to town'. And he himself was jobless, despite repeated attempts to find work. To be sure, he found it difficult to hold any work down, but there is in his poetry at this time a passionate desire to celebrate what he calls in 'The Lock Keeper' 'A net of craft of eye, heart, kenning and hand'.

'The Lock Keeper' is Gurney's 'Lob'. Not so great a poem, but a very fine one. There is no space here for the lengthy discussion the poem merits, but I need at the very least to remark Gurney's statement that 'to praise men' is 'still a luck and a poet's privilege'. And the man *he* praises 'goes in my dark mind / ... Might well stretch out my mind to be a frame – / A picture of a worthy without name'. The matter-of-factness with which he mentions his own 'dark mind' is as noteable as his feeling that such a mind could be 'stretched' to fit, like a picture frame, the full portrait of the anonymous lock keeper. The lock keeper is any and everyman, like Lob, in fact. And also like Lob he is a tutelary spirit: a countryman, a man of craft, cunning, and one who is free to wander, to work, and to 'talk with equals', among whom are included 'coalmen, farmers, fishermen his friends/ And duties without beginnings and without ends'. This man does not work by the clock, is not a hired 'hand'. He is in short the embodiment of that Morrisian dream of the truly free man.

That Gurney yearned for such freedom with its necessary if paradoxical – seeming commitment to work – of 'hands and brain together' – is evident from a number of remarkable poems, all of them written between 1912 and 1922. There is, for example, the following, which I quote in its entirety.

> The hoe scrapes earth as fine in grain as sand,
> I like the swirl of it and the swing in the hand
> Of the lithe hoe so clever at craft and grace,
> And the friendliness, the clear freedom of the place.
>
> And the green hairs of the wheat on sandy brown.
> The draw of the eyes towards the coloured town,
> The lark ascending slow to a roof of cloud
> That cries for the voice of poetry to cry aloud.

The echoes of Thomas ('Tall Nettles' and 'Digging') and of Housman's 'coloured counties' do not so much detract from this lyric as help secure its sense of a perfect harmony momentarily achieved in and through labour. In 'The Valley Farm' Gurney speaks of how the woodchopper 'in the sun/ Moves with such grace peace works an act through him,' and as with 'The Hoe Scrapes Earth' and 'The Lock Keeper', man, work and landscape are brought into a kind of visionary harmony which is to be found in some of Thomas's poems and is, of course, celebrated in Vaughan Williams' 'Lark Ascending'. (Gurney's use of the title as a phrase in 'The Hoe Scrapes Earth' is an instinctive act of homage to the contemporary composer whose work meant most to him.)

The same harmony prevails in 'Felling a Tree'. 'The surge of spirit that goes with using an axe', that wonderful poem begins; and it ends with the tree finally cut down:

> The axe fell from my hand, and I was proud of my hand,
> Crickley forgave, for her nobleness, the common fate of trees
> ... the tree that for long had watched Wales glow strong,
> Seen Severn, and farm, and Brecon, Black Mountains times
>   without reckon,
> And tomorrow would be fuel for the bright kitchen – for brown
>   tea, against cold night.

As with 'North Woolwich', so here: 'brown tea' has an almost sacramental value for Gurney because it is linked to what it may seem doctrinal to call productive labour and yet for which I can find no other useable term.

Gurney worried that his own insecurely-followed professions of musician and writer were far from productive. His career as a composer was stalled and although his two wartime volumes had sold reasonably well he couldn't get anyone to publish a third collection of his poems, to which he had given the title *Rewards of Wonder*. In view of his uncertain mental condition it isn't at all surprising that he should have come to feel desperately unsure of himself. But the poem 'Hedger', written in the autumn of 1922, rejects self-pity. It begins with a mingling of hand and brain: 'To me the A Major Concerto has been dearer/ Than ever before, because I saw one weave/ Bright patterns of green'. Art is redeemed, illuminated, by the craft of the hedger, whom the wandering Gurney tries to assist. 'But clumsy were the efforts of my stiff body/ To help him in the laying of bramble, ready/ Of mind, but clumsy of muscle in helping,' whereas 'his quick moving/ Was never broken by any danger, his loving/ Use of the bill or scythe was most deft, and clear'. Faced with such skill, Gurney is forced to think about his own work as a musician:

> Had my piano-playing or counterpoint
> Been so without fear
> Then indeed fame had been mine of most bright outshining;
> But never have I known singer or piano-player
> So quick and sure in movement as this hedge-layer
> This gap mender, of quiet courage unhastening.

Gurney's readiness here to make himself ridiculous – his acknowledgement of how he was 'clumsy of muscle' – is not mock modesty. His unawed certainty of the hedger's skill merely acknowledges the craft of hand and eye. And while praise of the man's 'quiet courage unhastening' seems at first excessive we may well feel on reflection that it pays its way. At all events, Gurney's recognition of the hedger's calm methodical ability to cope with recalcitrant material goes with the humbling acknowledgement of his own failings; and it ensures his refusal to consider the artist as innately superior to the artisan, to separate him off from those who are his fellow men, fellow workers.

This wish not to be separated comes out even more strongly in 'The Mangel-Bury', which will have been written at very much the same time as 'Hedger'. The poem begins with Gurney coming across a carter filling his cart with mangels, joins him in his work and 'We threw them with our bodies swinging, blood in my ears singing'. That last phrase is redeemed from cliché by the emphatic internal rhyme that records and celebrates this seized moment of utopian harmony. But then he and the man separate: 'my pain to more moving called/ And him to some barn business far in the fifteen acre field'. By 'my pain' Gurney must mean the terrible mental distress that forced him into those endless walks, by night as by day, about the Cotswolds, and which also expressed itself in the paranoid delirium that would lead to his institutionalisation. And we can then gauge the intensity of his distress when we note how the poem opens: 'It was after the war; Edward Thomas had fallen at Arras – / I was walking by Gloucester musing on such things / As fill his verse with goodness'.

For Gurney saw himself as taking over from Edward Thomas, of becoming the poet who celebrates the troublous life of ever day. And even more than it had been for Thomas, Gurney's was a peopled landscape. It was also more local, and more deeply known. I cannot here follow his intimate acquaintance with 'my two thousand year home', as he called the Gloucestershire country through, across and around which he walked; nor can I do more than suggest that his post-war poetry is much concerned with what would now be called Green Politics. But it can at least be said that Gurney's imagining a 'Golden Age' of England's past to be situated in Elizabethan England, where he claims there was 'some / Natural moving towards life's love / ... men working freely ... / ... On a free soil' ('The Golden Age'), is less a soft-focus appeal to some routinely conceived mythic past than a strategy as useful as Morris's appeal in *A Dream of John Ball* and *News from Nowhere* to a 'merrie England' which operates as utopian contrast to capitalist class-separations and the progressive de-skilling of workpeople.[22] For Gurney as for Morris and Thomas, England was to be most fittingly imaged as a field full of folk. And Gurney's loathing of the invasion into the fields of bungalow and villa has to be understood, not as snobbishness, but as fear of what happens to a society that loses contact with its history. As he says at the end of 'The Bargain':

> Waltheof's field will become a rubbish heap.
> Villas will stand there and look polite; with folk polite
> Where sedges stood for the wind's play and poet-delight,
> But Severn will be sorry and it can never be right.

Poet-delight is here, as so often in John Clare, for that congruence of nature and element, sedges and wind, which intimates a sanctioned propriety of relationship only to be broken at terrible cost. At the end of 'Possessions', a lament over the cutting down of trees for the War,

Gurney says 'It was right for the beeches to stand over Whitcombe reaches,/ Until the wind roared and softened and died to sleep'. Internal rhyme indicates a harmony of relationship which affirms its being right. The word 'right', with its clear implication of natural rights, is no more casually invoked than it is when Clare uses it to protest against the depredations of aggressive individualism.[23]

But as we have seen, Gurney's post-war experiences disabused him of his wartime hopes that in England such rights would be championed and might even succeed in toppling the Duke of Bilgewater and his kind. At the time of his breakdown he wrote 'Sonnet – eptember 1922,' a dark, impacted poem in which a terrible sense of defeat seems to be battling it out with whatever hope he retains for men working freely on a free soil.

> Fierce indignation is best understood by those
> Who have time or no fear, or a hope in its real good.
> One loses it with a filed soul or in sentimental mood.
> Anger is gone with sunset, or flows as flows
> The water in easy mill-runs; the earth that ploughs
> Forgets protestation in its turning, the rood
> Prepares, considers, fulfils; and the poppy's blood
> Makes old the old changing of the headland's brows.
>
> But the toad under the harrow toadiness
> Is known to forget, and even the butterfly
> Has doubts of wisdom when that clanking thing goes by
> And's not distressed. A twisted thing keeps still –
> That thing twisted easier than a grocer's bill –
> And no history of November keeps the guy.

I do not pretend to fully understand this poem. But in the first eight lines Gurney seems to be saying that those who have the energy to protest against injustice are those who enjoy independence or who nurture confident dreams of the future. Yet whether they do so or not, history rolls on and over them and they are sacrificed as it advances. In the sestet we have either to read toad and butterfly as compliant with their fate, and of no more importance than a paper spill used to start a conflagration – a Guy Fawkes' bonfire; or that they protest against their fate but are destroyed by superior forces. Bleakly terrible though this reading is, it does at least keep open the possibility of protest. It also allows us to sense how deeply Gurney felt the outrages committed on his fellow men by the post-war government, that government's mute, cynical denial of responsibility for any social and political vision, its ready toleration of mass unemployment among those who had fought 'the bosses' war'. And although I do not doubt that Gurney's experiences as a soldier had exacerbated his already precarious mental balance, it is surely demeaning to a great poet not to acknowledge how in the period 1919-1922 his imagination was seized by the violence he saw being done to his hopes for a just society – hopes he must have shared with many thousands of other soldiers. Out of such hopes he made poetry. Out of the defeat of those hopes he made more poetry. And the poetry he made offers a decisive rebuke to any reading of post-war writing which claims as unopposable the authoritative voices of Eliot and Yeats.

IV

A year before Gurney was shut away Edgell Rickword published his first collection of poems, *Behind The Eyes*. Like Gurney, Rickword had fought in the war. Unlike Gurney, he was an officer. A few of his war poems find their way into most anthologies. After demobilisation he entered Oxford intending to study French. He lasted at the university for no more than a year and then set out for London and a life of literary journalism. *Behind The Eyes* contains a number of fine love poems, a witty farewell to Oxford ('Complaint of a Tadpole Confined in a Jam-Jar'), and is characterised by an air of at best fastidious melancholy.

The exquisite note of ennui is however in the end debilitating.

Rickword's next volume, *Invocations to Angels and The Happy New Year* was published seven years later. (The collection is more often known as *Invocations to Angels* but as will become apparent later the full title is important and should be retained.) Some of the earlier poems in this collection would not be out of place in *Behind the Eyes*. But there are new strengths, as here, in 'Luxury'.

The long, sleek cars rasp softly on the kerb
and chattering women rise from cushioned nests,
flamingo-tall, whose coral legs disturb
the mirror-surface where creation rests ...

The churches' sun-dried clay crumbles at last,
the Courts of Justice wither like a stink
and honourable statues melt as fast
as greasy garbage down a kitchen sink.

Commercial palaces, hotels de luxe
and Banks in white immutable ravines,
life's skeleton unfleshed by cynic rooks,
remain to warn the traveller what it means ...

Time has no pity for this world of graves
nor for its dead decked out in feathery shrouds.
The ghoul must perish with the flesh he craves
when stars' hoarse bells of doom toll from the clouds.

According to Charles Hobday, 'Luxury' had its origins in a visit Rickword paid to Paris in the summer of 1924.[24] This may well be so, but the poem as we have it mingles vision and prophesy in order to speculate about the hidden but sensed decadence of city life – any city; and this hints at a larger, more inclusive decadence. It is therefore of immediate relevance to note that at the time he was writing 'Luxury'

Rickword was considering setting up the literary magazine which, when it began publication in 1925, would be called *The Calendar of Modern Letters*, and that, as Arnold Rattenbury has rightly commented, contributors to *The Calendar* were aware that they were attacking 'a largely moribund literature, and increasingly the issue was posed as to whether this was not because the whole of society producing it was moribund'.[25]

By no means all the poems included in *Invocations to Angels* can be read as sophisticated comments on contemporary society. But the most ambitious project of the volume, 'The Happy New Year', most certainly can; and Rickword himself clearly saw this 'Masque' as of signal importance. Hence, his including its title in the title he gave to his volume. And this must, I am certain, be connected to the fact that the masque was written between the spring and autumn of 1926. Rickword therefore was working on 'The Happy New Year' throughout the period of the General Strike and its immediate consequences. This needs to be pointed out, because otherwise we might be tempted to think that Rickword's real concern is the war and its aftermath. The evidence for this wider concern lies partly in the fact that Rickword chooses as epigraph for his masque some lines from Jasper Heywood's play, *Thyestes*, which takes for subject the murder by an uncle of three young nephews and his serving them to the boys' father. This provides an apt allegory of the butchery of a generation during 1914-18. The London setting of 'The Happy New Year' can therefore appropriately enough – though with a bow in the direction of *The Waste Land* – modulate into a phantasmagoric landscape of war: 'A fog-like poison drifts and whirls / such dreadful faces as the sun shone on/lying in fields, propped against walls, on beds / mottled with leaf-lights'. These are the dead of no-man's land but also of the contemporary city, where 'I had not thought death had undone so many'. (And although Eliot's image derives from *The Inferno*, it may also have been prompted by footage of war-film showing soldiers in their thousands slogging up the line to death.)

To say this brings me to what Hobday calls 'a very curious paragraph' in the issue of *The Calendar* for April 1926. Here, the unnamed writer, whom Hobday thinks must be Rickword, speaks of a poem which the editors have procured and in which 'the crops rot, the land becomes water-logged, and complete sterility ensues'. The author considers this an adequate symbol of the contemporary consciousness ... literary references are intended to enrich the texture of the verse with imagery, for invention risks being vulgar, and, besides, the success of several very cultured poems has recently approved the innovation'.26 It may be, as Hobday suggests, that Rickword initially intended his poem to be a burlesque on *The Waste Land.* The masque makes use of a city setting and a mythological sub-structure. In a prefatory note Rickword explains the action as spanning the course of the year, from the moment when the sun 'falls through the celestial map (of the Ptolemaic system) from the zenith through the astronomical signs, Houses, to the nowhere below the Arctic horizon'. The sun then 'retraces his steps and sequentially injects his vigour into the earthlings dwindling from his absence. This peregrination is observed with detachment expressed in an ironic commentary by the Sinisters who finally disassociate themselves'.

The tone of this suggests that Rickword stands at an ironic distance from his own scheme. It may even suggest that he is not at all sure how seriously he wants his masque to be taken. If so, that can only be because he is distrustful of poetry which uses myth as a way of foreclosing on the complexities of history – including the history of the present. In his opening speech, the Presenter provides a melange of faded poetic styles and mannerisms, ways of speaking about the falling /failing sun:

> Rosy-slippered dawn
> goes tripping down the spangled lawns
> but drab reminders dun insolvent streets ...
> where moribund the later sons of earth
> bask and chew up the remainders of their days,
> contemning Sol's archaic ways
> whose heaped bonfire in the romantic style

nurtures their candle-end of wit and wisdom.

There is no telling whether this is the sun of empire, of western civilisation, or of hope briefly aflare after the armistice. Most likely it is meant to suggest all these things. But now in 'the wall-eyed city' the Presenter announces that 'Sol falls weakly through his ruined house, / a dead coal in a rusty grate'.

Rickword was a member of the Labour Party. This does not mean that Sol's weak fall can be read as an allegoric statement of MacDonald's first, brief, ineffectual administration; but in 'The Happy New Year' the Presenter speaks of those brave hopes which have foundered because of 'vows rescinded, broken contracts,' and of the many who 'renounce complaints in wan waters' or who 'fall on pity's sword'. Their choice is between suicide and the death of self-regard. At which point, with wonderful inappropriateness, the Chorus intones 'London has many merciful instruments,' and the Presenter then speaks of these 'withered souls ... / with bands of music wailing through the streets'. This is followed by the direction '(*Here the Sinisters come on*)'. Hunger marches, marches of the unemployed, of strikers: these are all implied in the 'bands of music', as are the street bands of former soldiers. This is London, 1926.

And in this London 'The sunny side of the road / crawls with the aged like a lousy seam'. As a soldier himself, Rickword knew all about lice. Here, they function as relics of a discredited generation who, in a newly-risen sun (the defeat of the strike?) continue to bask in wealthy comfort and who include among their number such literary coteries as are unwilling to confront the political-social issues of the time. So at least I read the Presenter's next lines, indicting 'An embryo with dim reptilian brain/ womb-bound in Wandsworth, and the female flocks/ from dullest Kensington, and City ants and owl-wise Bloomsbury, [who] all send up a shout'. They are joined by the 'Dexters', who must surely be the Bright Young Things, for in their chorus they sing

We do not crave eternity
love's bowl of quintessential pearl,
since half an hour's propinquity
exhausts the meaning of a curl,
The Time, the Place, and a Girl.

The Sinisters, however, although they briefly assent to the triumph of the newly-risen sun, do so on different terms. 'New blood begets new forms / for comedies or tragic shows, / new vigour to confront old storms'.

Rickword's revival and adaptation of masque as an example of new form has then to be seen in the light of his review for the *Calendar* of Enid Welsford's The Country Masque where, as Hobday points out, he speaks of masque as developing from 'a rough, licentious ritual,' and as having as its primary impulse the celebration or inducement of 'fertility and felicity'.[27] In 'The Happy New Year' the Chorus's last lines are: 'Like begets like, immortal in each kind;/ through perishing units' union, death's defeat'. Units may die, but in union lies ultimate victory. The failure of the general strike was due to the collapse of union solidarity and, as the strikers saw it, the caving-in of union leaders before Baldwin's ambiguous and soon disowned promises. The choice of masque form for 'The Happy New Year' makes evident Rickword's intent to connect emergent political and social energies with new or at least revived and adapted cultural modes of expression.

Not that the masque ends on a note of triumph. After the Chorus's promise of death's ultimate defeat the Presenter makes a sombre concluding speech:

I see others who walk the earth tonight, homeless
throughout the city, pacing day's void suburbs
by unmade roads, raw gardens, blank-eyed lamps,
cinders and tin-cans and blown evening papers,
among refuse-pits and sewer-mouths,
wandering fires and voices of the swamp;

passing deliberately into the night
through the infinite extension of this landscape.

These lines powerfully blend images of contemporary London with an infernal Dantean landscape, where the poor who pass 'deliberately into the night' may be seen as offering a future threat to the sunny side of the road. Hobday quotes from a review of Trotsky's pamphlet, *Where is Britain Going?*, which appeared in the *Calendar* in July 1926. The reviewer, whom Hobday thinks may have been Garman, poses the question as to whether 'there exists a proletarian party to take advantage of the position of contemporary social malaise. The answer to it will decide whether England ... is to stay on the road of continually degenerating values, or to create a revolution as vital, potentially, as the inception of Christianity'.[28] For Rickword an achievable Happy New Year lies in the future, and his masque is an at once sardonic and deeply unsettling vision of contemporary society. And as with Gurney, so with Rickword: the prospect which filled Eliot with 'the blackest gloom' was for them lit by the sun of an achieved democratic state.

1996

Notes

To avoid littering the text of the essay with unnecessary references I have given beside relevant quotations the titles of all poems by Gurney and Rickword to which I refer. They can then be consulted in *Collected Poems of Ivor Gurney*, chosen, edited and with an introduction by P.J. Kavanagh, London: Oxford University Press, 1982, and *Edgell Rickword: Collected Poem*s, ed. Charles Hobday, Manchester, Carcanet, 1991.

1. I have borrowed this phrase from Lucy McDiarmid, who takes it as the title for her excellent book on 'Yeats, Eliot, and Auden Between the Wars,' Cambridge: Cambridge University Press, 1984.
2. The letter is quoted by Donald Davie in *Poetry Nation Review* May/June, 1991, 24.
3. In his *Ireland 1828-1923: From Ascendancy to Democracy*, Oxford: Blackwell, 1992, D. George Boyce remarks that although by the end of March 1921 the government was under increasing international and internal pressure to resolve the Irish question – especially in the light of the Black and Tans' brutal tactics – 'the cabinet felt it had no option but to stand its ground and meet war with war' (99).
4. Henry Pelling, *A History of British Trade Unionism*, Harmondsworth: Penguin, 1963, 165.
5. Quoted by Samuel Hynes in *The Auden Generation: Literature and Politics in England 1930s*, London: Faber, 1979, p.33.
6. For this, see an article by Patrick J. Keane on Burke, Wordsworth and the Genesis of 'The Second Coming' in B*ulletin of Research in Humanities*, Spring, 1979.
7. The phrase comes from *Within The Rim* – the title of both essay and book – which James wrote shortly after the outbreak of the Great War.
8. For this see my essay on New Polyolbions in *Critical Dialogues: Current Issues in English Studies in German and Britain*, eds. Isobel Armstrong and Hans-Werner Ludwig, Tübingen: The British

Council/Gunter Narr Verlag, 1995. (See the final essay in this collection.)

9. *The Calendar of Modern Letters* savaged most of the collections that came from The Poetry Bookshop and/or which found favour with Squire. As a result, the journal sometimes give the impression of denying the worth of any specifically English poetry produced in the post-war period. Siegfried Sassoon, for one, wondered why it must always be attacking everything.
10. For a fuller account of MacDiarmid's criticism see my essay on Sassoon in Lucas, *Moderns and Contemporaries*, Brighton: Harvester Press, 1985.
11. Robert Graves, *But Still It Goes On*, London: Cape, 1930, 293. In *Robert Graves: His Life and Works*, London: Hutchinson, 1982, Martin Seymour Smith reveals that Graves had been commissioned to write a play and that although he knew nothing about the stage accepted the commission because he and Laura Riding needed money to build a house on Majorca (208-210). I have no reason to query the truth of this, and this is no doubt why the play is choc-a-bloc with Graves' preoccupations of the moment.
12. Michael Hurd's *The Ordeal of Ivor Gurney*, Oxford: Oxford University Press, 1978 is a first attempt at a biography of Gurney but is notably lacking in information about Gurney's intellectual development and his social/political affiliations.
13. Quotations come from *Ivor Gurney: Collected Letters*, ed. R.K.R. Thornton, Manchester: Carcanet, 1991, 261, 288, 348, 151 and 352-54.
14. *Collected Letters*, 249.
15. See *Collected Letters*, esp. 391-441 and passim.
16. Edward Thomas, *The South Country*, London, Dent, Everyman, 1993 edn., 87.
17. Gurney, *Collected Letters*, 441.
18. See *Collected Letters*, 12-13 and *Collected Letters,* pp.382, 70 and 486.
19. The best discussions of this murky subject are to be found in William Greenslade's essay on Fitness and *Fin de Siècle/Fin du Globe*, edited by John Stokes, London: Macmillan, 1992 and the same

author's full-length study of the concept of degeneration at the turn of the century, published by Cambridge University Press in 1994.

20. I know nothing of Gurney's sexual proclivities. The letters indicate that while in war-time France he became briefly engaged, but the identity of the woman remains a mystery. In *The Great War and Modern Memory*, Paul Fussell has written well of the homo-eroticism of some war poetry but I do not see Gurney's work as particularly homo-erotic, unless we cite the dubious evidence of 'To His Love'.
21. It may be that Gurney had in mind the dreadful poverty of Poplar, which had led to the imprisonment in 1921 of George Lansbury and the Labour Councillors of the district. They refused to levy rates which they knew their constituents could not meet.
22. *Merrie England* was the title of Robert Blatchford's work, first published in his socialist newspaper, *The Clarion*, in 1893, then in book form the following year. In this widely-read and frequently reprinted work, Blatchford, an avowed disciple of Morris, sets out an account of the blight of capitalism on the lives of workers and offers a socialist alternative. I find it difficult to imagine Gurney hadn't at least heard of Blatchford's book, and his own version of a genuine '*Merrie England*', which he locates in Jacobean times, is, for all its a historicality, important for his acute understanding of the ways in which Shakespeare and other dramatists of that period draw on common speech and idiomatic expressions and of how they imagine an England remarkable for its 'whole' living. It should be noted that between 1900-1914 several Arts and Crafts communities established themselves in the Cotswolds.
23. Gurney's concern with such rights cannot be disentangled from more general fears of the despoliation of England in the post-war period, a matter taken up by Clough Williams-Ellis in a book called *England and the Octopus*, which, when it was published in 1928, was enthusiastically reviewed by D.H. Lawrence, whose own attacks on 'ugliness' in his writing about Nottingham and the Mining Villages and in a famous passage of *Lady Chatterley's Lover* are also germane.

24. Charles Hobday, *Edgell Rickword: A Poet at War*, Manchester: Carcanet, 1989, 24.
25. Quoted by Hobday, *Edgell Rickword*, 102. For more on the *Calendar* see Hobday, esp. chapter 6, and my essay on Edgell Rickword in *The Sewanee Review*, 52.1 (1994): 112-121.
26. Hobday, *Edgell Rickword*, 96-7.
27. Hobday, *Edgell Rickword*, 99.
28. Hobday, *Edgell Rickword*, 95.

EDGELL RICKWORD

According to received opinion, Edgell Rickword gave up writing poetry in the early 1930s, either because the Communist Party of Great Britain – which he had newly joined – told him to, or because his own political conscience made him regard poetry as a bourgeois luxury and therefore an unworthy pursuit for a committed writer. Clive James holds this view and it has been voiced by writers a good deal more cautious than James. Thus Roy Fuller, in his excellent introduction to Rickword's *Fifty Poems: A Selection* (Enitharmon Press, 1970), remarks that Rickword's career in the 1930s makes sense only if we assume that he had decided to 'devote himself to the regeneration of society rather than the regeneration of literature', presumably choosing to allow Leavis and *Scrutiny* to try to bring about the latter regeneration; and Fuller mourns 'the truncation or deformation of a talent so outstanding'. Fuller, however, adds a note of caution that is unlikely to recommend itself to a man of James' brash absolutes: 'How far the Marxism he embraced led to his abandonment of poetry we cannot say, but his verse anyway quite quickly began to develop towards satire, epigram, and the kinds of topicality that only a few great poets – a Pope or a Swift – have been able to make of permanent interest'.

I met Edgell Rickword only once, in the Winter of 1975, when he was old and physically frail. But there was nothing wrong with his mind, and he made a very firm reply to my hesitant question about whether being a Party member had had much to do with his giving up poetry. (My interview can be found in *The 1930s: A Challenge to Orthodoxy*, Harvester Press, 1978.)

> No, not at all. It was just because I hadn't any impulse to write poems. I would have quite liked to but I was getting into rather a different mood, less subjective I suppose, and I think poetry must have much of the subjective in it. I had stopped writing poetry well before I became a Party member so all that stuff about how being a communist killed me off as a poet is nonsense.... My acquaintance with Marxism didn't act as a psychological brake on my writing life. Lyric poets tend to finish early, you know.

I think we need to weigh these words carefully, because they do much to dispel the simplistic argument that Rickword's decision to give up poetry can be explained in terms of his political commitments. The hidden bias of such an argument is that art and politics can never have anything to do with each other, which is and ought to be seen as nonsense. Dangerous nonsense, too, for it finally implies that art ought to be indifferent to ideas. Yet in a sense Rickword seems to be in agreement with it. 'Lyric poets tend to finish early, you know'. Yes, but Rickword was never an entirely lyric poet; and as Fuller says, he quickly began to develop towards satire. On the other hand, it is undeniably the case that certain poets do exhaust all they have to say in a comparatively brief span; the entire combustible world of their poetic material swiftly burns itself out. (Of poets roughly contemporary with Rickword we might note William Empson and Kenneth Allott, whose oeuvres are even slighter than his, and whose prolonged silences have led to much speculation as to their causes: e.g. Christopher Ricks on Empson, and Donald Davie on Allott.)

It is in the nature of things that speculation cannot be other than tentative, provisional. Nevertheless, a careful reading of Rickword's work, poetry and prose, may go some way towards helping us grasp the probable reasons for his decision to give up poetry. And in case it should be thought that I beg the question in speaking of a decision – for mightn't it simply be that poetry deserted him rather than he poetry, that he had no choice in the matter? – I should add that in his interview with me he remarked that he didn't try very hard to write poetry in the 1930s because 'for some time I had had the news that it had ceased'. Which, if it admits that the necessary fire was out, also makes it clear that he chose not to hammer cold iron.

Rickword published three separate collections of poetry: *Behind the Eyes* (1921), which contains some of the most remarkable poems to have come out of the First World War, poems that are still underestimated; *Invocations to Angels* (1928), which I agree with Fuller, contains his finest work; and *Twittingpan* (1931), dominated by satirical verse. There is in addition a so-called *Collected Poems of 1947*, which omits a good many poems, and the Enitharmon *Fifty Poems*, which restores fifteen poems withheld from the 1947 volume and adds two which had been previously uncollected.

Anyone coming to Rickword's work for the first time is bound to be struck by the fact that he belonged to the generation for whom Grierson's great edition of Donne acted as the discovery of a new-found land. 'Our ears have been opened', Rickword wrote in the course of a savage review of a bad critical study of Donne, 'and it would be profane now to think of [him] as less than a master of English verse .... If we are to compare 'purest utterances', those of Donne on sacred and profane love are, it has been granted, excellent by no poet in the language'. Those sentences were written in 1924, and the extent of Rickword's debt to Donne is plain to see in *Behind the Eyes*, which appeared in the same year as Eliot's famous essay on 'The Metaphysical Poets'. It is customary to assume that Eliot defined those poets for his generation; and to an extent he did. 'A thought to Donne was an experience; it modified his sensibility .... The poets of the seventeenth century, the successors of the dramatists of the sixteenth, possessed a mechanism of sensibility which could devour any kind of experience'. I do not deny that Rickword would wish to assent to those words, and it is certain that some of his own work exemplifies the hope for poetry which they embody. His poems can glitter with brilliantly deployed ideas, handled with a grace that is perhaps justifiably described as toughly lyric. (Rickword's skill in handling ideas in verse gives him the right to attack Wyndham Lewis's irresponsible way with them. As he justly remarks, 'To have a lot of ideas is no more to be a good thinker than to have a lot of soldiers is to be a good general.)

Yet this side of Rickword's work always seems to me somehow sport; it is more than merely dutiful because the nature and scope of his gifts never allow him to write a dull or unmusical verse. But in the last resort Donne surely matters to Rickword less for the reasons that appealed to Eliot than for his love-poetry (which was also why he appealed to Empson)? So that when Rickword writes, in 'Beyond Good and Evil',

> Her thoughts haunt that duplicity
> and perch alike on tree and star,
> in calm, white-winged simplicity,
> innocent as angels are.
>
> Since, in those blissful powers at least,
> thought and act are identified,
> it is a part-angelic beast
> sleepily smiling by my side

– when he writes this, he is not merely asking us to remember Nietzsche's famous remark that whatever is done out of love takes place beyond good and evil, he is also identifying with Donne the spaceman, in Empson's famous formulation; he is emotionally and intellectually at one with the poet who insists that lovers create their own universe, free from the moral and religious considerations of a post-lapsarian world. And this is the voice that speaks in 'Intimacy'.

> Since I have seen you do those intimate things
> that other men but dream of; lull asleep
> the sinister dark forces of your hair
> and tie the bows that stir on your calm breast
> faintly as leaves that shudder in their sleep;
> since I have seen your stocking swallow up,
> a swift black wind, the flame of your pale foot...

> I have not troubled overmuch with food,
> and wine has seemed like water from a well...

But here another comparison inevitably suggests itself. The tone of these lines echoes the work of English poets of the decadence, of Symons and Dowson, perhaps; and behind them, of course, loom the greater figures of certain French poets, above all Baudelaire. For although we shouldn't place undue stress on an isolated phrase, that 'sinister dark forest' may well signal woman as Salome, as fatal attraction; and in its characteristic deployment of such images Rickword's love poetry is the nearest thing I know in English verse to an attitude, a habit of mind that is to be found in much of Baudelaire's poetry. Fuller notes qualities that link Rickword to the characteristic virtues of seventeenth-century verse, but it is the French connection that I would rather stress. Poems such as 'Obsession', 'Chronique Scandaleuse' and 'Necropolis' ('Decayed fertility now wraps me close / in darkness of no-more-desire, / in damp and fusty sheets of fallen rose / rust-edged at touch of fire / expired, and staring coldly as the moon... The essence ravished from the pudic rose/ oozes from Memory's fallen flask') – such poems are inconceivable without those French poets of the decadence whose work Rickword knew and about whom he wrote: Baudelaire, Laforgue, Corbière and Rimbaud. Whether he knew equally well the work of the English decadents is unclear, but it is at least likely.

This is not to say by this that Rickword set out to imitate these poets. But I think it obvious that they meant a great deal more to him than even Donne, and I suggest that they did so because his modern sensibility was more attuned to their sardonic, disillusioned view of love than to the one he found and cherished in Donne. The only poem of Rickword's which utters an unqualified 'yes' is a remarkable lyric, 'The Cascade', which is, or so I think, at once a brilliantly ingenious description of a waterfall and also a metaphoric evocation of the female orgasm. And even this poem ends with a bitter twist:

The iron beaks that seek her flesh
vex more her lovers' anxious minds,
in whose dim glades each hunter finds
his own torn spirit in his mesh.

If I understand this stanza aright, and the conceits are uncomfortably compacted, Rickword sees man as both aggressor and victim: he is in fact hurt by his own lusts, tortured by his own flesh.

This sad, sour account of love has to be set beside Rickword's sense of universal disorder that finds expression in such poems as 'Earth and Age' and the wryly named 'Regret For the Passing of the Entire Scheme of Things':

Whilst now in dusky corners lovers kiss
and goodmen smoke their pipes by tiny gates –
these oldest griefs of Summer seem less sad

than drone of mowers on suburban lawns
and girls' thin laughter, to the ears that hear
the soft rain falling of the failing stars.

Such accidie is unmistakably modern. Which is to say that it is of the 1920s. It is easy to forget how that decade was marked by a deep-rooted cynicism, a feeling (and perhaps no more than a feeling, since the best lacked all conviction) that life had become a kind of posthumous existence without purpose or value. And if we are tempted to dismiss such feelings as youthful excess, or indulged rancour, we ought to remember that they were shared by most of the best writers of the time. 'The man of today has inherited a nervous system which cannot withstand the present conditions of life'. That is Montale. And this is Rickword, on Corbière: '[His] is the poetry of rhythmic agitation of the subconscious'. The point I wish to make is simply this, that Rickword's sensibility was one that made it impossible for him to be other than grievously shaken by the world he came into and fought through – and although he was physically injured in the Great War the poems that come out of that experience record the equivocal mastering of a deeper hurt. His finest work expresses a rhythmic agitation of the subconscious in which delight and disgust are blended in about equal proportions, but in which the equilibrium always threatens to give way to vicious cynicism, hatred, self-loathing. Rickword's poems have an outer suavity and an almost dandaical control of cadence which he was certainly helped to achieve through his reading of French poets, and which at a very deep level he needed because formal orderliness helped him cope with the otherwise intolerable disorder he found about him. And although love might seem to offer a stay against confusion in fact it proved to be a further or even major source of confusion, yet further evidence of a world falling apart.

Rickword, in short, found himself deeply divided. On the one hand, there was the promise that Donne's poetry seemed to epitomize: the promise of a world elsewhere, which makes one little room an everywhere; on the other, the fact of disillusion, of 'spirit sunken, girls undone' ('Complaint After Psycho-Analysis'). How far was he prepared to face the fact of that division? 'It is often in the artist himself that the enemy to creation is most deeply entrenched, in distrust of his own intuitions; in fear of, resulting in contempt for, aspects of his own emotional life'. Rickword wrote those words in the course of an essay on Wyndham Lewis, and I think they may tell us a good deal about himself. They may, that is, explain why he began to move towards satire and away from the more lyric, though guarded, personal poetry of his early period. For it is at least possible that Rickword came to feel that he had to direct his attack towards the outer world, to find in its horrors an explanation for disorders within. 'The churches' sun-dried clay crumbles at last, / the Courts of Justice wither like a stink / and honourable statues melt as fast / as greasy garbage down a kitchen-sink'. These lines come from 'Luxury', and if we recall the earlier meaning of the word as well as its modern one, we can, I think, gain some sense of Rickword's seeing in the sins of the flesh a releasing metaphor for a distinctly modern malaise. Given this, he was bound to turn towards satire, and to the wish for 'explosions of the spleen' as he put it in his fine essay on 'The Re-Creation of Poetry', where he makes plain that such explosions are of value because they 'bring about that relief and cleansing of the mind which is one of the functions of expression'.

Why then did Rickword stop writing poetry? Because he had sufficiently cleansed his mind? Perhaps. Yet I think it truer to say that the best of his work answers to his claim that 'We need a poetry in which the moods [of pure ecstasy and sheer revulsion] are subtly balanced'. The difficulty comes in holding that balance, once you have achieved it. Rickword achieved it in a handful of lyrics that are of a quite unique value. I do not know that we have the right to expect any more.

1982

MAKING THE 1920S NEW

There is a long-established view of the 1920s according to which novelists hung out a sign saying business as usual, whereas for poets it was all change. Bennett, Gibbs and Walpole managed to cling to the cult of briar pipes, tweed suits and monogamy (to paraphrase George Orwell) while English poets – but of course there were no English poets. They had been killed in the Great War. The following decade was therefore dominated by the non-English – Yeats, Pound and, above all, Eliot. Then, at the end of the 20s, came Auden. English poetry was back on the rails, although the best of it would travel by unfamiliar routes (from Birmingham to Wolverhampton).

Like all generalizations, this blends truth and falsehood in about equal proportions. To see why we need look no further than that key year, 1922, the year of Bennett's *Mr. Proback* and Eliot's *The Waste Land* – traditionalism versus modernism. But then it was also the year of Hardy's *Late Lyrics and Earlier* and of *Ulysses*, and before we rush to adopt that other familiar generalization according to which the English stayed loyal to traditional virtues while the rest of the world got on with being modernists, we need to recall that 1922 was flanked by *Crome Yellow* and *Antic Hay*, and that *Mrs Dalloway* would appear in 1924. Besides, Robert Bridges's *New Verse* (1925), most of which had been written in 1921, revealed a poet deeply affected by the war and its traumatizing effects on the consciousness of Europe. Hence 'Low Barometer' which despite, or perhaps because of, a faded vocabulary and strict metres, can barely contain its horrific vision of a world given over to death:

Some have seen corpses long interr'd
Escape from harrowing control,
Pale charnel forms – nay ev'n have heard
The shrilling of a troubled soul.

That wanders till the dawn hath cross'd
The dolorous dark, or Earth hath wound
Closer her storm-spredd cloak, and thrust
The baleful phantoms underground.

'That corpse you planted last year in your garden, / Has it begun to sprout? Will it bloom this year. / Or has the sudden frost disturbed its bed?' It says much for Bridges's deep sense of the destructive powers unleashed in 1914 that he should have come so close to anticipating Eliot's famous lines; and his fear of the baleful phantoms helps to explain his public endorsement of closer relations with post-war Germany (for which *The Times* gave him a severe verbal caning). It may also go some way to account for the urgency with which he worked on the unreadable *Testament of Beauty*, published in 1929, the year before his death. I suspect this was a final, honourable but forlorn attempt to produce a work which would affirm the continuing vitality of that humanist sense of European culture he had earlier evoked in his war-time anthology, *The Spirit of Man*. Sadly it ended up as a wagonload of 'timeless' speculations on the beautiful, hauled by plodding hexameters. These fragments I have shored against my ruin.

As to Hardy. Three years after *Late Lyrics and Earlier* he brought out *Human Shows*, and then, in 1928, the year of his death, *Winter Words*. This final volume includes the epigrammatic 'Christmas: 1924':

'Peace upon earth!' was said. We sing it,
And pay a thousand priests to bring it.
After two thousand years of mass
We've got as far as poison gas.

Hardy wasn't surprised by the horrors of a war that had so shaken others. Nor, it should be said, was he being wise after the event. His grimly laconic reading of history had found pre-war utterance in his great work *The Dynasts* as well as in such individual poems as 'The Convergence of the Twain' (about the sinking of the *Titanic*) and 'Channel-Firing', the latter of which, dated 'April 1914', ends: 'Again the guns disturbed the hour, / Roaring their readiness to avenge, / As far inland as Stourton Tower, / And Camelot, and starlit Stonehenge'. But of course this very refusal to be taken aback by the events of 1914-18 could be a source of comfort to others. Hardy had foreseen it all. He could therefore be claimed as the most eloquent and persuasive voice of a vital English line of poetry which the deaths of Owen and Edward Thomas might have been supposed to have broken. And so when Robert Graves cycled down to visit Hardy in 1920, he famously reported the old poet to have told him that '*vers libre* would come to nothing in England' and that 'all we can do is write on the old themes in the old styles, but try to do a little better than those who went before us'. There are good reasons for doubting that Hardy said any such thing, but he couldn't contest Graves's account because by the time it appeared in *Goodbye to All That* he was dead. What is beyond dispute is that Graves, who loathed Pound, chose to brandish Hardy's presumed remarks in his personal battle against imported modernism; and this has subsequently been turned not so much against him as against Hardy. Hence, Donald Davie's well-known accusation that Hardy sold English poetry short, an accusation which has behind it an assumption that Hardy didn't much care for the grandly confident poetry of his younger contemporaries, that he was in fact a little Englander, and as such could be used by a later generation of English poets to justify their sneers at 'abroad' and everything to do with modernism. I am certain this accusation is unfair – Hardy had always maintained a keen interest in French poetry, and he even spoke politely about Pound's *Homage to Sextus Propertius* – but the point to grasp is that Graves spent the 1920s battling against most modernist tendencies in poetry.

Graves's campaign got under way in his critical essay, *Of English Poetry* (1922 – that year again) and then in *Contemporary Techniques of Poetry* (1925) he went on the attack against virtually all contemporary poets. Only Hardy and Frost were spared, because only they understood what poetry was about. Traditionalism's last stand? Perhaps. And yet although Graves's own poetic practice is undoubtedly based on those regular metres and stanza forms which he praised Hardy and Frost for using, and although his *Poems, 1926-1930* may at first glance seem contentedly to exist within Georgian conventions, some key poems voice a bleak recognition that the prewar world is gone for ever. 'Lost Acres', for example, feels to be a threnody for that heart of England Edward Thomas had so persistently sought out – 'A plot of undiscovered ground', so Graves says; but the lost acres cannot be recovered:

> They have no doubt, their flowers, their birds,
> Their trees behind the phantom fence,
> But of the substance of mere words:
> To walk there would be loss of sense.

Graves's traditionalism can perhaps best be thought of as the last-ditch strategy of a poet trying to solder together a past and present which he senses have finally broken apart. His saying *Goodbye to All That is*, then, a way of turning his back on actual history in the interest of constructing a poetic vocation that can be located within an ideal 'timeless' history. Once out of England he manages, against the odds, to produce a body of first-class poems, although as with Landor's, you feel that the marmoreal perfection of the best of these has much to do with their having been sealed against the encroachments of the actual.

But for other poets who had fought through and survived the war, history would not go away. Edmund Blunden's post-war verse is haunted by wrecked landscapes of primal joy, lost Edens. Between 1920 and 1930 Blunden published at least nine volumes of poetry, plus *Undertones of War*, which, like several key writings about the war, appeared in 1928. (It took a decade for many to come to terms with the traumatic effect of the years 1914-18.) In all of these volumes, *Undertones* not excluded, there are poems whose subject is war or memories of war. *The Shepherd and other Poems Of Peace and War* which came out in – yes – 1922, is haunted by what seems to be inescapable mental torment as in the driven, obsessive poems 'Festubert 1916' and 'Third Ypres: a Reminiscence'. And in 'Death of Childhood Beliefs' Blunden writes of his own lost acres:

> Drummers jumping from the tombs
> Banged and thumped all through the town,
> Past shut shops and silent rooms
> While the flaming spires fell down, –
> Now but dreary thunder booms.

Here, an 'innocent' rumble of thunder in the English countryside springs a memory of the heavy guns of war and of a weird, phantasmagoric Armageddon which is also the landscape of an actual battle: 'Drummers jumping from the tombs'. Infantrymen as the souls of the dead.

Death operates as a dominant force in Blunden's poetry of the 1920s. In the justly celebrated 'The Midnight Skaters' (*English Poems*, 1926), it lurks within the pond's secret waters:

> What wants he but to catch
> Earth's heedless sons and daughters?
> With but a crystal parapet
> Between, he has his engines set.

These lines pick up on a distinctive feature that can be found in much writing of the 1920s: the sense of living on borrowed time, which therefore licenses a frantic and even joyless hedonism. Hence the last stanza of Blunden's little masterpiece:

Then on, blood shouts, on, on,
Twirl, wheel and whip above him,
Dance on this ball-floor thin and wan,
Use him as though you love him;
Court him, elude him, reel and pass,
And let him hate you through the glass.

At roughly the same time this fine poem was being written, Evelyn Waugh was noting in his diary that 'I received a letter from Richard Greene telling me that he is becoming definitely engaged with Elizabeth. It makes me sad for them because any sort of happiness or permanence seems so infinitely remote from any one of us'. There is a posturing about this (though not in *Vile Bodies*, Waugh's novel about a society literally wheeling to its death) which is absent from Blunden's poetry. And this prompts the question as to why is there still no adequate account of Blunden's work, given that in the 1920s in particular he produced any number of outstandingly good poems. Every so often someone notes that he's shamefully neglected; but there the matter rests.

Perhaps we need a proper edition of his poems, of the kind we now have for Ivor Gurney and as a result of which we can see that in the poetry he produced between 1919 and 1922 (when he was shut away in an asylum), and even in a handful of poems of later years, Gurney became a great poet. In the key years he unshackled himself from the Georgianism of his early verse. Like Patrick Kavanagh, Gurney began to write poetry more or less as a pastime – he was trained to be a musician – and only gradually discovered that it was his way of life. This in essence meant that he found the means to break out of the undue constraints of those formal metres which had at first contented him, while keeping a most powerful sense of rhythmic propulsion, and in this he was aided by learning how to use a loose, casual syntax and springboard rhymes that bounce you from one line to the next. Gurney had an intense admiration for Whitman and for the blank-verse of Elizabethan writers. He probably came to these through musician friends and teachers: Vaughan Williams's *Sea Symphony*, which Gurney, his pupil, loved, uses lines from Whitman (although Whitman, the homoerotic poet of democratic vistas was 'in the air' among many young writers and intellectuals in the first decade of the century); and the recovery of Elizabethan writers and musicians is part of that complicated attempt to vindicate a native English culture which also preoccupies English writers in the pre-1914 years. Gurney, who admired the music of, among others, Downland and Byrd, developed an intense, reverential love for the poetry of Elizabethan and Jacobean poets, and he came to them quite independent of Eliot's 'vindication' of such writers in *The Sacred Wood*, which incurious literary historians have wrongly taken to mark the modern rediscovery of that 'English' line. Gurney knew nothing of Eliot's work when he praised, in terms Eliot could anyway hardly have used, 'the football rush' of Chapman's blank verse. But the phrase could well be applied to Gurney's own headlong energy. The writing of his great period is characterized by a voracious determination to see and 'express' his England – of Gloucestershire and the Cotswolds – before that becomes impossible. For Gurney is haunted by a terrible sense of loss; he too mourns lost acres.

There's an almost desperate ardency in his recording the acres he walks – and walks and walks.

> One comes across the strangest things in walks:
> Fragments of Abbey tithe-barns fixed in modern
> And Dutch-sort houses where the water baulks
> Weired up, and brick kilns broken among fern,
> Old troughs, great stone cisterns bishops might have blessed
> Ceremonially, and worthy mounting-stones;
> Black timber in red brick, queerly placed
> Where Hill stone was looked for – and a manor's bones
> Spied in the frame of some wisteriad house
> And mill-falls and sedge pools and Saxon faces;
>
> ('Cotswold Ways').

The restless eagerness of this is reminiscent of John Clare, as is the refusal to sort out or tidy up his impressions. Gurney reads his landscape in terms of a complex history whose very higgledy-piggledyness disbars him from 'ordering' it. But this isn't to say that it amounts to no more than fragments shored against ruin. Gurney's England, like Thomas's, is to be interpreted in terms of a human history. At the same time, it can be read with greater familiarity and love than even Thomas, that displaced wanderer, could achieve. Gurney's acres are at once more local and more of a knowable palimpsest. Knowledge such as this necessarily includes within it a tragic sense of loss.

> Sand has the ants, clay ferny weeds for play
> But what shall please the wind now the trees are away
> War took on Witcombe steep?
> It breathes there, and wanders at old night roarings;
> October time at all lights, and the new clearings
> For memory are like to weep.
> It was right for the beeches to stand over Witcombe reaches
> Until the wind roared and softened and died to sleep.
>
> ('Possessions')

This miraculous little lyric, while it grieves over a gap made in nature, also celebrates consonance, relationship, mutual possession: true love. The last two lines, with the passionately stressed internal rhyme emphasizing and so celebrating mutuality, nevertheless relegate 'possessions' to the past tense. And in many of his greatest poems Gurney shifts uneasily between past and present in an attempt to bridge gaps which the poems themselves end by recognizing cannot be reconnected. 'The Lock Keeper' (a poem which will stand comparison with Thomas's 'Lob') begins with Gurney remarking that 'Men delight to praise men; and to edge / A little further off from death the memory/ Of any noted or bright personality / Is still a luck and a poet's privilege'. But not only is the lock keeper 'unnoted' until Gurney writes about him, he is inevitably housed in the past tense. And this is not because Gurney indulges a sentimental longing for some mythic 'essential countryman', but because his sense of a decisive and terrible change within a culture's history requires him to confront as fact his sense of dislocation and severance.

Gurney shares this apprehension with another poet and survivor of the war, Edgell Rickword. But there is a difference. It is not only that Rickword (born in 1898) was eight years younger than Gurney, nor that he was a city poet. (His early heroes, Donne apart, were Baudelaire and Rimbaud.) The fact is that, put together, these matters become more than the sum of their parts. Rickword belongs to a post-war generation of whom it's possible to say that they are sons in revolt against their fathers. He is therefore a more directly political poet than Gurney. It's true that he didn't join the Communist Party until the early 1930s, but in his first fine volume, Behind the Eyes (1921) Rickword cultivates a weary disdain for the culture he has inherited but wishes to disown. This pose owes something to his reading of French poets, but the knowing, dandiacal, mocking-melancholic note he most often strikes is very much his own creation. For example, 'Regret for the Passing of the Entire Scheme of Things':

> Whilst now in dusky corners lovers kiss
> and goodmen smoke their pipes by tiny gates –
> these oldest griefs of Summer seem less sad
>
> than drone of mowers on suburban lawns
> and girls' thin laughter, to the ears that hear
> the soft rain falling of the failing stars.

Yet Rickword's technical panache is put to best use in a number of love poems, chief among which are 'Intimacy', with its stunning opening ('Since I have seen you do those intimate things/ that other men but dream of; lull asleep/ the sinister dark forest of your hair'); 'Dead of Night', 'Desire', 'Dalliance; and several others.

I don't intend to scant the early war poems by which alone Rickword is far too frequently represented in anthologies of 20th century poetry. 'Winter Warfare', 'The Soldier Addresses his Body', 'Trench Poets', are all fine poems, but it is important to remark that readers who only know him by these poems (and possibly by his Spanish-Civil War squib, 'To the Wife of a non-Interventionist Statesman') can have no idea of his range. There are poems in his second volume, *Invocations to Angels* (1927) which are among the best work to have come out of the 1920s. The equable but mordant stanzas of 'Luxury', for example, show why Rickword's social awareness amounts to a political vision of real depth and scope.

> Time has no pity for this world of graves
> nor for its dead decked out in feathery shrouds.
> The ghoul must perish with the flesh he craves
> when stars' hoarse bells of doom toll in the clouds.

By the time Rickword was identifying this world of graves he had decided to bury some of the 'fathers' he so despised. In 1925 he co-founded the *Calendar of Modern Letters* with Douglas Garman. 'We were discontented with all the established novelists and the literary cliques', Rickword was to recall many years later, and this discontent led to the journal's regular 'Scrutinies'. Here, such eminences as Arnold Bennett, Sir James Barrie, and Galsworthy, were put through the shredder. Yet although 'Scrutinies' was undoubtedly important I don't see it as being of any greater significance than the journal's internationalism, for which Rickword deserves most of the credit.

In nearly all literary histories of the decade it's taken for granted that Eliot's international outlook has to be seen as a decisive rebuke to the insularity of the English. But if you compare Eliot's *Criterion* with *The Calendar* it soon becomes clear that, of the two, the latter did more to alert English readers to good writing by non-English authors. Quite apart from contributions by Forster, Lawrence, and Aldous Huxley and such new writers as Edward Muir and L.P. Hartley, *The Calendar* also published stories by Leonov, Nievierov, Isaac Babel,

Pirandello and Remizov, poems by the Americans John Crowe Ransom, Allen Tate and Hart Crane; translations and reviews of work by Trotsky, Valéry, Gide, Proust; and Andre Breton's 'Manifeste du surréalisme' was also carried in translation.

The Calendar's editorial policy – hampered, it must be admitted, by Rickword's absolute indifference to efficient management (on one occasion he had to pawn his typewriter) – shows that, contrary to much that has been assumed about the 1920s, there is no justification for thinking that the choice of literary journals lay between *The Criterion* and whatever Sir John Squire happened to be editing in any particular year. Nor does *The Calendar* shine alone. In the later years of the 1920s Cambridge's small magazine, *Experiment*, was publishing early work by, among others, William Empson, Kathleen Raine and Malcolm Lowry; and in 1929 the *Fritillary*, an Oxford journal for women writers, was edited by the young E.J. Scovell.

This is of some importance. If the 1920s sees the emergence of a new generation of women prose writers – Woolf, Rhys, Bowen, for example – it is also remarkable for the number of women poets who began to publish. There are good reasons for this upsurge of women writers. They include the fact that during the war women had taken over work previously thought of as reserved for men and this had given them a measure of independence they weren't prepared to surrender, especially when it was reinforced by a long overdue act of parliament that enfranchised all women over the age of 30. In addition, the 1920s, that decade of Marie Stopes and 'married love', was also the decade when not merely the sons but the daughters revolted against their fathers.

New freedoms became the norm: new styles of architecture, a change in relationships. Carrington, Strachey, Partridge; H.D., Richard Aldington and their various lovers; the Woolfs and Sackville-West; Mary Garman, Roy Campbell and Sackville-West; Sackville-West, Violet Trefusis and her husband; Winifred Holtby, Vera Brittain and *her* husband; Laura Riding, Robert Graves and Nancy Nicholson; Sylvia Townsend Warner, Valentine Ackland and their various male and female lovers; to say nothing of the Sitwells and their hangers-on and off-droppers. There are women poets in each of these groupings, and I wouldn't claim that all of them are worth making a fuss over. Nor can I see why Anna Wickham is thought to be much good. Charlotte Mew is a very different matter but most of her good work seems to have been done by 1920. As for H.D., the best of her work is in prose.

Laura Riding, on the other hand, is a poet of real worth, though the nature of that worth is very difficult to pin down and deserves an essay to itself. Her pared-to-the-bone verse makes just about every other poet of the decade look unduly rhetorical; and her astringent lyricism clearly made a deep impact not only on Graves but, as Graves was later to remind people, the young Auden. Her 1930 collection, *Poems: A Joking Word*, is, as Michael Hamburger has remarked in The *Truth of Poetry*, 'outstanding ... for its intellectual tautness, its sophistication and its psychological searchingness'. No account of the poetry of the 1920s can afford to ignore this collection. Riding's major concerns have to do with the problematic nature of words as conveyors of truth-to-reality; and they are most teasingly and effectively explored in such poems as 'The Quids' – 'the little quids, the monstrous quids, / The everywhere, everything, all quids' – where quids are, I assume, a kind of verbal monad, a vocalized quiddity, the flesh made word; and 'The Troubles of a Book', whose last stanza runs:

> The trouble of a book is chiefly
> To be nothing but book outwardly;
> To wear binding like binding,
> Bury itself in book-death,
> Yet to feel all but book;
> To breathe live words, yet with the breath
> Of letters; to address liveliness
> In reading eyes, be answered with
> Letters and bookishness.

That Laura Riding's poetry should be so little discussed is pretty disgraceful. The poetry of Sylvia Townsend Warner, though nowhere near that level of achievement, ought also to be better known than it is. It's of course true that with the success of *Lolly Willowes* (1926) Townsend Warner became an accepted novelist; and later successes such as *Summer Will Show* (1936) and *The Corner That Held Them* (1948), to say nothing of numerous collections of short stories, means that she can be regarded as essentially a prose writer. But this is to ignore the fact that during her life she went on writing and publishing poetry. It's also to skate past her remarkable volume of poems, *The Espalier* (1925). *Time Importuned*, which followed three years later, is far less successful, perhaps because, as her editor Claire Harmon suggests, Townsend Warner had allowed her imagination to be affected by T.F. Powys's love of 'graveyards and dark, empty houses'. But the second volume is also formally dull. In the collection's final poem, 'The Decoy', Townsend Warner claims that 'I have tamed two birds, / Called metre and rhyme'. She has indeed, with the result the poems end up as stuffed linnets.

The Espalier is, however, a very different matter. It includes a number of poems which, if they occasionally anticipate the faux-naif note of Stevie Smith, nevertheless breathe a genuinely new and heady air: a kind of beady-eyed deviltry which goes with formidable narrative skills. 'Nelly Trim', for example, about a woman who gives herself to a demonic lover, is a truly original poem, and one of cherishable sexual candour: 'He breathed her to him / With famished sighs, / Against her bosom/ He sheltered his eyes, / And warmed his hands / Between her thighs'. The same can be said of a handful of other poems in the volume, while 'Peeping Tom', which is dedicated to Powys, turns out to be a teasing meditation on that tutelary figure of the possibly 'essential' countryman whom Thomas and Gurney had evoked. As an embodiment of 'Englishness', however, Townsend Warner's character is even more elusive than either Lob or the Lock-Keeper. Unlike them, he has no place to call his own. At the end of the poem, having pulled up a weed that he thinks may be a sign of his spot of hallowed ground, he 'peered at it / Full steadfastly – and then/ Throwing it down,/ Limped on again'. He must survive without the consolation of dwelling which both Thomas and Gurney had sought for their Englishmen. The poem can therefore be read as an expression of Townsend Warner's growing awareness of social and political crisis which would eventually lead her, like Rickword, into the Communist Party.

I can't follow her that far. Nor can I do more than suggest that a comparable awareness is almost certainly responsible for the handful of terrific poems which Elizabeth Daryush wrote in the 1930s, especially the two sonnets, 'Still Life' and 'Children of wealth in your warm nursery' – work whose quality certainly couldn't be anticipated from the tepid verses she published during the previous decade. Nevertheless, English poetry in the 1920s was a great deal more various and more accomplished than is usually allowed. This isn't to make a 'little Englander' claim. Eliot, Yeats and Pound are still the big three, although Gurney is of their company and so, probably, is Riding. But that shouldn't mean that we have to ignore or slight the work of other poets. A good anthology would show us what we've been missing.

1993

SYLVIA TOWNSEND WARNER AS POET

In 1925 Sylvia Townsend Warner published her first book, a collection of poems to which she gave the title *The Espalier*. Over half a century later, two years after her death in 1978, *Twelve Poems* saw the light of day. From first to last, then, Townsend Warner can be thought of as a poet. But the publication in 1926 of *Lolly Willowes* and, a decade later, of *Summer Will Show*, more or less guaranteed that her abiding reputation would rest on her novels. I see no point in protesting about this. Townsend Warner wrote wonderful prose fiction, and her best (and sometimes her worst) work as novelist and writer of short stories is increasingly acknowledged and discussed. It would, however be a pity if the attention paid to her prose meant that her poetry was pushed into sidings and left there.

For Townsend Warner is a true poet. Yet to the best of my knowledge her poetry rates barely a mention in studies of twentieth-century poetry. This may be connected to the fact that whereas her major novels are in print or easy to come by, her *Collected Poems,* which Claire Harman edited for Carcanet, and which was published in 1982, has long been unobtainable. Moreover, it was published on paper so shoddy that it quickly became as discoloured and friable as wood-shavings, almost as though the publishers hoped the book might go up in smoke. Since then there has been a not very good *Selected Poems*, and Jane Dowson included six poems in her 1996 anthology of *Women's Poetry of the 1950s*, among them verses Townsend Warner wrote out of her principled support of the Spanish Republic. Dowson also prints 'Drawing You Heavy With Sleep', which ought to be in every anthology of love poetry but isn't. But then you will not find Townsend Warner represented in any of the recent anthologies of twentieth century poetry, no matter that they find space for poets who haven't an ounce of her talent.

Both Harman and Dowson make helpful remarks about Townsend Warner's poetry, as does Jan Montefiore in *Feminism and Poetry* (1987). There are also brief, illuminating essays by Donald Davie and Peter Scupham. Davie, who for all his pugnacious and, I think, wrong-headed defence of Poundian modernism, was, like Pound himself, capable of wide-ranging generosities, twice offered critical notes on Townsend Warner's poetry, both of which are to be found in his collection of reviews and more substantial pieces, *Under Briggflatts: A History of Poetry in Great Britain 1980-1988* (Carcanet, 1989.) In the first of these, Davie worries at the question of whether Townsend Warner's style is better thought of as out of date or out of fashion, and perhaps not surprisingly concludes that it's now the one, then the other. On the whole, however, he thinks of her as a late Georgian in that her style is for the most part pre- or even anti-modernist. This can even be detected, he says in poems whose matter ought to require a modernist approach. Thus in *Opus 7*, one of the fruits of what Davie calls 'her long dalliance' with the Communist Party, 'her village is, as never before, firmly a post-l919 village. And yet this new-found responsibility to the date on the calendar has the effect of highlighting more than ever the incongruity between the matter and the manner, the impression of new wine in old bottles'.

In fact, *Opus 7* was begun in 1929 and published in 1931, four years before Townsend Warner joined the Communist Party of Great Britain (CPGB). But Davie is quite right to register the poem's radical politics. Whether he is also right to consider that the politics undermined or anyway compromised by the poem's style is a matter to which I will return. Here, I will only say that Davie deserves credit for acknowledging in what is essentially a three-page note that Townsend Warner's politics mattered very much to her.[1]

In his second, rather longer piece, called 'Sylvia Townsend Warner, Posthumous', Davie is, however, concerned purely with matters of style.[2] Taking his cue from a remark she let fall about why Dryden appealed to her, Davie now suggests she is best understood if we recognise that her style is a matter of conscious choice and not something she simply fell into. He is struck by her suggestion that there is something 'sublime' about Dryden's handling of the animal-myth in 'The Hind and the Panther', his fable of Church and State, as evidence of which Townsend Warner quotes the line 'The Lady of the spotted muff replied', and about which she comments: 'Now that is a line which is purely nonsensical and yet Dryden is so stately in his control of the medium and so sublime that one hears it almost with awe'. This, Davie suggests, is Dryden consciously making use of the only version of the sublime open to him, namely the baroque. It is a mannered style. By the same token, Townsend Warner's style is deliberately mannered, knowingly out of kilter with its subject-matter, maintaining an on-guard, even at times ironic distance which can as easily modulate into social or historical distance. In this sense Townsend Warner is to Georgian poetry what John Crowe Ransom is to Thomas Hardy. I am not sure that Davie sufficiently allows for the self-conscious comedy of Townsend Warner's procedure but he is surely right to insist that her style isn't a matter of hapless eccentricity, a blend of Miss Tox and Margaret Rutherford. On the contrary, it is intellectually and imaginatively astute. (The OED definitions of the word include 'shrewd, sagacious, *crafty*'.) [My italics]. Sylvia Townsend Warner's poetry is both carefully crafted and full of craft.

Peter Scupham also focusses on matters of style.[3] His essay makes any number of deft suggestions about Townsend Warner's tactics or what might be called her poetic signature. Thus, having quoted a stanza from 'The Story of a Garden', Scupham notes:

> The stanza has many of the marks of her style: the just-askew rhymes, the stresses that make artfully memorable cadences by setting up a threatening tremor in the heart-beat, the spare, unmetaphorical diction, the habit of ending a poem by introducing a cloud no bigger than a man's hand … .

He also draws attention to her 'unillusioned way of seeing, feeling, and thinking demonstrated in plain style – her poetic vocabulary never mines the more *outré* veins of the dictionary, her deceptive simplicities and occasional archaisms made enticing by a sure and strange fitness of cadence'. We might jib at the phrase 'plain style', if only because Townsend Warner's poetry is hardly that plain cooking made still plainer by plain cooks about which Auden complained. But for the rest, Scupham is spot on. As here, where, having quoted the opening stanzas of 'Vale' with its listing of

> Roxeth and Kenton
> Greenford and Mutton Lane,
> The gasworks and the canal:
> These were my ports of call
> Between the autumnal and the vernal equinox

he says: 'There's a special pleasure in the taste, the saying of a poem like this: the tongue's lilt lightening the head, creasing out a smile'.

Fitness of cadence, poetry on the tongue. Such phrases remind us, if reminder is needed, that Townsend Warner studied music, was a distinguished musicologist, and that from 1917 she worked for a decade as editor on the ten volume Oxford History of *Tudor Church Music*. Equally important – perhaps indeed more important – she became, as Arnold Rattenbury has pointed out, a familiar of the 'New Elizabethans'.[4] A composition student of Vaughan Williams, she was, as how could she not be, alert to the Royal College of Music's vivid interests in the folk song tradition and in the setting of poem-texts, interests which were to loom so productively in the careers of, among others, Herbert Howells, Gerald Finzi and Ivor Gurney. 'Elizabethanism of this sort was a love of newness, poetic invention, verbal and imaginative adventure, rather than something historically exclusive'. None of this guarantees that Townsend Warner would herself be able to make use of those interests. On the other hand, given the qualities that Scupham rightly identifies, her grounding in folk-song and in the setting of Elizabethan poems was sure to be of immense benefit to her.

With a wide face
And an anxious nose
The owl sits in the ash tree
Thinking of all he knows –
Thinking of all he knows,
And his quiet feathers
Sit duteously around him
Like good scholars.

This may start from cliché – the wise old owl – but it took a rare poet to spot the 'anxious nose', still more the possibility of transforming those fustian 'quiet feathers' by the miraculous wit of 'duteously'. In addition, the wavering, or perhaps more accurately, undulant pulse of rhythm, together with the repeated line, 'Thinking of all he knows', indicates just how much Townsend Warner's poetry profited from her musical background.

There is, though, another aspect to all this, one to which Rattenbury importantly draws our attention when he remarks that the new Elizabethans and their associates were socialists. 'Vaughan Williams had been a socialist since his student days at Cambridge', and for him, as for others in his circle, radical politics were inseparable from art. Whitman, that seer of Democratic Vistas, was a key figure for all of them. Hence, most famously, Vaughan Williams's *The Sea*, with its quotations from Whitman. Far less famous but worthy of note, there is Townsend Warner's student 'Requiem', a setting of Whitman for string quartet and voice. This is not to suggest that in any sense Townsend Warner writes like Whitman. She does, though, in *The Espalier*, frequently try on the loose-limbed couplets practised by Ivor Gurney, another Whitman devotee, whose influence is unmistakeable in such poems of hers as 'The Vinery Has Been Broken', 'A Man in a Landscape' and 'Mangolds' – 'unstirred the last / Flecks of the motoring soil. Day-long lumber past / Lorries and farm tumbrils with the mangold load,/ And the cars spurn the spillings along the road'.

And the radicalism which so shapes the course of *Lolly Willowes* and which would eventually lead Townsend Warner into the CPGB is, from the first, stirring powerfully within her.

As Rattenbury has also noted, a radical impulse is manifest in her writing about Rosa Luxemburg.[5] The same holds for the anti-prudential sexual generosity of 'Nelly Trim'. This ballad about a woman who welcomes a cold stranger into her house and sends him, warmed, into the night, is remarkable for its entire lack of coy evasion, or of the reliance on stock effects that does, I find, limit the achievements of Robert Graves' strictly contemporary ballads about sexual love.

> With looks unwavering,
> With breath unstirred,
> She took off her clothes
> Without a word,
> And stood up naked
> And white as a curd.
>
> He breathed her to him
> With famished sighs,
> Against her bosom
> He sheltered his eyes,
> And warmed his hands
> Between her thighs.

Conventional opinion insists that the woman is 'A wanton'. The poet's answer is that Nelly Trim has behaved well, has offered comfort to 'a stranger, bound / She knows not where. / And afraid of the dark, / As his fathers were'. I don't want to lay too much stress on what is after all a slight ballad, but it is to be noted that 'Nelly Trim' acts as an implicit rebuke to that encounter between house-agent's clerk and typist in *The Waste Land*, which was for so long taken to typify the sterility of sexual relations in the modern world. Nelly is in some ways an anticipation of Polly Garter. David Holbrook was outraged by

Dylan Thomas's readiness to imagine and then celebrate Polly's sexual liaison with Captain Cat. 'Is it likely she would have consented to sex with this drunken old reprobate?' Holbrook demanded to know. 'Yes,' William Empson wonderfully replied, 'We love her for being so unlike Mr Holbrook'.

Nelly is one of several outsiders in *The Espalier*. Her behaviour denies the propriety of utilitarian, prudential value. It alerts us to, or at least glances at, the fact that in the 1920s many of the young rejected those values they associated with an older generation which, in the eyes of that generation's sons and daughters, had elected for and then rejoiced in the terrible destructiveness of the First World War. Down with the old, down with their morality. A new sexual candour, generosity, permissiveness – call it what you will – became almost a norm and was the more asserted the more it was identified by that older generation with the 'decadent' or, even more horrendous, the radical.[6]

The long shadow cast by the war is also the subject of 'Cottage Mantleshelf', one of the most unsettling poems in the volume. I am astonished that this poem isn't better known. Peter Scupham's reaction may, however, help to explain its neglect. 'Almost an oddity in the richness of its bric-a-brac,' Scupham says of it, although he adds, 'How well I knew such mantelshelves [sic]; how curious and how right seems her half-whimsical, wholly moving recreation of the paired marriages of black, pink-rose-painted vase and vase, flower-basketed dog and dog, stencilled fan and fan – and then the dissonance: the unpaired clock 'rocking its way through time' and the photograph of the dead young soldier'. The sentimental Georgian clutter becomes electric, he goes on: 'the last stanza with its risky re-write of Lawrence Binyon's 'To the Fallen', holds the scene in that mordant equipoise which is her trade-mark'. All of which is well said, as far as goes. It doesn't, however, go nearly far enough.

Here, then, is the last stanza.

> Uncomely and unespoused amid the espousals of beauty,
> The cats with their plighted noses, the vases pledging their roses,
> The scapegoat of the mantleshelf he stands and may not even cleave
> To the other unpaired heart that beats beside him and apart,
> For the pale-faced clock has heard, as he did, the voice of duty
> And disowns him whom time has disowned, whom age cannot
> succour nor the years reprieve.

The soldier who did his duty and is dead, is disowned in the sense that Ivor Gurney recognised and railed against in poem after poem of the post-War period. A 'grateful nation' was all too quick to forget what debt it owed those who fought and died, fought and, more troublingly, survived.

> Where are they now, on state-doles, or showing shop-patterns
> Or walking town to town sore in borrowed tatterns
> Or begged. Some civic routine one never learns.
> The heart burns–but has to keep out of face how heart burns
> ('Strange Hells')

The pale-faced clock is therefore doing no more than is habitual in turning its back on the unespoused soldier. He is dead, speak no more of him.

But there is more to it than just this. To understand why the poem is unsettling and, I would say, important in a way that Scupham doesn't acknowledge, we need to have before us the two preceding stanzas. For it is just here that we are enabled to understand why the young soldier is a 'scapegoat' who must go 'unespoused'. Townsend Warner has acknowledged that among all the clutter of 'love and beauty' are 'two uncomely whose sorrows / Isled in several celibacy can never, never be mated, / One of them being but for use and the other useful no more'. The two are the clock and 'young Osbert who died at the war'.

Against the crumpled cloth where the photographer's fancy
Has twined with roses the grand balustrade he poses,
His hands hang limp from the khaki sleeves and his legs are bent.
His enormous ears are pricked and tense as a startled hare's,
He smiles–and his beseeching swagger is that of a nancy,
And plain to see on the picture is death's indifferent rubber stamp of assent.

As though through gathering mist he stares out through the photo's
Discolouring, where the lamp throws its pink-shaded echo of roses
On the table laid for supper with cheese and pickles and tea.
The rose-light falls on his kin who sit there with a whole skin,
It illumines through England the cottage homes where just such ex-voto
Are preserved on their mantleshelves by the living in token that they are not
    as he.

'His beseeching swagger is that of a nancy'. So *that's* why he couldn't belong in the world of pairings, of espousels. *That's* why he's a scapegoat. 'I am a tainted whether of the flock'. Antonio's sad self-loathing in *The Merchant of Venice* is a recognisable variation on the dead soldier's 'beseeching swagger', his being imaged as hare and scapegoat, hunted or banished animals. The obtrusive rhyme on 'fancy'/'nancy', which can't possibly have been unintended, is there in order to draw attention to the young man's 'unmentionable' homosexuality. The shock of this even manages to take away from the undoubted clumsiness of the line with which the following stanza opens.

Whether Sylvia Townsend Warner knew the poetry of Charlotte Mew I don't know, though it seems highly likely. *The Farmer's Bride* had, after all, been well received on its publication in 1916, and an enlarged edition appeared in 1921. Like Townsend Warner, Mew is interested in writing about those marginal figures who shun or are shunned by conventional communities. Hence, the title poem of her famous volume, about a woman who rebels against the confinements of domesticity. Hence, too, 'The Changeling' and 'Ken', whose eyes 'looked at you / As two red, wounded stars might do', and whose 'voice broke off in little jars / To tears sometimes. An uncouth bird / He seemed .../ ... arms thrust out as if to beat / Always against a threat of bars'. I bring in Mew, not to argue for influence, but to suggest common interests – ones that were shared by others at the time. And as that time was the 1920s, a decade when young writers were, not surprisingly, in revolt against their elders, the hope and/or need for change prompted much of what they wrote. Scupham implies that on the whole Townsend Warner means to endorse the worth of the cottage life she depicts. I am certain she means to do no such thing. The poem is about poisonous suppression, the denial of commonalty. The 'norm' of this cottage life is as rigid, as deadly, as the town life of *Lolly Willowes*' family. Both cottage and town house are massively resistant to the change which can alone make for a good society.

But knowing that change is needed isn't the same as knowing how to achieve it. Eccentricity is all very well, but more is required in order to bring about new styles of architecture, a change of heart. Townsend Warner obviously realised this – it is there in *Lolly Willowes* – but in her early poetry the possibilities for change seem only faintly glimpsed or end in defeat. 'Peeping Tom', for example, a long poem – it covers eight pages of the *Collected Poems* – looks as though it might be about a man's desire to be of 'independent means' (that state John Clare so ardently desired), someone who, in radical Spencean terms, owns enough land to live by. Instead of working for the farmer in whose interest he has to rise up early and go home tired, Tom yearns

To have some land of my own,
To be my land
And mine alone.

Say, half an acre –
More would outdo my means –
To grow potatoes
And a few beans.

This longing for land of one's own was not merely still common at the time, it had been turned to practical ends by, among others, the Whiteway Colony, which had set itself up as a kind of Tolstoyan community in the late nineteenth century, and which by the 1920s was located in the Cotswolds, five miles north of Stroud, where Townsend Warner would almost certainly have either come across it or heard of it. The community even attained a brief notoriety when it was investigated by MI5 agents in the post-War years, on the grounds that its members were 'thought to be practising free love in the English countryside [and] were considered to be a Bolshevik threat'.[7]

Whether Townsend Warner initially meant her Peeping Tom to become a communitarian, I don't know. But after a promising beginning the poem turns into a portentous meditation on the fatal lure of 'the bride/ Nature, hidden under her dark veils of Time and Space and Causation'. That the poem should be dedicated to T. F. Powys is sufficient cause for alarm, at least if, like me – and Peter Scupham – you are immune to what Scupham calls 'the welter of character, mystification and rurality of Powys-land'. All too soon 'Peeping Tom' traipses off into that land, to become, predictably enough, lost in the rhetorical wastes of 'ah' and 'parteth' and 'brooketh' and 'hearken', and a general tangle of deadhead blossoms.

At a casual glance *Opus 7* looks as though it might lie open to a similar charge. Not, however, because of the apparently coy, if mysterious title, the explanation for which is simply that *Opus 7* was Townsend Warner's seventh book-length publication. (Although we should not forget that at the time there was a taste for severe titles: Group X, and Auden's *Poems* 1930, each poem identified by number alone.) But as we have seen, Davie thinks the poem written in an out-moded style, and Scupham confesses that *Opus 7* 'with its visionary alcoholic heroine Rebecca Random of Love Green is not for me – I find it too much a conflation of Powsyery and the Georgian trudge of such a poem as 'Miss Thompson Goes Shopping', by Martin Armstrong'. I know what he means and I can also understand Davie's feeling that the poem is improperly 'quaint'. Not that this is a word he uses, but it lies behind his charge that although the matter may be new, the manner creaks. If I also think there's more to the poem than either will allow it is because of elements to which they don't attend. And these need to be given due weight if we are to come to a fairer estimate of the poem's worth.

In the first place, then, we need to knock on the head the routinely-made and deeply misleading assumption that Townsend Warner's poem is somehow reminiscent of Crabbe's work. Crabbe is a great poet – a greater poet, to be blunt, than she is – but only someone who wasn't prepared to look steadily at either could think they had much in common. It certainly won't do to say that as both used couplets and were fascinated by social outcasts, he has her in his grip. Crabbe adapts his verse narratives from the heroic couplet of his great predecessors, Dryden and Pope. 'Pope in worsted stockings', he was sneeringly dubbed, although Byron, a great admirer, rightly praised him as 'Nature's sternest painter and her best'. In Crabbe's couplet poems each distich is complete in itself, run-overs are infrequent, and every verse paragraph is a free-standing block. In contrast, Townsend Warner's more fluid narrative couplets have an onward impetus which is derived from a very different tradition, one that starts with Shelley and finds a fit successor in Browning. It is true that Crabbe greatly appealed to nineteenth-century novelists, including Dickens, George Eliot, Elizabeth Gaksell and Hardy, because from him they could learn ways to manage an intense scrutiny of individual lives and their social circumstances. Nobody has bettered Crabbe in 'reading' a character through his or her domestic arrangements, ways of speaking, of dress, of decor, of all those involuntary revelations of who and what we are. For all I know, Townsend Warner may have learnt from him in this respect, but if you want to see how well she handles such material, read her prose fiction. *Opus 7* is about something else.

It is of course mostly about its heroine. 'A visionary alcoholic heroine,' Scupham calls her. Well, yes, but this is to ignore the significance of her name. It is inconceivable that so self-conscious a poet as Townsend Warner could have been unaware of the resonances set up by 'Rebecca Random'. She would certainly have known that the rioters in South Wales of the 1840s who were protesting against unfair toll charges levied on public roads, and who were either led by women or by men dressed as women, took, less as their motto than as their inspiration, that moment in the Good Book where men 'blessed Rebekah, and said unto her, Thou art our sister, be thou the mother of thousands of millions, and let thy seed possess the gate of those which hate them' (Genesis 24 ix). Every band of rioters who seized possession of tollgates throughout South Wales was led by a captain called 'Rebecca', and the members of the band were known as her 'daughters'. As to Roderick Random, in the words of one commentator, the hero of Smollett's novel pits his 'furious small wits against the monumental and massively organised depravity of the existing social order'.[8] Townsend Warner would have known that, too.

Still, Rebecca Random isn't a heroine of the people. That kind of romantic individualism belongs to an earlier moment. (Or ought to: but there would be intendedly radical novels of the 1930s which try to reinstate the ideal.) Townsend Warner began writing her poem in 1929, the year that saw the election of the second minority Labour government and of the Wall Street Crash The previous year all women over the age of twenty-one had become enfranchised, but in that same year Radclyffe Hall's lesbian novel *The Well of Loneliness* was banned. 'I would rather give a healthy boy or girl a phial of prussic acid than this book,' James Douglas told his readers in the *Daily Express*. The best of times? The worst of times?

In addition to these confusing signals we need to keep in mind that 1928 and the following year saw the publication of many of the key writings about the Great War: *Death of a Hero, Undertones of War, All Quiet on the Western Front, Journey's End, Goodbye to All That*, all belong to these years. That the aftermath of war matters in *Opus 7* is made very plain in the episode where an Anzac soldier asks Rebecca for some wallflowers and then tells her about himself:

> ' … great-grandfer
> was bred up hereabouts, and here he courted
> a girl, and married her, and was transported
> for firing ricks . . .
>
> … When I was a pup
> I felt to come to England I'd give up
> all I could ever have–and here I am,
> her soldier. Now, I wouldn't give a damn
> for England. She's as rotten as a cheese,
> her women bitches and her men C3's.
> This silly soppy landscape – what's the use
> of all this beauty and no bloody juice?
> Who'd fire a rick these days?' 'Farmer Lee
> fired his for the insurance once,' said she.
> He heard not, and spoke on. 'I've come too late,
> and stay too long. Ruin can fascinate
> a man like staring in a cattle-hole;
> that still, black-waterlook pulls down his soul.'

These lines surely indicate that the poem isn't the indulgence Scupham takes it to be. Nor is it, as Davie contends, an attempt to decant new wine into old bottles. The narrative couplets are a perfectly effective means of conveying, among much else, the vigour of the soldier's speech. They also, and artfully, allow us to recognise that much as we might want to accommodate the poem to the Georgianism of which Scupham convicts it, we are here dealing with a poisoned pastoral. Rebecca's is no idyllic village. It is deeply, you could say incurably, infected by greed, snobbery, bourgeois fear – masquerading as contempt -of any mode of living that challenges its own timid acceptance of Ruin. I use the word the soldier uses because it is certain that he is to be regarded not merely as one voice among many but as diagnostic of England's ills.

And to say this is to suggest that we do Townsend Warner and

Opus 7 in particular a great disservice if we fail to register the poem's concern with England at the end of the 1920s. Other poets shared the concern. 'Get there if you can and see the land you once were proud to own,' Auden was writing at the same moment as Townsend Warner began work on *Opus 7*. There is a glee in his challenge to what he perceives as the wasteland of post-War England that's very different from the dark pessimism of Eliot's poem. And this is to be accounted for not merely by the fact that 'Get There If You Can' is a young man's work, an iconoclastic pastiche of Tennyson's 'Locksley Hall', with its encomium to a glimpsed future greatness of Empire, but because whether that glee is sardonic or exuberant – and it is both by turns – Auden's glimpsed alternative to ruin requires new styles of architecture, a change of heart. Such an alternative is also tentatively present in Edgell Rickword's masque, 'The Happy New Year', published in his 1928 collection, *Invocations to Angels* and the *Happy New Year*. But Rickword understands how difficult it will be to achieve the change of heart that lies beyond the confines of the wasteland. Opposed to those who want Change are the powerful forces of reaction he characterises as 'the Dexters'. Moreover, Change, to be effective, cannot be merely cosmetic. Above all, it cannot be a retreat to some dream of rural England. This has a particular bearing on Townsend Warner's poem.

For at the end of *Opus 7* the couple who buy and renovate Rebecca's cottage and who think they'll be able to set it up as a 'picturesque' tearooms – an image of olde-England- – fail dismally.

> I passed the cottage some few weeks ago.
> Where once the flowers had been there was a row
> of tottering iron tables where no one sat …
> and at the inn I heard it told that these
> newcomers did so poorly with their teas
> that they had set out cots, one in the pantry,
> to house the well-dowered by-blows of the gentry.

Opus 7 is, quite deliberately, pastiche Georgianism, as the opening of *Lolly Willowes* is pastiche realism. It undermines the form's claim to present vitality. That Townsend Warner would have been persuaded of the need to confront such a claim becomes evident as soon as we note that in 1929 Longmans began a series of books on 'English Heritage'. Individual volumes were dedicated to Folk Song and Dance, the Parish Church, and Wildlife. The series carried an introduction by Stanley Baldwin in which he famously claimed that 'England is the country', and, believe it or not, Longmans were able to induce a commendation for the series from Ramsay MacDonald. The following year Batsford began its own series, with volumes on the Countryside, Villages, Inns and Cottages, all those well-dowered infestations of the gentry.

Given such rottenness, such Ruin, it is clear that Rebecca Random, outsider though she undoubtedly is, cannot be a vehicle for change. On the contrary, her name is carefully chosen in order to remind readers that each generation must find its own fit image of protest against and opposition to rottenness. From now on, Townsend Warner will discover her fittest images in prose fiction. In particular, as Arnold Rattenbury has, I would hope definitively, noted, there is 'her great novel of middle-class desertion towards revolutionary engagement, *Summer Will Show*'.[9] But to say this is not to question the originality of *Opus 7*. If anything, it reinforces the poem's originality. She had done battle against Baldwin and MacDonald's reactionary appeal to rural circumstance as evidence of a still healthy England. Other battles had now to be fought.

2000

Notes

1. Donald Davie, *Under Briggflatts*, Carcanet, 1989, 58-60.
2. Davie, 229-233.
3. Peter Scupham, *Poetry Nation Review*, 26.5: 63-5.
4. Arnold Rattenbury, *London Review of Books*, 14 October 1999, 15-19.
5. Arnold Rattenbury, 'Literature, Lying and Sober Truth: attitudes to the work of Patrick Hamilton and Sylvia Townsend Warner', *in Writing and Radicalism*, ed. John Lucas, Longman, 1996, 210.
6. For a further discussion of these matters, see John Lucas, *The Radical Twenties Aspects of Writing*, Politics and Culture, Five Leaves Publications, 1997, and Rutgers University Press, 1999, see chapters 3 and 4.
7. See an article in *The Independent*, Friday, March 3, 2000.
8. Donald Bruce, *Radical Dr Smollett*, Gollancz, 1964, 73.
9. Rattenbury, *Writing and Radicalism*, 209.

COMPULSIONS OF A CODGER

Roy Fuller, *New and Collected Poems, 1934-84*. 557pp. Secker and Warburg in association with London Magazine Editions. 557pp. ISBN 0436 167905

For so widely praised a poet, Roy Fuller is strangely difficult to bring into focus. At first glance this may look to be no more than a problem of classification, of just where to place him in literary historical terms. Born in 1912, Fuller is too young to be put among the 'Auden Group', even though he shares (or shared) many of their concerns. By the same token, he is too old to be brought into the Movement, even though some of his characteristic virtues make him sound like a composite, Larkamie, poet, with his respect for form, social observation and wry humour. As for the 1940s, it is clear that Fuller has nothing in common with the tepid excesses of the neo-Apocalyptics, and his war poetry is of less interest than that of Alun Lewis or Keith Douglas.

All attempts to fit poets into the pigeon-holes of literary history inevitably involve a good deal of lopping and wrenching, and it shouldn't matter that as far as Fuller is concerned the attempt hardly seems worth while. On the other hand, it is odd that there seems to be very little agreement as to which poems – or periods – represent his best work. D.J. Enright prints ten poems in his *Oxford Book of Contemporary Verse* (they include 'The Unremarkable Year', 'Autobiography of a Lung-worm', 'Consolations of Art'); in the Oxford *Twentieth-Century Verse* Larkin prints six different poems (for example 'The Image', 'The Day' and 'Faust's Servant'). Larkin's selection seems to me by far the better, and yet it would be difficult to argue that it is the one on which Fuller's reputation will eventually come to rest, or that the half-dozen poems he has chosen make you impatient to read Fuller in bulk. On the evidence they provide, Fuller is optional rather than required reading.

It is a fate for which most poets would perhaps be content to settle, Fuller included. So at least you feel as you begin to read your way through the *New and Collected Poems*, and note the many occasions on which he says or implies that there are things important beyond all this fiddle, or that he doesn't think he's the stuff of which poets are made, or his life the stuff out of which poems are made.

> According to a TLS review
> Franck 'led an uneventful life ... was not ...
> Prolific'. Might have been describing me

Yet by the time you have finished reading, and noted that the nearly 550 pages don't by any means amount to a *Complete Fuller*, you realize both that he is extremely prolific (there are novels, autobiography and criticism to be taken into any final account); and that when in 'Family Matters' he speaks of the 'true joy of life, creativeness', he means it. Fuller is, in fact, a compulsive poet; and by the 1970s he has come to think so naturally and easily in verse that such volumes as *Tiny Tears* (1973) and *From the Joke Shop* (1975) can best be thought of as verse journals. Indeed, in a much earlier piece, 'Poem to Pay For a Pen', he says, 'it seems/ That any old subject fits into my verse'.

Of course, putting it this way is to imply that 'any old subject' mustn't be taken too seriously, or that Fuller as poet is incapable of giving it serious treatment. And again and again this is precisely what Fuller *does* say. Or rather he implies that some failure in himself, some unbreakable reserve, makes it impossible for him to respond as a good poet should to the material he handles. In the 'Obituary of R. Fuller', he writes that he is 'so unemotional and shy / Such friends as he retained would cry / With baffled boredom, thankful they / Were not part of his family'; and although in the much later 'Family Matters' this self-scrutiny or self-presentation has been altered to an account of himself as 'Ironic, emotion-hiding', it is clear that Fuller has always chosen to image himself as a poet who lacks passion.

But the matter of choice is important. In the wartime sonnet sequence 'Winter in Camp', he notes that 'Beyond the word, the chosen images,/ Painful and moving as they are, I feel/ Unutterably the epoch's tragedies'. At first glance this is so wet that it seems to be an attempt to set Godfrey Winn to verse. But then you notice that 'unutterably' is, after all, not uncunning (to use a Fuller locution): it is an almost blatant apology for not being able to write better, rather than an amateurish declaration of emotions. Or it may be. It begs the question of how far and in what ways you can trust the statements of a poet who so astutely asks to be taken on trust. All Cretans are liars … .

> Says his life to the poet: "Can you make verse of this?"
> And the poet answers: "Yes, it is your limitations
> That enable me to get you down at all."

'Rhetoric of a Journey', from which these lines come, is a good poem (too long for most anthologies, though); and in lifting the lines out of context I am being slightly unfair to them. But they carry the odd, unsettling note characteristic of much of Fuller's work: a note of blue-eyed candour which does not mean entirely to conceal the tease. You cannot tell whether the lines are confessional or wittily self-scornful; and the problem is compounded by the fact that the syntactic inversion in the first line feels proper to a poet who so oddly talks to himself, or who feels himself to be talked to: who is, in short, a codger (or, in Fuller's own formulation, 'Buff').

The oddest of all features of 'Rhetoric of a Journey' is that it comes from *Epitaphs and Occasions*, published in 1949. Fuller was therefore in his mid-thirties when he began playing the role of codger. If we need any more evidence of this extraordinary gimmick we can find it in a poem from the same volume, 'Youth Revisited', where Fuller writes of 'A war more innocent, an age of man/ Removed, my poem thick with formal doom/ and baseless faith in humans'. Such lines tell us not only that long before 1956 Fuller was keen to renounce an earlier commitment to Marxism, but that he found a way of presenting himself that would deflect imputations of bad faith. For how can you take seriously someone who speaks of a 'baseless faith in humans'?

Not that the faith had ever been particularly strong. Where the young Fuller tries his hand at socialist verse, as in the Audenesque 'Follower's Song', you sense how inauthentic it is:

> Oh to be mad with marching and May,
> To be bold, to be brutish,
> To dream in the night and by day
> To delight in duties ... .

The tone of this shows how far Fuller is from wanting to be such a follower. Whenever in his earlier poetry he claims to be speaking for and/or with others he sounds remarkably unFuller-like:

> But where the many are there is no death,
> Only a temporary expedient of sorrow
> And destruction, today the caught-up breath –
> The exhalation is promised for tomorrow.

– 'Autumn 1940'. No trouble in identifying where those lines come from. But 'expedient'? Coming across this word, in this context, it is tempting to say that Fuller's brand of amoralism is only possible if you are always somewhere else when the trigger is pulled. It's a temptation that has to be resisted; apart from anything else, Fuller served in the wartime navy. But my point is that for all his later renunciation of the early adherence to the dream of collective man, Fuller's Marxism never feels more than dutiful. At all events, when, in 'The Divided Life Re-Lived', he looked back to the pre-war dream, he confessed:

How we innocently thought that we should be alone no more,
Linked in death or revolution as in war.
How completely we have slipped into the same old world of cod,
Our companions Henry James or cats or God....

And the best that we can wish for is that still the moon will rise
Enigmatic, cracked and yellow to men's eyes,
And illuminate the manuscripts of poems that foretold
All the ruin and survival of the old.

Anyone writing a history of the *trahison des clercs* after 1945 would be well advised to study this poem. Its MacNeice-like manner goes well beyond stylistic echoes. The pose is one of assumed world-weariness, where 'we' have turned into a quietistic, sensitive few, withdrawing into a world of art, heads averted from the problems of a wider world where 'demon scientists and rulers of the land/ Pile the bombs like fiddler-crabs pile balls of sand'.

That Fuller was alert to the possible charge of bad faith is clear, I think, from his extremely clever and tactically adroit poem, 'Translation', which Larkin includes in his Oxford book, but which feels much better when it is read in the context of other Fuller poems of the immediate post-war years.

Now that the barbarians have got as far as Picra,
And all the new music is written in the twelve-tone scale,
And I am anyway approaching my fortieth birthday,
        I will dissemble no longer.

I will stop expressing my belief in the rosy
Future of man, and accept the evidence
Of a couple of wretched wars and innumerable
        Abortive revolutions ....

The ruling class will think I am on their side
And make friendly overtures, but I shall retire
To the side farther from Picra and write some poems
About the doom of the whole boiling.

Anyone happy in this age and place
Is daft or corrupt. Better to abdicate
From a material and spiritual terrain
Fit only for barbarians.

It is easy to see why Larkin would enjoy the crapulous tone of this, which is very close to one he himself has employed. It is also worth noting that he may have borrowed the phrase 'the whole boiling' for 'Going, Going', that Fuller's 'A long-dead negro plays through a machine', in 'One and Many', may have suggested a moment in 'Reference Back', and that the ending of Fuller's 'On Reading a Soviet Novel' – 'naive, old-fashioned tears / Which once it shed itself by bucketsful /In nascent, optimistic, long-dead years' – is close to the tone and cadence of more than one Larkin poem. But the important point to make about 'Translation' is that the element of self-contempt is both genuine and potentially a let-out, because there is no way of knowing whether the poem's real subject is the speaker or what he rails against. What we have here is a version of the codger, self-condemned to a life of retirement, of 'Henry James or cats'.

He turns up again in 'Expostulation and Inadequate Reply', where Fuller writes that 'posed against / [The active world's] harsh demands for truth and sacrifice / The useless poet must arrange himself / With care if he is not to be an adjunct/ Reactionary or irrelevant'. Here the mask is impeccably and impenetrably adjusted. Where does Fuller stand in relation to what the poem says, to the cliché of those 'harsh demands', for example? Does he mean to imply an allusion to 'Hugh Selwyn Mauberley'? Is the poet 'useless' in that he makes nothing happen, or in the Paterian/Wildean sense of creating pure art? Does he 'arrange himself' as poseur or contriver? And so on, and so on.

There can be no certain answers to the many questions which Fuller's post-war poems habitually throw up or leave us feeling the need to ask, all of them having ultimately to do with how the poet chooses to regard his own subject-matter. This elusive knowingness is epitomized in 'The Ides of March', which makes cunning use of the alternatives of private and public life, and the limitations – and perhaps delusions – of choice that seem available to the speaker. And yet the man who speaks this poem is, though trapped by circumstance, committed to very little; and even that little is deliberately compromised by a manner that disowns what it affirms. As an evocation of the self-deprecatory, self-doubting mode that many commentators have identified as somehow definitive of contemporary English consciousness, 'The Ides of March' is both brilliant and, I think, betraying.

For the codger stance can and does become wearisome in its evasiveness, and as a result there are long stretches of Fuller's post-war poetry which feel simply dull. That is why, I imagine, his discovery of syllabics was so important, for it released in him the kind of casual but rather grand eloquence which in his more conventional iambics he had to guard against. (An earlier attempt to take over the conversational metrics of MacNeice's *Autumn Journal* was understandable, but had understandably to be dropped.) Such poems as 'Reading *The Bostonians* in Algeçiras Bay', 'The Visitors', 'Departures' and several more besides are deft, witty, exploratory ruminations in a manner which, while it inevitably owes something to later Auden, feels independently assured. All of the poems I have in mind are to be found in the volume Fuller published in 1968 and to which he significantly gave the title *New Poems*. They really are new: new in their ability or readiness to take their subject-matter with an unforced seriousness, new also in the aplomb with which Fuller takes command of a mode that can loosely be called Horatian.

Tiny Tears and *From the Joke Shop* very obviously benefit from this new start, although in the later volumes Fuller returns to the iambic pentameter, and many of the poems are written in an unrhymed three-line stanza which, while it produces a number of cherishable successes

– among them 'In Praise of Wakefulness', 'Family Matters' and 'Watching TV' – runs the danger of tilting towards mere garrulousness. I imagine that Fuller realized this danger, because still later poems come in the form of 'ABBAs'. Their terseness brings to mind Auden's 'Shorts' but, although enjoyable, many of them feel like not much more than the mildly interesting observations of one of Henry James's valetudinarians. They typify the difficulty that Fuller seems to have sensed with so much of his poetry, of needing to persuade the reader, no matter how sympathetic, that he really is worth reading, and yet of hesitating to presume. The fact that the hesitation is frequently a mask doesn't finally help, because the strategy of courteous deference or ironic self-doubt often hardens into routine. The mask settles on the face so firmly that it cannot be removed. Except, that is, in the case of *New Poems* and some others I have mentioned. They at least are required reading.

1985

CHOOSING THE SPARTAN WAY

Warren Hope, *Norman Cameron: His Life, Work and Letters*. London: Greenwich Exchange, 2000.

Norman Cameron seems always to have been a fully paid-up member of the Awkward Squad. He was born in India in 1905 – his father was a military chaplain stationed in Bombay – and his delicate health was offered as the reason for him being packed off as a five-year old to make a home in Edinburgh with his grandmother. Three years later she threw him out. It wasn't that she bore any resemblance to the sadistic bitch Kipling wrote about so wrenchingly in *Baa Baa Black Sheep*. She was in fact 'pretty and charming and generous and kind', Cameron's sister recalled, but she was also vain and expected people to flatter her. 'This was quite alien to Norman's soul as he was a most direct person'. So off he went, to board with a family connection.

From the moment he arrived at Fettes, 'the Eton of the North', Cameron was marked out as an 'odd lad'. For one thing, he towered above all his contemporaries (in adulthood he stood well over six feet), was physically ungainly, and 'dreamy'. For another, he was hopeless at team sports. The only game for which he showed any aptitude was golf. (He's one of four poets I can think of who have taken golf seriously.) By all accounts, he suffered from much bullying, but by the time he left Fettes he was a published poet. 'A Bowl of Wine' appeared in *Public School Verse*, as did 'Woods in Rain' by a poet whose name was given as W. H. Arden.

After Fettes came Oxford, where Cameron was soon contributing excellent, fully-accomplished work to *Oxford Poetry*. Hope points out that Samuel Hynes, in his overrated study of *The Auden Generation,* characterises Oxford poets at that time as taking for models 'Edith Sitwell, Hardy, and perhaps De la Mare', which certainly won't account for Cameron. This doesn't bother Hynes, or perhaps it does, for Cameron, that awkward customer, is entirely absent from his survey of the period's poetry. Yet the author of such poems as 'Decapitation of Is' and 'Marine Lament' was already in control of great gifts, in which intellectual stringency goes together with lyric grace to make for a quite distinctive, lapidary, near-epigrammatic mock of utterance. Shades of Landor, perhaps? But Cameron is more intelligent, or perhaps more modern: more quizzical, testing, sceptical. Edgell Rickword's poems must, I think, have been congenial (the poets shared a dedication to Rimbaud and translated him), as Graves and Laura Riding's were to become, but this isn't to underestimate Cameron's originality, in particular his characteristic note of 'ironic exactitude', to borrow Peter Scupham's fine phrase, a habit of mind that ought to have made him a natural model for the Movement poets. (One poem in particular, 'Punishment Enough', written sometime in the 1940s, could have been slipped into the pages of *New Lines* without anyone noticing.) 'He taught us thinking was a kind of feel,' G. S. Fraser wrote of William Empson, who *did* influence the Movement, and Fraser's words apply as aptly to Cameron, whose poems love to 'argufy'.

That love is evident in the poems of his included in Auden and Day Lewis's 1927 *Oxford Poetry*. As Roy Fuller perceptively noted of this famous anthology, Cameron's contributions are such that 'Even the undergraduate poetic brilliance of William Empson rather pales ... beside such an achievement .... The collection is prefaced by an amusingly portentous piece of prose above the initials W.H.A. and C.D.L. As in the ensuing decade, Cameron's work cuts, with its clarity, shapeliness and neutrality, right across any pontifications'.

I'm not sure about neutrality, though. Cameron was in the Awkward Squad because he refused to take the fashionable side, ever. As Graves noted, he was 'alternately a Presbyterian and a moralist; and a pagan poet and boon-companion'. The poet and companion got drunk and lavished money on others. (Graves and Riding, Dylan Thomas and Ruthven Todd were among those who benefited from Cameron's open handedness.) The Presbyterian and moralist had no time for log-rolling. Cameron saw straight through Stephen Spender. 'The Rupert Brooke of the Depression', he called him, and he once remarked that the proof that England wasn't an intellectual nation was that it thought Spender was an intellectual. He also dubbed him 'King Sensitive the First' (in the poem 'The Votive Images'). This benign contempt probably has as starting point the contrasting experiences of the two as President of the Oxford Literary Society. Cameron invited the then barely-known Laura Riding to speak to the society. Spender invited Sir John Squire.

During the 1926 General Strike Cameron went up to Preston with his friend A. J. P. Taylor, whose father was active in the Labour movement and chairman of the local strike committee. Taylor reports that he and Cameron were walking through the town's darkened streets after one meeting when they were joined by 'a very superior person', who called the strikers 'poor, ignorant people'. According to Taylor, 'Norman stood still, very tall ... You little shit! You bloody little prig! Those people – and his voice roared over Preston – are worth a thousand of you'.

Hope, who has co-edited with Jonathan Barker Cameron's *Collected Poems and Selected Translations* (Anvil Press, 1990), and who for the most part writes very well about the poetry, thinks that at least one of the poems in the 1927 Anthology, 'The Thespians at Thermopylae', comes from the Preston experience.

> The honours that the people give always
> Pass to those use-besotted gentlemen
> Whose numskull courage is a kind of fear,
> A fear of thought and of the oafish mothers
> ("Or with your shield or on it") in their rear.
> Spartans cannot retreat. Why, then, their praise
> For going forward should be less than others'.
> But we, actors and critics of one play,

Of sober-witted judgment, who could see
So many roads, and chose the Spartan way,
What has the popular report to say
Of us, the Thespians at Thermopylae?

There actually was a troupe of Thespians at Thermopylae, who chose not to desert the Spartans. Cameron's moral fable is grounded in real history. I suspect that his Presbyterian imagination required that, for a poem to be any good, it had to be alert to fact. It had also to encounter the devil-in-the-flesh: hence, for example, 'Naked Among The Trees', a brilliantly achieved poem which might in some sense be thought of as a verse commentary on Hawthorne's *Maypole of Merrymount*, although with an uncanny resemblance to John Crowe Ransom. Moreover, the moralist in him – out of the quarrel with whom his poems came – required Cameron to acknowledge that we live by choice. His anti-determinism was as unfashionable, then, as his contempt for those 'oafish mothers' – a giveaway phrase, mothers had little to do with what went on at Thermopylae – who'd sent sons to war in 1914, hoping that their deaths would reflect glory on those who had 'sacrificed them to the greater cause'. Later, this view would undoubtedly become fashionable. (See for example the early writings of Isherwood, Upward and Auden, among others.) But when Cameron wrote 'The Thespians at Thermopylae' he couldn't have known that.

What he did know was that the kind of poem he wanted to write was close in temperament to the work of Graves and Riding. After leaving Oxford he mooched about London for a while, then followed them to Majorca. But it didn't last. He gave them money to help in the building of a hotel they planned, then came back to London under the lash of Riding's denunciation.

Both 'Forgive me, Sire' and 'A Visit to the Dead', which ends 'I, Marco Polo, traveller, / Am back, with what a tale!', though written some years later, are at least partly about his refusal to be conscripted by Riding and Graves. He found work as an advertising copy-writer (the famous Horlicks advertisement for combating 'Night Starvation' was his invention), wrote poems when they demanded to be written, and in 1935 published his first (and only) full collection, *The Winter House and Other Poems*. Packed with wonderfully good poems, the volume was indifferently received. The age demanded a different kind of poem from such minor masterpieces as 'The Compassionate Fool', 'The Disused Temple', 'Comical Men', 'Release From Fever', 'Naked Among The Trees', and at least a dozen others, all of them possessed of that deep intelligence and scrupulous attention to metred cadence that make him so exemplary a poet.

Two marriages came and went. 'Norman adored women and women adored him to an extent which could make it rather hard for a wife to keep her poise', Hope quotes a friend as remembering. Then, in 1942, he joined the wartime Political Intelligence Unit, which took him to Algeria and Vienna. From the first experience came the marvellous 'Green, Green is El Aghir', and from the second a meeting with the woman who was to become his third wife.

Back in drab, post-war London, he made a living from the world of advertising, saw few friends from the 30s and wrote fewer poems. ('One poem a year Cameron', he dubbed himself.) He did, however, spend much time on his translations, especially of Villon, which Richard Wilbur has gone on record as greatly admiring, and of Rimbaud, which I wish I could like more than I do. (Anvil Press published *A Season in Hell and Other Poems* with a preface by Michael Hamburger in 1994.) *Forgive Me, Sire*, a 24-page pamphlet in the 'Key Poet' series, was put out by Fore Publications in 1950. Besides reprinting a number of poems from *The Winter House*, it contains the justly well-known 'Three Love Poems', 'A Hook For Leviathon', 'The Firm of Happiness, Limited', and 'EI Aghir' (as it is here called). It was barely noticed.

Three years later Cameron died of a brain haemorrhage, as had his father and a younger brother. Hope records that 'A spontaneous, private funeral, a kind of poet's wake, took place in a Greenwich Village Bar, when word of his death reached Dylan Thomas and Ruthven Todd in New York. They gathered as many of Cameron's poems as they could find and took turns reading them aloud to a crowd of truck drivers, longshoremen, painters, sculptors, and writers, what Todd described as 'a remarkably appreciative audience'. It would be good to believe that this critical biography, which, despite Hope's maddening refusal to identify his sources, is a first-rate piece of work, will bring Cameron the enduring appreciative audience so fine a poet deserves.

2001

A LIFETIME'S CATCH

The Nightfisherman: Selected Letters of W. S. Graham. Edited by Michael and Margaret Snow, Carcanet, 1999.

Praise where praise is due. There was a time when Carcanet's logo was a virtual guarantee of poor production: cheap paper, ugly type-face, shoddy binding. No longer. In recent years they've been getting steadily better, and with *The Nightfisherman* they have excelled themselves. On the front cover is a painting by Alfred Wallis. I haven't seen the original, but there's not much reason to doubt the quality of this reproduction. In particular, the blues – always difficult to get right – look as close to the mark as even the most demanding critic has the right to expect. Open the book and you find that the text is set in Bembo, an unusually elegant type-face which I first became aware of when helping Ian Fletcher with a number of slim volumes he saw through Reading University's Press in the late 1950s.

More importantly, the author of these letters would also surely have approved the publisher's decisions and the scrupulousness with which they have been realised. A book's overall appearance was a matter of great importance to Graham. Of the New York Ecco Press's *Selected Poems* (1980) he wrote to his editor at Faber, Charles Monteith to say, 'Isn't it a lovely looking book and to handle, the yellow and black'. There's a barb lurking within this apparently innocent remark. Three years earlier he'd had a run-in with Monteith over Faber's proposed setting of *Implements In Their Places.* 'The type is all right but the moustache between the title and the first line of the poem should surely be taken out. The title is part of the poem. And the space between the title and the first line is part of the poem. If I had wanted to put something in that space I would have'. Monteith must have demurred because Graham writes again, at length, and insistent:

> The ornament (or whatever name we give it) will have to come out .... It is wrong on so many counts.
> 1 – After the title the poem begins and the space between the title and the poem is the writer's. What if I had wanted to put a zodiac sign or an ideogram in that space?
> 2 – The look of it on the page offends the eye aesthetically and makes that small page slightly more difficult to deal with. In the poem in your 'rough tracing', IMAGINE A FOREST, I see the title in caps. and when my eye manages to scurry round the 'tache and begin 'Imagine a Forest' my eye is still conscious of the disturbance before.
> 3 – The ornament there is Victorian. Surely it is not conscious Victoriana. If I'm supposed to be sky-trekking new frontiers of language on the blurb, what will the reader think of that corny fancy-work?
> 4 – You have no right to put a mark between the title and the poem.
> 5 – It is in bad taste. It is vulgar. It is not worthy of Faber and Faber. Anyhow I did not write it.
> Dear Charles, to shave the moustache off can't be too difficult. Anyway, off it must come. Love and from Nessie.
>
> Yours unhirsutely, Sydney.

"It is not worthy of Faber and Faber'. The rebuke is magisterial and without doubt true. Goodness only knows what Graham would have said about the slovenly way collections of poetry are for the most part now pushed out into the world. I haven't seen any of his early collections, but would guess that at all events *2nd Poems*, published by Poetry London in 1945, was worthy of both him and the publisher, Tambimuttu. Tambimuttu is usually recalled in histories of the period as an improbably absurd part of Fitzrovia, poseur, scrounger, louche drinking pal of Dylan Thomas and Thomas's hangers-on. 'Tutti-Frutti', Geoffrey Grigson cruelly but memorably called him, and Graham himself, in a letter of 1949 to his friend, the poet David Wright, remarked of 'poor Tambi' that 'he was useful and did some good things at the beginning. Now I'm afraid he is, in his late position, a retarding force and I don't know if he ever had any critical standard of his own'. Probably not. Yet Tambimuttu certainly worked hard to make the books he published aesthetically pleasing. There is, for example, the comparatively plain but clean-cut *Home Town Elegy* of G. S. Fraser (1944), there is Fletcher's 1947 collection, *Orisons Picaresque & Metaphysical* (in which different sections are introduced by decorated head-pieces and the acrostic 'Aromatic Ballade: in lieu of three brandies and a soda' has the initial letters of each line picked out in red). There is also, quite spectacularly, Nicholas Moore's elaborate *The Glass Tower* (1944). Here, an unlettered black and yellow cover features a striking design of a spikily-leafed plant reminiscent of work by Graham Sutherland, although it's in fact by the young Lucian Freud. Freud is further represented inside by a number of line drawings as well as several colour plates. In entrusting *2nd Poems* to Tambimuttu's Editions Poetry London, Graham must have felt he was in good hands.

He was by then in London, having chosen to escape the effects of what, in a letter of 1944, he calls 'the National bias' that opts for a poetry 'of heather and homerule and freedom' rather than 'of words'. London meant Fitzrovia and Fitzrovia meant Dylan Thomas. There was and I think still is widespread agreement that while Graham may have escaped the lure of MacDiarmidry he fell into the sticky web of the Apocalyptics. Years ago I recall Charles Tomlinson saying that 'The Nightfishing' was a good poem all but wrecked by Thomas's malign influence, and Graham himself was sensitive to this charge, which began long before the publication of that poem in 1954. In a letter of 1945 to David Wright, he commented ruefully, 'THE SEVEN JOURNEYS [his second collection; *Cage Without Grievance*, his first, had been published in 1942] is having a bad time. O the reviewers certainly go their mile. 'It's the forgery of the poetic currency and of Dylan Thomas'. But I suppose it's to be expected. But I expected maybe one or two favourable reviews'.

The question of Thomas's influence is so important that it needs to be discussed here, however briefly. In his lengthy review of *The Nightfisherman*, (*PN Review* 135, 27.1) James Keery takes Dennis O'Driscoll to task for saying that '*Cage Without Grievance* ... displayed some of the worst obfuscatory characteristics of the time. A Dylan Thomas accent was, no doubt, a licence to consume alcohol in the 'sodality of Soho' … Graham … was proud to display his early symptoms again and again'. For Keery, 'the quality of Graham's early poetry has been obscured by fifty years of anti-Apocalyptic orthodoxy', and he quotes Graham's letter to Michael Schmidt in 1977, in which Graham importantly says 'I know how I struggled up through my early poetry to gradually get better and clearer ... I am getting better I hope. But it is not like a graph saying 'he started out not knowing what he was doing and then he went through his Dylan Thomas phase (Which I got a great deal out of) and now he [is] refining himself ... Of course I think there is an advance, but if I put out 'Here Next the Chair I Was' now, I would be proud ...'.

The poem Graham refers to was first published in *Cage Without Grievance*. This collection was apparently made up of poems written later than *The Seven Journeys* although published two years earlier, when Graham was 24. In her prefatory note to the posthumously published *Aimed at Nobody: Poems from Notebooks* (1993), Graham's widow, Nessie Dunsmuir, says that 'time and time again he said that he did not disown any of his poems. When commenting on his work, he remarked that every poem was relevant; that it was integrated into the whole body of his writing'. 'Here Next the Chair I Was When Winter Went' (to give it its full title, which is also its opening line), is undoubtedly a young man's poem, one that combines a certainty of poetic calling with a Romantic sense of apartness and of being chosen, perhaps cursed. The second stanza runs:

> I was what the whinfire works on towns
> An orator from hill to kitchen dances.
> In booths below bridges that spanned the crowds
> Tinkers tricked glasses on lips and saw my eyes.

Tinkers, those Yeatsian outsiders with the gift of telling fortunes, can presumably see in the orator's eyes a knowledge withheld from the crowds and all those who attend kitchen dances. In a letter to *PN Review* about Keery's review, Matthew Francis notes that the collection's title comes from a poem to be found in *The Seven Journeys*. 'The cage is the text itself,' Francis says, 'which [Graham] regularly depicts ... as a prison, cut off from community .... Any grievance, then, is Graham's own when confronted with the isolating properties of text'. And, he adds, this was to provide him with a theme for the rest of his career. We might perhaps baulk at that word 'text', that ok word of current critical orthodoxy. Graham is after all writing poems, whose formal properties and requirements are not usually associated with the issues that preoccupy such orthodoxy. Nevertheless, Francis's remark can be linked to Keery's claim – and here I need to quote a little more fully – that

> The influence of Dylan [Thomas], the right precursor for this poet, is profound (not least in mediating that of Mallarmé, Hopkins and Joyce), but so is Graham's originality. Thomas too insisted that his poems were 'hewn' and 'made' ('the last thing they do is flow') but they are nevertheless obsessed with 'process', 'The force that through the green fuse drives the flower'; Graham's obsession is with the construction of an 'abstract cage' ('I Leave This at Your Ear'.) Already in *Cage Without Grievance* he is speaking of 'tilting planes' ('There Was When Morning Fell') and capable of an uncanny abstraction: 'We fell down darkness in a line of words' ('No, Listen for This I Tell').

I wondered at first about the propriety of that word 'obsession' but concluded that Keery is justified in using it. The dictionary definition of 'obsess', 'to preoccupy completely', feels exactly right to account for Graham's regard for poetry. Everything else came second and not much was allowed to rattle the bars of his cage. If between the years of 1939 and 1945 you'd asked him whether he knew there was a war on, you feel he'd have had to think before replying. True, in May 1945, at the time of V.E. Day, he wrote to the artist John Minton to say that 'the only good thing about this victory is that the soldiers who were fighting will be saved'. He then adds: 'It is an ominous peace and but conceals the germs of something worse than before'. But me no buts. The self-consciousness of that sentence suggests that war and war's alarms aren't really his concern. And sure enough he continues

> But on such a highskyed blue and green day what is there to greet about. It is hard enough to blow the time by the dandelion clocks and scare off the lesser emerald backed chariotbeetle. 3d of ham bones scraped makes a tidy wee breakfast and then boiled with split peas and you have soup.
>
> My long poem is coming on well ...

Then, as always, it was the poetry that mattered.

O'Driscoll is nevertheless right to note a difference between early and later Graham. The Apocalyptic-like claim that 'My tongue is a sick device' (in 'Here Next the Chair'), surely comes dangerously near to the kind of toe curling vaingloriousness which damns so much writing in the 1940s. 'You're a writer? Show me your wound'. Or, in the ineffable words of Wrey Gardiner (to be found in his autobiographical *The Dark Thorn*, in which the war is cursed as a personal affront to Gardiner's sensibilities), 'Too much work bows me down ... Too many hopes fly like blind swans into the sun .... We cannot know the massed inferno of our times without feeling close to us the imprint of the strange iron kiss of death. In the limited avenues of our cities we plunder the moment in the desperate ending of a diseased world'. There is all the difference in the world between this kind of vatic posturing and the question, 'What is the language using us for?' And that Graham himself knew how in his earlier work he'd been lured towards the former is evident in a letter he writes to Edwin Morgan in 1949, when he says:

> So many of those early poems are 'difficult' – but as well as 'difficult' they are often lazy offerings, with the 'suggestive' serving as that dazzling stroke of communication which they should be. There is obscure poetry and lazy poetry and, of course, often a poem is both but is more often lazy than obscure. I am, I think, specially supplied with a facility for the lyrical and memorable phrase and I've exploited it, as a sole power in the poem, overmuch.

This is admirable in its unsparing honesty, and it explains why, a little earlier, he should have told another correspondent that 'In spells of the poetry I've been trying some drawing. Only to help me to see better'. (Interesting that he should use 'spell' as jazzmen and women do, to mean a period of rest: the OED – wrongly – says that this use is 'chiefly Australian'). To see better, to get better and clearer: Graham is in endless pursuit of a lucidity that will enable him to understand what the language is using him for. And this means leaving 'poetry' behind. Hence, in the same letter to Morgan – a letter which I'm tempted to say is for students of his poetry perhaps the most important he ever wrote – he remarks:

> The only ones whose sympathy to my poetry I respect are those who write poetry also and in whose poems there is evidence of that relation to language as a dialogue taken part in, going on in the very centre of loneliness ... Art can not be fake. It either unites with us to our advantage or doesn't unite with us at all. By 'to our advantage' I mean to our enlargement of spirit. So, more and more, I realise the aloneness is a joy to live in and talk there to the most marvellous listener which is within my imagination and the limitations of that listener are the limitations of my poetry. So certainly now I think – if I hadn't poetry – that place to be in the act of making poetry – what would I do? Where would there be the least peace in my life?

In another letter of the same period he tells that he's been seeing something of T.S. Eliot and that

> ... it is good to realise that, if one had been lazy or deceitful (though I am guilty enough and should try harder) in one's verse he would have known. We talked a lot about the structure of the long poem (I've just finished mine) and the 'purity of criticism' which I am almost a crank about. I mean that the criticism of poetry in Britain today is so bad and trite often through the 'critic' not bringing pure critical canons to bear on the subject, but bringing in outside values (which I admit have to do with values in the 'poem' but which are incidental) of morality, ethics or even politics. Or they write about everything but the object because they have no elementary knowledge of what such an object is made of or how it works.

I'm not sure why, in the second parenthesis, Graham hedges the word *poem* about with quotation marks. Perhaps it's because he thinks a poem is only its true self when it is quite free of incidentals – those 'outside values'. Everything else, everything which has designs on us, or is self-consciously aware of an audience beyond the 'listener which is within my imagination', is a 'poem'.

Given this absolute concentration of imaginative energy – it is what I understand Lawrence to have meant when he called true thought 'a man in his wholeness wholly attending' – it isn't surprising that Graham should have added that Eliot thought his (Graham's) poetry 'would go slow because people just were lazy about thinking'. Nor is it surprising that he should have seemingly cared little about this. He not only never made a poorer song that he might have a heavier purse, he'd have been incapable of doing any such thing. And if the consequences included having to eat pancakes made of flour and water, seasoned with whatever herbs he and Nessie picked in the fields, then so be it.

He was, without doubt, blessed to have had her by him for most of his life. They met in the 1940s, lived together and then apart, and finally married in 1954. In one of many helpful interventions – and what good editors they are, how unfussy, how alert to what needs to be said and no more – the Snows point out that 'Sydney Graham had a fortunate ability to endure and even derive great pleasure from very simple surroundings and was fairly indifferent to ordinary domestic comforts. Nessie was just able to support them both by seasonal work in St. Ives, and there were the widely separated cheques for his poems, but most of the time they were extremely poor'. And, they add, 'His need for freedom of movement, association and experiment took precedence over any need for everyday security'. True enough. On one occasion, when they moved to a new cottage from the unheated, unlit coastguard's cottage at Gurnard's Head where they'd survived for several years, 'Graham appears to have made the move ... by abandoning everything not immediately needed and walking out leaving the door open and clothes, books, papers behind'. Such behaviour is reminiscent of Lawrence or of Edgell Rickword, another who travelled light. But Rickword, a fine poet in his earlier years, was later preoccupied with political journalism and critical and editorial work. Graham was, in all senses of the word, and as these wonderful letters attest, purely a poet (as undeflectable in his concern for his art as, in a different medium, Gwen John, with whom he shares certain characteristics). Once he'd worked through his debt to Thomas it is difficult to think of him as other than an entirely original, *true* poet. Lyric and memorable phrases, though they don't disappear, are subsumed into the keener, more exact, sustained poems *of Malcolm Mooney's Land* (1971) and *Implements in Their Places* (1977). These collections are like no-one else's at all, although others – chief among them David Wright and C. H. Sisson – must have learned a good deal from them. But even Wright's best poems, clean and spare as they are, scrupulously though they are worked, lack the unremitting concentration of Graham's finest work.

As his passage-of-arms with Charles Monteith shows, Graham was intensely professional in pursuit of his calling. There was nothing of the dilettante about him. Writing to that fine poet, Matt Simpson, some time before Simpson's first book came out, Graham, having told him 'you are to my measurement a very good poet', advised him to do 'Everything you can think of to get your poems before magazine editors, publishers, any poetry platform. I can think of nothing but the long slog of sending poems out again even to magazines in America … .

Try everything and keep writing and don't let yourself harden up with despair'. Good, practical advice, as, in a different but related manner, is his telling David Wright that he should avoid the word 'wisdom' because it is 'so difficult a word. Almost like 'death or hate'. The best phrases, or lines, about say death or hate usually haven't the words in them'.

The Collected Poems 1942-1977, run to over 260 pages. The fragments and fuller drafts of poems gathered in *Aimed at Nobody* add another 60. Given the hysterical, brawling, drunken community of artists among whom Graham and Nessie lived for so many years (late on he thought of returning to Scotland, but nothing came of this), it may seem surprising that he managed to produce so much and that the best is so good. But he had a steely will. Moreover there was poetry, its peremptory demands, its fathomless appeal. After days of frenzied, often violently competitive shenanigans with Bryan Winter, Terry Frost and the almost certainly insane Roger Hilton, he had always the joy of aloneness to withdraw into. From there came poems which 'Through the lens of language' ('The Don Brown Route') make a body of work for which 'essential' seems the most appropriate term. The same can be said of *The Nightfisherman*.

2001

HARD CIDER AND SPAM

George Fraser (1915-1980) published three full collections during his lifetime. In 1944 Tambimuttu's Editions Poetry London brought out *Home Town Elegy* and this was followed by *The Traveller Has Regrets* (Harvill Press, 1948). Then, after a gap of more than twenty years, the Byron Press, which Allan Rodway and I had set up in 1965, published *Conditions* (1969). And that, fugitive pamphlets apart, was that. Yet when in 1980 Ian Fletcher and I came to edit Fraser's poems for Leicester University Press, we found a mass of good poems from all periods, and especially from the 1970s. The result was a substantial volume that ran to very nearly two hundred pages of poems and which even so fell some way short of being 'Complete'. *Poems of G S Fraser* was warmly received, as *Conditions* had been. There was good reason to believe that the later poems alone – the 'real riches' as Robert Nye described them – would guarantee Fraser a permanent place in twentieth century poetry. Martin Seymour Smith, a hard man to please, was emphatic in his praise. 'Not only are the poems from his earlier volumes enormously impressive when seen together', he said in his review of *Poems*, 'but there was also a remarkable late flowering in the 1970s. Fraser was a major Scottish poet of great versatility'. This view was endorsed by J B Pick, who called Fraser 'the most technically accomplished Scottish poet of his time'. And yet Fraser's work is not represented in any of the recent anthologies of Scottish poetry. How on earth did this come about?

There are two possible explanations. One is that, W S Graham apart, the reputations of poets who are thought to be 'of the 'forties' have still not recovered from the often malicious battering administered by those who succeeded them. Some of the victims got more or less what they deserved, although swatting the likes of Wrey Gardiner, say, hardly requires you to break sweat. But the clobbering of Fraser and his great friend and fellow poet, Ian Fletcher, is a different matter, not only because their anthology, *Springtime* (1953), importantly introduces most of the poets made famous by Conquest's narrower *New Lines* (1956), but because they were happy to share with others their prodigious learning in matters of prosody. Fraser's *Metre, Rhyme and Free Verse* remains a first-class guide to its subject. (Though the first edition contains a number of misplaced scansion marks, not the fault of Fraser's ear but of his eye.) They were in fact fare more disinterested in serving the cause of the art they practised than most of those who sneered at them.

There is the ghost of a sneer hanging about Donald Davie's famous remark that for years 'Literary London had to make do with the occasional aperçu from George Fraser'. In the post-war years, Fraser became well-known and admired as a critic. He was generous, discriminating, his sympathies stretched wide and deep, and he was usually quick to spot the bogus. But his regular work as reviewer and critic, together with his important study *The Modern Writer and His World*, seems to have convinced many that he wasn't truly a poet. He certainly worked very hard and wrote much prose for comparatively little. In her as yet unpublished Memoirs, his widow, Paddy Fraser, recalls the young Burns Singer's horror when he discovered that Fraser, with a family to support, made in the early 'fifties at best between £900 and £1000 a year. This 'drudging', to borrow Dryden's term, persuaded others he was a mere hack. Hence, for example, the mean-minded and odiously snobbish attacks on him in Ian Hamilton's *New Review*.

Yet Fraser was far better read than most of the coterie associated with Hamilton's journal, and I suspect he was a better linguist, too. In addition to Latin, he had Italian and French, and he translated well and abundantly from all three languages. (Fletcher and I at one time hoped to be able to publish a collection of the translations, and I still think such a collection would be a good idea.) He once startled pub conversationalists into silence with his declamation of Villon's 'De

Dames du temps jadis' ('Mais ou sont les neiges d'antan'), in which he stressed with particular relish the fricatives and gutturals so as to demonstrate how Rossetti's famous version traduced the original's spiky harshness.

Still, the years in London as freelance writer undoubtedly took their toll. He confronts the cost in 'Lenten Meditation'

> The fools and rogues whose boots I had to lick
> To earn a pittance: the possible young poets
> Who ate my heart and spat away the gristle:
> The Great Master, a bibulous charlatan:
> The White Goddess, in the end a blowsy whore:
> The Teachers, vain, tetchy, malicious pedants:
> The Old Chums, pilfering one's books and bottles
> And chumbling one's fame to death over their cups:

Yet although he found little time to practise his art – at least until he took up a lectureship at Leicester in the late 1950s – Fraser always thought of himself as a poet. In a late, beautiful poem, he says 'Madness, illusions of omnipotence!/ I am a poet. I have known them too'. This poem, 'A Napkin With Veronica's Face, Not Christ's', Is an elegiac tribute to Veronica Forrest-Thompson, a young poet who had worked for a PhD under Fraser, and who killed herself in 1975, at the beginning of her twenty-eighth year. The poem, as he himself notes, 'is an attempt at the kind of artefact she might have liked, with allusions to her favourite poems, and poets. The form is the mock-sonnet in terza rima of Shelley's "West Wind"'.

Poem and note are alike deeply instructive about Fraser. He was temperamentally drawn to elegy, he loved writing poems which made considerable formal demands on him, he was fascinated by ideas (he read a good deal in philosophy and theology and put that to good use in a number of poems, including 'The Insane Philosophers'), and, in his own words, if as a young man he was 'an agnostic of deeply religious sentiments', he became 'an Anglican with few religious sentiments:

I need the sacraments but hate the sermons and false good-fellowship. In 1947, I was better and wiser'. In addition, many of his finest poems are written to and for women. 'Only Robert Graves has written love poems as beautiful as those in this book', Seymour Smith says of the *Poems of G S Fraser*. This may well be true, although in the typescript version I have of 'Estrangement', Fraser has written in his clear, surprisingly child-like hand, 'A love poem, written after I had been reading a lot of Hardy. William Empson disliked it so much that he hurled it across a room. The subject never recognized herself in the poem'.

Empson, a friend and admirer of Fraser's work, preferred Fraser the 'argufier', creator of such poems as 'The Human Situation' and 'Yin and Yang: A Dialogue'. These are good poems, certainly, but Fraser wasn't entirely happy with what he saw as the limits of Empson's appreciation. Hence the barbed ending of his warm 'For William Empson's Fiftieth Birthday': 'He taught us thinking is a kind of feel/ And how to read, and wonderfully misread, a page!/ But who has plumbed the poet's narrow sound?' 'Flash Harry', his poem for George Barker's sixtieth birthday is just as witty, and equally acute. It starts:

> Flash Harry I used to call that one,
> The man for the three-card trick,
> The thimble-rigger, the con-man
> With a loverly golden prick –
>
> Does George write 'poems' or 'poetry'?
> Nobody doubts he has balls!

Though 'Flash Harry' isn't an epistolary poem, it strikes the note of familiar address that sounds through many of Fraser's poems, including the Letter Poems for Anne Ridler and Nicholas Moore, in which, as Roger Bowen remarked, there is often great tenderness. This can sometimes sink into an unguarded nostalgia, as in the intermittently vivid 'Christmas Letter Home (To My Sister in Aberdeen)': 'And I remember the dances, the scarf and cane,/ Strolling home in the cold with the silly refrain/ Of a tune by Cole Porter or Irving Berlin'. The debt to MacNeice is, however, more than Fraser can repay.

'Christmas Letter' was written in Cairo, where he spent his war years. The city prompted a number of good poems. Time abroad also sharpened an already quizzical gaze at what, in 'Letter to Hugh MacDiarmid' he called 'the broken ghosts of Gael', and it allowed him to hone his abilities as the at-an-angle-celebrant of literary and other friends. (Hence 'Elegy for Keith Bullen', with its acid-sweet account of how Bullen 'bobbed incredibly in our modern air'.) Yeats was his favourite poet, but Fraser avoids the Yeatsian imperative of identifying friendship with Glory. His often elegiac poems are in a wryer, more modest mode. Yet they, too, subtly intertwine individual lives with social history, and one, 'For Tilly, Sick, With Love', is so good that I feel an awed fury at all those anthologists who have managed to overlook it. 'People don't give such parties now' it begins, before developing into a fond-sardonic account of post-war London, a city of 'Fringes and dirndls... weak, wersh beer,/ Salami, Algerian wine-cup, hard cider and spam', and a lovingly attentive account of Tilly herself, the 'gay Muse', of the 'green-gold cascade of [her] merciful hair'.

It's an exemplary poem because it's about how to write fittingly: how to judge tone, how to rhyme, how to carry off a complicated metre (a weave of anaepest and iambic) without a hint of strain. A minor masterpiece.

2001

APPROPRIATE FALSEHOODS:
ENGLISH POETS AND AMERICAN JAZZ

> He breathed in air, he breathed out light,
> Charlie Parker was my delight.

Adrian Mitchell's celebrated couplet defines a minority response, at least as far as English poets who claim an interest in jazz are concerned. They may not agree with Philip Larkin's even more celebrated anathematizing of the three Ps (Parker, Pound, and Picasso) but on the whole their devotion is given to the so-called traditional styles and masters, and for most of them 'modern jazz' is a contradiction in terms. The music of New Orleans and Chicago, of Armstrong, Beiderbecke, Condon, Ellington, Ory, and Waller: this is what jazz means for those predominantly middle-class, university-educated poets who, during the 1940s and 1950s, proclaimed their devotion in prose and verse. I want to offer some suggestions as to why this should be so, but before I do it will be as well to say something about the reputation of jazz in pre-1940s England.

The year to begin with is 1919. Before then there had been much talk of 'ragtime', but I do not think that anyone had much sense of what that word really meant, and since they had little more to go on than Irving Berlin's 'Alexander's Ragtime Band' this is not very surprising. What does seem to be true is that during the war years, 1914-18, army officers home on leave or due to be sent out to the Western Front included among their diversions regular attendance at dinner-dances; at such dinner-dances, interspersed with the newly-fashionable and 'shocking' tango, and other, rather more acceptable, dance-music, there would be an occasional bow in the direction of 'ragtime'. This seems to have meant up-tempo numbers with a fairly solid four-to-the-bar rhythm. Given that most orchestras were largely composed of violinists, the results must have been pretty excruciating.[1]

Then in 1919, the Original Dixieland Jazz (or Jass) Band came to England. These 'Untuneful Harmonists playing Peppery Melodies', as they rather oddly styled themselves, produced what has been called a 'phenomenal impact' on British audiences, and numbers such as 'At the Jazz Band Ball', 'Bluin' the Blues', 'Clarinette Marmalade', and above all 'Tiger Rag' soon entered the repertory of English dance bands of the period.[1] For many people, however, even those who did not know the original meaning of the word 'jass', this was the music of a decadent society, of sexual promiscuity, of drink and drugs. Dances such as the charleston and blackbottom were widely thought to be quintessential jazz dances, and the music became a kind of do-it-yourself affair, since all you needed to make it with was a banjo or ukelele. Sheet-music, setting out simplified chord sequences for these instruments, sold in their thousands, and the Bright Young Things of the Jazz Age set about destroying themselves and others to the accompaniment of 'You're Nobody's Sweetheart Now', 'Mississippi Mud', 'Margie', and other, similar, numbers, turned out as fast as Tin-pan Alley could supply them. To put the matter this way is of course to parody it. (Although not outrageously, as Evelyn Waugh's Diaries of the 1920s and Martin Green's *Children of the Sun* between them make clear, and anyway it is difficult to parody the kinds of self-parodying people who occur in their pages.)[3] More important is the fact that the vast majority of those who jigged and hopped and crossed hands over knees in or out of time to 'Nagasaki', 'Has Anybody Seen My Girl?', and the rest, had no real interest in jazz as such. Nat Gonella is on record as saying that when he went to hear Louis Armstrong at the Palladium in 1930 the fashionable audience left in droves. Gonella, a genuine enthusiast, was so enraged by this response to his hero that he did his best to trip up those who passed him on their way to the exit.

Nevertheless, for most writers in the 1920s ragtime equalled jazz equalled decadence. Eliot's 'Shakespeherien Rag' ('It's so elegant/ So intelligent') echoes eerily round the room of the neurasthenic, bored wife of 'A Game of Chess', and the syncopated speech-rhythms of *Sweeney Agonistes*, as well as the song 'Under the bamboo tree', imply a world whose devitalized routines ('You'd be bored. / Birth, and copulation, and death') can be known and judged through its devotion to ragtime, and this, for Eliot, meant Jazz.[4] We know this is so because in 1924 he consulted Arnold Bennett about a 'drama of modern life (furnished flat sort of people)' which he wanted to write 'in a rhythmic prose "perhaps with certain things in it accentuated with drum beats"'.[5] Three years later Bennett wrote to Eliot to ask what had happened 'to that Jazz play'.[6] (A fragment, called 'Wanna Go Home Baby', had in fact been published in Criterion for January 1927.)

You would expect attitudes to change with the coming of a younger and politically radical group of poets, and of course they did. What had been seen as decadent now became subversive. Yet for the writers of the 1930s jazz wasn't the influence it might and perhaps should have been. Auden, for example, never seems to have been much interested in it. True, a number of his songs and the *Dance of Death* show how excited he was by the cabaret and revue work of the Weimar Republic which he had had a chance to experience at first hand, and some of that work was undoubtedly influenced by American jazz. But once you have taken note of his approval of such song-writers as Cole Porter and Rogers and Hart, and of the fact that he includes a generous selection of spirituals and bar-room and chain-gang songs in his great *Oxford Book of Light Verse* of 1938 (they include 'John Henry', 'Stagolee', 'Frankie and Johnny', 'Casey Jones', and 'This Train'), you have exhausted the matter of Auden's interest in the music. When Geoffrey Grigson commissioned various writers to contribute to *The Arts To-day* (London, 1935) he invited Edward Crankshaw to write about 'Music'. Crankshaw's piece avoids any mention of jazz, even though it aims to be as up-to-date as possible. At one point in his essay he notes that 'Mr Constant Lambert in his admirable book was the first to point ... out' the parallel between the progress of Schönberg and James Joyce (174). He does not, however, note Lambert's remark that Duke Ellington is probably one of the finest and most influential of modern composers and arrangers. Even Louis MacNeice, the one poet you might think would be much interested in some aspects of jazz (not least in the clubs where it could be found uncertainly surviving, and where late drinking, the conducting of illicit affairs, and a general air of cigarette-ash bohemianism provided the kind of atmosphere that seems made for him), uses the word in a vague, if vaguely approbatory, way.

But at this point I need to say that I am not at all sure just how much jazz any of the writers of the 1930s could have heard or of what they could have been aware. It is not simply that confusion over the word was still wide-spread. (Two important details about the first sound-picture, *The Jazz Singer*, are that Al Jolson wasn't black and he couldn't or anyway didn't sing jazz.)[7] More important, perhaps, is the fact that if you were in England it was never very easy to hear American musicians playing the new music. In the first place, from the mid-1930s the Musicians Union banned visiting musicians playing with their own groups, which meant that any American jazzman booked to appear in Britain had to be accompanied by British musicians, an understandable move to preserve jobs but a disaster in that it led the majority of jazzmen to stay away. (Still, Fats Waller came to England in 1938 and recorded a half-hour programme for BBC television, with a group that included the trombonist George Chisholm. Unfortunately the BBC either lost or destroyed the recording.) In the second place, records of the jazz bands were not easy to come by, although those who lived in the port towns fared better than most, if only because visiting American seamen would frequently bring records ashore with them for barter or sale. This helps to explain why cities such as Belfast, Bristol, Liverpool, and Glasgow have always been jazz strongholds, and places from which some of the best British bands and musicians have emerged.

All this means that anyone wanting to listen to jazz in the 1930s, whether in clubs, on records, or sitting by the wireless in kitchens in the lonely fens, would not have had an easy time of it, and that what they heard might well be no more than a parody of the real thing, especially if it came from such dance bands as those led by Jack Hylton,

Ambrose, Henry Hall, and Ray Fox, which were nationally famous, had regular time on the radio, and made many records.

> They were in almost no sense 'jazz' bands, but about every sixth piece they made a 'hot number', in which the one or two men in the band who could play jazz would be heard. The classic 'hot number' was 'Tiger Rag':....Harry Roy had a band-within-a-band called the Tiger-Ragamuffins. Nat Gonella's stage show had a toy tiger lying on the grand piano. Trombonists and tuba-players became adept at producing the traditional tiger growl. I found these hot numbers so exciting that I would listen to hours of dance music in order to catch them when they came.[8]

This is Philip Larkin, in the introduction to *All What Jazz* (London, 1972, 2), and he goes on to tell of how he slowly began to build up a record collection which could 'bear all the enthusiasm usually directed at more established arts. There was nothing odd about this. It was happening to boys all over Europe and America. It just didn't get into the papers'. At Oxford, he continues, 'my education grew. I met people who knew more about jazz than I did, and had more records, and who could even parallel my ecstasies with their own' (3). Larkin names no names, but among the Oxford near-contemporaries who shared his enthusiasms were Kingsley Amis and John Wain, and the 'ecstasies' of all three were to spill over into poetry and prose. There will be more to say about this, but as a way into discussing the poems I need to ask why this *particular* enthusiasm was happening, if not 'to boys all over Europe and America', at least to Larkin and many of his contemporaries.

The most obvious explanation is that jazz recommended itself to Larkin's generation precisely because it wasn't seen as an established art. Since Auden's generation (within which there would have been some who taught Larkin's) had no great interest in the music, beyond annexing its name and vaguely-understood contents in the cause of subversive social and political stances, the way was clear for Larkin and his contemporaries to strike a rebellious pose through their adoption of jazz as an art form. If they did not want to claim that much for it they could at least justify an interest in jazz because it was 'unpretentious'. This unpretentiousness is, in fact, one of the most widely-presumed characteristics of jazz and its exponents. A story (almost certainly apocryphal) which jazz-buffs of Larkin's generation never tire of telling is of Louis Armstrong (or, in some versions, Fats Waller), replying to the inevitably white, upper-class lady's enquiry as to what swing is (in some versions swing becomes rhythm): 'Lady, if you has to ask, you jest ain't got it'. And when jazz musicians tune up (usually to A natural) they famously remark, as they finish adjusting slide or string, 'near enough for jazz'.

This self-deprecatory element, which could be found among jazz musicians and which, in America at least, had a lot to do with the fact that most of the musicians were black and working in white men's clubs, hotels, and restaurants, becomes one of the most remarked-on elements of the generation of Movement poets. This may also explain why Larkin and others so took against Parker and the jazz musicians of *his* generation, simply because they refused to be 'unpretentious': that is, they were prepared to be aggressive champions of their music, to take pride in their great technical mastery, to scorn their (often white) audiences, to play unfamiliar tunes or radically alter familiar ones. Parker's creative or, some would say, destructive treatment of 'How High the Moon' is an obvious example.

Jazz also recommended itself simply because it was the almost private/secret possession of the young. The fact that the records were hard to come by meant that they acquired an almost legendary status; labels and matrix numbers were memorized, rare buys were jealously guarded. The fact that the wax 78 rpms were frail, easily scratched and broken, added to their rarity value. In general there was the heady feeling that in learning to appreciate jazz you were coming in on a sub-culture. As a devotee who joined this sub-culture in the early 1950s, I can speak with the authority of one who recalls the thrill of buying a black-Brunswick-label recording of the Hot Six playing 'Potato-Head

Blues' which *must*, so my elders and betters told me, have been a pirated version. I can also recall the thrill of joining my school's Rhythm Club (I don't suppose there was a school in the country which, throughout the 1940s and 1950s, failed to have such a club) and hearing my very first jazz record: Dizzie Gillespie's 'Cognac Blues'. The music itself meant little, the title everything. It suggested a society of dimly-lit cafés, a night-life of sex and poetry, and, perhaps most importantly, an escape from the Light-Programme. I bring my own experience in at this point in order to suggest that for at least twenty years (roughly from 1936 to 1956) jazz music was the music you could, if you were young, associate with mild rebelliousness, with striking the father dead, with an argot known only to the *cognoscenti*.[9]

There was also the fact that jazz became increasingly admired by those who could identify it with a mild form of socialism. It was, after all, the music of the down-trodden, and was therefore ethnically respectable; there were those who claimed to hear in it the voice of the oppressed slave striking back at his or her oppressor (for the great Blues singers, Ma Rainey and, pre-eminently, Bessie Smith were idolized by my generation and I suspect by Larkin's). There is a particularly nauseating moment in Osborne's *The Entertainer* (1957) when Archie Rice recalls an old negress 'singing her heart out', and the idea that jazz simply (very simply) spoke equally for joy, heartache, and deprivation was one of the more enduring myths of the period I am now considering. This is not to say that the music lacked social content, or that it was devoid of political comment; but it is to say that one of the motives behind the identification with jazz was that it could be seen as expressive of the admirer's political and social radicalism. It is worth adding that, although Larkin (before his comparatively late and almost parodic lurch into Thatcherism) seems never to have been prepared to declare a political point of view, Amis and Wain were milk-and-water Fabians for whom an identification with jazz might well seem appropriate to their political positions. More generally, and perhaps more seriously, jazz could be seen as the 'people's' music, a possibility that would have been strengthened by the meetings of British men-at-arms with their American counterparts, many of whom were black and some of whom were the very musicians the British had worshipped and imitated from afar. Support for and interest in jazz could therefore be seen or adopted as a sign of political solidarity, and it is no accident that during the 1940s and 1950s the *William Morris Society Bulletin* should have carried jazz material.

To admire jazz could also be seen as a sign of intellectual daring, or of wanting to shock the bourgeoisie. The post-war euphoria will have had something to do with this heady determination of clearing out the old in order to make way for the new. After all, it was daring to prefer Armstrong to 'filthy Mozart', or to pretend to do so, or, more seriously, to find room for both. In addition it became another means of scorning the insular philistinism of previous generations. Jazz was eminently acceptable on the Left Bank. France had been the one country in Europe prior to the war where jazz and jazz musicians were made very welcome. Albert Nicholas, Bill Coleman, Sidney Bechet (who had first toured in a revue in 1925 which included Josephine Baker), Tommy Ladnier, and others had all made at least temporary homes in Paris; and Paris was famously the adopted home of Django Reinhardt and the Hot Club. After the war many of these musicians returned. Jazz was now the approved music of the literary avant-garde. Sartre and Camus regularly and casually mentioned jazz musicians and quoted the titles of their 'classic' recordings. In 1947 Henri Matisse issued a series of lithographs named, simply, *Jazz*, and although the inspiration for the title had less to do with Matisse's interest in the music than in the fact that he was responding to a renewal of hope, of light, of freshness, this in turn meant that jazz could be enjoyed as carefree music that dispelled the gloom and shabbiness of war-shattered Europe. It really *was* Europe which took to the music. In Paris Claude Luter's band gained extra *cachet* because Bechet so often played and recorded with it, but it attracted large audiences on its own account. There was the Dutch Swing College Band, the White Eagle New Orleans Band of Berlin, there were bands aplenty spread across Belgium; and so on.

In addition there was now a steady growth of literature on the subject. In Britain *Jazz Journal* was an established and respected magazine, *The Melody Maker* gave regular and increasing space to jazz commentators, Eric Hobsbawn wrote a jazz column in the *New Statesman and Nation* under the pseudonym of Francis Newton: Frankie Newton was a negro jazz trumpeter who had died young, of tuberculosis, just before the war. Then there were the books. Rex Harris's *Jazz* was first published by Penguin (as a Pelican book) in 1952, and by 1957 was into its fifth edition. André Hodeir's highfalutin *Jazz: Its Evolution and Essence* was translated into English in the early 1950s. As the decade wore on biographies, criticism, and general histories piled up on the bookstalls. Jazz, it seemed, was everywhere.

Yet this is an exaggeration. For although in Britain any number of jazz bands, professional and semi-professional, came into being, and although most towns had a jazz club where local bands could perform each week and where there would be occasional guest nights featuring out-of-town musicians, these were invariably British. The Musicians Union did not relax its ban on foreign groups until 1956. Before then, if you wanted to hear the great and not-so-great American bands, you had to cross either the English Channel or the Irish Sea. (*The Melody Maker* ran excursion specials for those wanting to hear live such orchestras as those of Woody Herman and Stan Kenton when they visited Ireland.) Then, in 1956, the Musicians Union decided on a policy of exchanges. American bands could come to England on condition that English bands were allowed to tour the United States. They got Freddy Randall and his band and we got Louis Armstrong and his All Stars. You would think that this would have increased jazz's popularity. Quite the reverse: 1956 marked the beginning of the end for the music's mass popular appeal. There were still many tours to come, jazz-band balls and concerts at the Festival Hall and halls throughout the country (nearly all of sell-outs in both senses of the word), and the traddy-pop boom was as yet some years off. But George Melly recalls that in 1956 he recorded a 'novelty number' of the 1920s, 'My Canary's Got Circles Under His Eyes', which was a total flop (it deserved to be), and that the week it went on sale a 'boy' called Tommy Steele released a record called 'Rock with the Cavemen' (*Owning Up*, Chapter 11). A new kind of do-it-yourself music, born from the skiffle bands which themselves had been born out of the jazz bands, was on the way.

Jazz had always been a do-it-yourself music, or so legend reported. The negroes of the deep south made guitars out of cigar-boxes and broomsticks, bought reach-me-down brass instruments from hock shops; and away they went. Of course, it wasn't at all like that, but this appropriate falsehood made it easier for young people in Britain (predominantly male) to buy up odd instruments and learn to play them (a new brass instrument could easily be 'improved' by a few well-placed dents). Philip Larkin says that after an early and brief flirtation with drumming he became a listener only, and he remarks that only one person in his circle at Oxford could play a musical instrument: the saxophone. I do not know whether this was typical of his class but it certainly wasn't typical of his generation, for many young working-class men were learning to play instruments so that they could copy the bands and music they loved.

The first British jazz bands were therefore almost entirely made up of working-class musicians, and they continued to be so throughout the 1950s. There were exceptions: Humphrey Lyttleton, of Eton and the Guards, was the most spectacular; and everyone knew that Chris Barber and Johnny Dankworth had been to the Royal College of Music, and that Sandy Brown (almost certainly the most original talent among British musicians) was Scottish and formidable in argument. On the other hand, when he played he usually wore a vest or dirty old grey V-neck sweater and in this respect looked little different from the musicians who made up his and countless other home-grown bands. The only exception to this, for a while at least, was Ken Colyer, who had a penchant for requiring his band to wear evening dress, as an act of homage to King Oliver's bands of the 1920s whose music he idolized and rather beautifully reproduced. But this did not last for long, and for most of the time his band, too, was wearing the classless uniform of cords, check-shirts or sweaters, and cracked leather shoes (they were sometimes replaced by 'desert boots') which like the rest of the outfit typically came from Millett's or the Army and Navy Stores.

For a while, at least, classlessness might even have seemed to be the crux of the matter. Everyone dressed more or less the same way and went to the same places to hear live jazz and danced in the same manner and followed the same bands and used the same forms of transport; for all of these reasons jazz fans were keen not to be identified as hooray Henries. 'Did we really talk like this, / With such absurd self-consciousness?' The question John Mole puts, wonderingly, in his charming poem 'The Jazzmen' (*The Instruments* (London, 1971)) is directed at the fact that he and his schoolfriends, jazz *aficionados* all, did their best to disguise their public-school accents by adopting the jazz patois, speaking, for example, of 'cats' who 'grooved'. They may have been 'Young gentlemen from public school', a minor one, 'deft at turning out a bore', but they knew that the music they loved was rooted and flowered in the most underprivileged of all levels of American society; if they wanted to hear it in England ('Humph at the Conway, Ken at Mac's'), Eel Pie Island, where Sandy Brown's band played to vast, delirious audiences, or anywhere else, for that matter, it was advisable to put on a protective voice along with the protective uniform.

Yet as Mole's poem reveals, middle-class and upper-class boys were now not merely listening to the music; they were trying to play it. He and his friends formed a jazz-band:

> Honour, though, our little clique,
> That dinned the Music Room each week,
> Us practising musicians who
> Thumped as grossly as we blew;
> Authentic every turgid sound
> Issuing from that hallowed ground.

For the cornet-player authenticity meant taking pains 'Not to sound slick like Harry James'. For Mole himself it meant learning the classic Alphonse Picou solo on 'High Society'. Mole still plays clarinet, and in fact you could easily make up a jazz band from the writers of our generation who learnt to play the music they loved.[10] Throughout the 1950s there was an annual Universities Jazz-Band championship, and jazz meant 'traditional', that is, non-modern, jazz. Oxford in 1957 had a very George Lewis-like outfit, the Loughborough Colleges band managed a fair imitation of Eddie Condon's group, the band I played in took Bunk Johnson as hero, and so on.

The point about all this is that the amorphous classlessness of the immediate post-war days was giving ground before the growing confidence of public-school and grammar-school products who were quite likely to be using traditional jazz as a stick with which to beat not only modernism (the three Ps) but also the vague radicalism that had earlier seemed an integral element in jazz appreciation. I need to tread carefully here. Some of my best friends are jazzmen and most of those are politically on the left. Some went to public school and others, like myself, came out of the grammar school system. Still others were products of secondary moderns and some of them were and are to the political right. Nevertheless, there can be no doubt that as the 1950s wore on so traditional jazz became increasingly identified as 'apolitical' (that is, conservative) and that some of its eloquent champions emerged as themselves increasingly conservative: which is why they rejected the newer jazz, for that signified a new-found confidence and aggressiveness on the part of black people which was part of the story of the emergence of black consciousness in America. And in Britain? I think it fair to say that only one kind of modern jazz ever really caught on here, and that, significantly enough, its adherents were working-class (Glasgow and London were the centres where it grew). They admired Parker but they imitated the 'cool' jazz associated with the Gerry Mulligan quartet, and their uniform featured button-down shirts and Italian suits; as far as I know, just because this jazz was working-class it was never much written about.

Traditional jazz, by contrast, never lacked for articulate middle-class supporters, who could look back to the early 'innocent' days as a kind of golden world before the fall into modernism and Birdland, Art

Blakey's Jazz Messengers, Charlie Parker and, worse and worse, John Coltrane and free form. I have to say that the jazz I love best belongs to the period stretching from early Armstrong through to the death of Fats Waller in 1943 (this period does, after all, contain a mass of beautiful and exciting music), but I know that the social-political context in which jazz exists, at least in America, made it inevitable that musicians such as Parker and Miles Davis and their followers would turn their backs (often literally) on audiences who asked for more of the same and who, as they rightly saw, essentially wanted black musicians to go on being Uncle Toms to white audiences. The uncomprehending contempt directed at modernism by Kingsley Amis is, therefore, an essential part of the condescension with which he gives his approval to the more traditional forms of jazz, as in his 'Farewell Blues', a pastiche of Hardy's great poem 'Friends Beyond':

Bongo, sitar, 'cello, flute, electric piano, bass guitar,
Training Orchestra, Research Team, Workshop, Group, Conservatoire,
Square Root, *Nexus*, *Barbaresque*, *Distortions*, *Voltage* – bloody row,
For Louis Armstrong, Mildred Bailey, Walter Page and Sidney Catlett
lie in Brunswick Churchyard now.

Trumpets gelded, drums contingent, saxophones that bleat or bawl,
Keyless, barless, poor-man's Boulez, improvising on fuck-all,
Far beyond what feeling, reason, even mother wit allow,
While Mugsy Spanier, Floyd O'Brien, Sterling Bose and Henry Allen
lie in Decca Churchyard now.

Dead's the note we loved that swelled within us, made us gasp and stare,
Simple joy and simple sadness thrashing the astounded air;
What replaced them no one asked for, but it turned up anyhow,
And Coleman Hawkins, Johnny Hodges, Bessie Smith and Pee Wee Russell
lie in Okeh churchyard now.

(*Collected Poems, 1944-1979* (Harmondsworth, 1980), 152)

A revealing point about this poem is that Amis's adherence to traditional jazz, which had earlier made him seem faintly radical, can now go hand-in-hand with a tetchy conservatism. 'Farewell Blues' reads almost as a parody piece, its snarling, ignorant dismissal of the new music very similar to the peevish anger with which Somerset Maugham tried to dismiss the young iconoclastic post-war writers among whom was, of course, Kingsley Amis. Another point is that in most of its claims and assertions the poem is plainly wrong. When Amis says that 'no one' asked for the new music he's talking nonsense. The fact that he didn't want it hardly counts against the fact that Charlie Parker, for example, became a hero to millions of young blacks in America and to a sizeable number of people in Britain. The gap that Amis tries to open up between then and now is made ludicrous as soon as you realize that Parker's music, as he himself always acknowledged, owed a great deal to the examples of Coleman Hawkins and Johnny Hodges.[11] Larkin, more astute and truthful than Amis, had grudgingly to admit the fact of Parker's genius when, reviewing a Parker memorial album, he wrote:

> It is Parker's solos that carry these records and have caused an alteration in the course of jazz. Granted that his technique and musical instinct for innovation were unrivalled, what was he like? His talent was indivisible; one cannot say that he would have been better if he had played more simply or with fewer rhythmic eccentricities; these are features of the wild, bubbling freedom that characterises him, and that some say earned him his nickname. But freedom from what? As one listens to Parker spiralling away 'out of this world', as the phrase goes, one can answer 'humanity', and that is a fatal thing for any artist, or any art, to be separated from. (*All What Jazz*, 96)

On the other hand, the two writers are not far apart in their prejudices. What Larkin here means by 'humanity' can be glossed by Amis's phrase 'simple joy and simple sadness'. Jazzmen and women are then a kind of stand-in for a contented peasantry in Amis's vision of an ideal past where music is the token of uncomplicated lives, uncomplicated relations. But you have to shed a great deal of history before you can arrive at the belief that there was anything simple about the sadness of Bessie Smith or the joy of Louis Armstrong. ('Laughin' Louis' was an invention of the Mafia, who forced the great genius of the music into excruciatingly embarrassing roles, on stage, on screen, and on record, because he was good business – at least as long as he kept laughing, kept on pumping out the simple joy.)

Like Amis and Larkin, John Wain's preference is for the more traditional forms of jazz. Nevertheless, Wain's 'Music on the Water' (subtitled 'to Bill Coleman in Paris') is alert to some of the historical tragedies out of which jazz emerged:

> Out at sea, the slave ships were coming.
> Sound reached out across water:
> dead-smack of corpse, gull-scream,
> chop of the settler's axe, gun-crack and
> whip-crack: in the steamy fields
> the black backs bend, the long dark song goes up:
> the American earth, no longer Eden:
> and sound moves out across water.[12]

Unfortunately, as this passage illustrates, Wain's poem is not much more than a plodding Janet-and-John rehash of a part of American history; his efforts to characterize Coleman's music, and that of Django, with whom Coleman sometimes played in Paris, is clogged with the same kind of clichés as deaden *Strike the Father Dead*, his well-meaning novel about jazz musicians. ('I brought up my hands and let them fall on to the keys. Instinctively, they formed a chord,... a lovely rich chord, which welled up out of the piano and rolled out, in ever-widening circles, till it filled the whole world' (52).) I have to say that I have never known a jazz musician who talks and thinks as Wain's are made to do.

In their different ways both Amis and Wain want to make absolute claim for the jazz they like. If this feels less than convincing it is because you realize that they aren't in fact in a position to speak with the kind of inwardness, or knowingness, that they pretend. Their writings about jazz therefore create some decidedly inappropriate falsehoods. Philip Larkin, on the other hand, from whose marvellous poem 'For Sidney Bechet' the phrase comes, knows how to keep his distance while at the same time finding the right way to praise the music he loves.

> The note you hold, narrowing and rising, shakes
> Like New Orleans reflected on the water,
> And in all ears appropriate falsehood wakes,
>
> Building for some a legendary Quarter
> Of Balconies, flower-baskets and quadrilles,
> Everyone making love and going shares –
>
> Oh, play that thing! Mute glorious Storeyvilles
> Others may license, grouping round their chairs
> Sporting-house girls like circus tigers (priced
>
> Far above rubies) to pretend their fads,
> While scholars manqués nod around unnoticed,
> Wrapped up in personnels like old plaids.
>
> On me your voice falls as they say love should,
> Like an enormous yes. My Crescent City
> Is where your speech alone is understood,
>
> And greeted as the natural noise of good,
> Scattering long-haired grief and scored pity.
>
> (*The Whitsun Weddings*, London, 1964, 16)

I do not know which particular record of Bechet's Larkin may have had in mind when he wrote the poem, and it is entirely possible that the description of 'the note', although it accurately catches Bechet's great powers of wide-vibrato glissand, is not meant to refer to a specific track. Nevertheless, it is worth remarking that on at least two occasions Larkin picked out 'Blue Horizon' as one of his favourites: 'six choruses of slow blues in which Bechet climbs without interruption or hurry from low to upper register, his clarinet tone at first thick and throbbing, then soaring like Melba in an extraordinary blend of lyricism and power that constituted the unique Bechet voice, commanding attention the instant it sounded'.[13]

The title of that great recording is appropriate to the meaning of Larkin's poem, which is after all about travelling across to an entirely imaginary New Orleans, the Crescent City where jazz first began and where, so various legends had it, the good times endlessly rolled. Hence the attractions of the Latin Quarter, its fantastic creole freedoms held in check by 'Oh, play that thing!', a phrase that can be heard on one of the classic jazz records, King Oliver's 'Sugar Foot Stomp', where it is exuberantly shouted by banjoist Bud Scott, after three choruses of the master's muted cornet and as a lead into a joyous ensemble closing sequence. In Larkin's poem the phrase, placed as it is, sounds with a rueful self-mockery which reminds us of the distance between the world of those 'antique negroes' (to quote from another Larkin poem which alludes to King Oliver) and the fact that Larkin, the jazz-buff, is listening on his own to the music that seems to hold out the promise of making love and going shares.

New Orleans was also famous for the fact that in 1917 the police closed down Storeyville, the red-light district where many of the early jazz musicians were hired to entertain punters waiting their turn with the Sporting House girls. In scripture it is, of course, a virtuous woman who is priced far above rubies. Larkin's joke testifies both to the fact that some of the Storeyville brothels were extremely lavishly got-up and very expensive, and that the solitary listener can in his licentious imagination (but only there) reissue licences to the sporting houses. The brilliant image of the scholars *manqués* 'wrapped up in personnels like old plaids' points to the efforts of rival jazz historians and discographers to put a name to each musician taking part in the early recording sessions – they were often left unnamed by the record companies concerned.

In the 1950s these attributions brought the historians into sharp conflict and provided them with a no-doubt welcome opportunity to assert their erudition on record-sleeves and in the columns of the musical press. In short, Larkin evokes, generously and wittily, a number of very English preoccupations with a city and its music that have attained the status of myth. It is this which saves the poem from falling into sentimentality at the end, for, although at first glance 'the natural noise of good' may seem uncomfortably close to 'simple joy and simple sorrow', in fact Larkin is aware, as Amis isn't, of the mythicizing qualities of that 'enormous yes'. It is another appropriate falsehood, and because he knows this he is able to indulge a dream of a world free of 'long-haired grief and scored pity'. In the 1950s 'long-hair' was a term of genial contempt directed by jazzmen at classical or 'serious' musicians. Larkin brilliantly puns on this to imply that Bechet's music cancels a world of sorrow, of Niobe and her misfortunes; and, in a further pun, that such improvised (unscored) music dispels the deep-hatched lines of pity and suffering that mark her woes. But this dream can last for only so long as the record itself. The poem has about it the neat containment of the kind of jazz number that fits perfectly into the limitations of a 78 rpm record.

Once Larkin had written his poem it became inevitable, I think, that other poets would try to pay tribute to the virtues of their jazz heroes, or to empathize with their hard-luck lives. This will explain Michael Longley's 'Words for Jazz Perhaps', a sequence of poems contained in his first volume, *No Continuing City*, in which he writes of Fats Waller, Bud Freeman, Bessie Smith, and Bix Biederbecke, just as it will explain Douglas Dunn's rather better 'Billie 'n' Me', about the tragic life and death of Billie Holiday. 'And silent now', it ends, 'As the saxophones in Harlem pawnshops, / Your voice that meant how tough love is'.[14] There are other such poems, but it is hardly necessary to list them here. Instead, I want to close by mentioning a far more original poem than any so far discussed: Roy Fisher's 'The Thing About Joe Sullivan'. This is the title-poem of a volume Fisher brought out in 1978, and it has been subsequently republished in his *Poems 1955-80*, London, 1980, 52).

Joe Sullivan was a pianist who, having learned much of his craft from Earl Hines, began his career with Eddie Condon before branching out into solo work and occasional recording sessions and work with other groups. (There is an affectionate account of him in Condon's *We Called It Music*, London, 1948; Corgi Paperback, 1962.) Jazzmen have always had a great respect for Sullivan, yet he never achieved the fame of other, less talented, musicians, perhaps because he never stayed for long with any one group; this was almost certainly due to his restless desire to push his music further, to test himself against harder obstacles. Sullivan, in other words, was not a 'one style' man; I imagine it was this which attracted Fisher, himself a talented pianist and very fine poet, to him. It is significant that Fisher is more aware of developments in post-war American poetry than most English poets, Charles Tomlinson and Donald Davie excepted, and both in style and subject-matter he is *sui generis*. 'The Thing About Joe Sullivan' is at once a poem in praise of an outstanding pianist, a subtle probing of his art, and at the same time an example of how to write the kind of poem that, perhaps like Sullivan's own music, starts from certainties and moves off into more exploratory and tentative statements.

> The pianist Joe Sullivan,
> jamming sound against idea
>
> hard as it can go
> florid and dangerous
>
> slams at the beat, or hovers,
> drumming, along its spikes;
> in his time almost the only

one of them to ignore

the chance of easing down,
walking it leisurely,

he'll strut, with gambling shapes,
underpinning by James P.,

amble, and stride over
gulfs of his own leaving, perilously

toppling octaves down to where
the chords grow fat again.

In jazz talk 'to jam' is to improvise, and in a sense the poem is improvising with possibilities of language and rhythm that Sullivan's own daring seem to have required of his admirer. You have only to compare this language, and the handling of pause, of pace, with the passage I quoted from *Strike the Father Dead* to sense how authentic Fisher's recreation of Sullivan's manner is. Yet it isn't just recreation that's at stake here; for the poem is an act of considering, a way of thinking about and enacting the daring perilousness of improvisation, while recognizing that there must always be the possibility of control. Thus when Sullivan struts, 'with gambling shapes', he is both playing and playing with the kind of music called a 'strut' (or, as variation, a 'cakewalk'),[15] which accompanied or summoned up black mimicry of the white man's way of walking or dancing, and at the same time gambling with ideas that might not come off were it not for the fact that he has not entirely forsaken the solid left-hand rhythm he learned from listening to James P. Johnson, the acknowledged king of 'stride' piano. As a result Sullivan can 'stride' over 'gulfs of his own leaving' (the enjambment reinforces the stride), and to do this is both an act of great daring and a way of employing artistic means that offer him a firmness of purpose: of jamming sound against idea.

Towards the end of the poem Fisher brings himself in. 'The thing about Joe Sullivan', he says, is his mood:

> a feeling violent and ordinary
>
> that runs in among standard forms so
> wrapped up in clarity
>
> that fingers following his
> through figures that sound obvious
>
> find corners everywhere,
> marks of invention, wakefulness;
>
> the rapid and perverse
> tracks that ordinary feelings
>
> make when they get driven
> hard enough against time.

The strange hesitancy of the poem's title is now justified as Fisher more deeply and personally explores Sullivan's way with music, his use of form to take risks that threaten to become formless but which are always rescued by a shaping purpose that discovers itself through the very act of creation, through the artist's mixture of daring and determination not to waste or idle with his art. At the same time he can place his trust in hard-won techniques which, traditional themselves (in the sense that Sullivan was brought up in the era of, and learnt from, a great generation of jazz pianists, especially Johnson and Hines), allow him, indeed require him, to move forward, tracking feelings that become eloquent with ideas as they are 'driven/ hard enough against time': the time a tune takes to be played, the musical time it is played in, and the time in which the artist lives, all of which form resistant mediums that his restless spirit must challenge.

Fisher's deep, inward understanding of how an art form cannot stand still makes 'The Thing About Joe Sullivan' not merely a far better poem than 'Farewell Blues' or several of the same breed; it also shows a far more tactful and alert awareness of how we all must live in time. Not, of course, that this will seem a recommendation to those for whom the three Ps spell the death of civilization.

1987

Notes

1. I do not know when drummers, bass-players, and banjoists (or guitarists) became a regular feature of hotel orchestras, but what later became identified as the 'rhythm section' certainly wasn't common in those war-time orchestras, any more than a 'brass' or 'reed' section. These terms come into their own with the big bands of the 1930s, and such bands did not play ragtime.
2. See Rex Harris, *Jazz* (Harmondsworth, 1952), 73-74.
3. See *The Diaries of Evelyn Waugh*, edited by Michael Davie (Harmondsworth, 1979; this edition makes minor revisions from the London edition of 1976), especially 155-303, passim; Martin Green, *Children of the Sun* (New York, 1976).
4. In *Recollections*, London, 1984, Geoffrey Grigsons claims to have heard T.S. Eliot sing 'Frankie and Johnny', but I do not suggest that this amounts to evidence that Eliot had an interest in jazz.
5. *The Journals of Arnold Bennett*, 1921-28, edited by Newman Flower, London, 1973, 52.
6. *The Letters of Arnold Bennett*, edited by James Hepburn, 3 vols, London, 1966, III, 124.
7. *The Jazz Singer*, the first example of a film to have sound on disc, came to London in 1928. Two reels are accompanied by sound, and on them Jolson sang 'Mammy' and 'Sonny Boy'. The film toured the provinces during the following two years.
8. For a fuller, more sympathetic account of the frustrations of would-be British jazz musicians of the 1930s, see the interviews conducted by Richard Sudhalter, under the title of 'Yesterday's Men: The Generation Gap in British Jazz', in *Jazz Now*, ed. Roger Cotterall, London, 1976.
9. John Wain's novel *Strike the Father Dead*, London, 1962, deals with the rebellious son of a university professor, who, despite his father's wishes, becomes a jazz pianist. In Owning Up, London, 1965; rpt. Harmondsworth, 1970, George Melly produces an hilarious autobiographical account of his years as a jazz singer with Mick Mulligan and his Magnolia Jazz Band, and also provides a very full

glossary of jazz argot.

10. Here is one such possible jazz-band: Humphrey Carpenter, brass bass; Roy Fisher, piano; Norton Smith, banjo; Russell Davies, trombone; Douglas Dunn, tenor sax; John Mole, clarinet; John Lucas, cornet; Terry Hawkes, drums.
11. For Parker's debts and sources, see Ross Russell, *Bird Lives: The High Life and Hard Times of Charlie 'Yardbird' Parker*, London, 1973, especially pp. 58-60.
12. 'Music on the Water' was first published in *Letters to Five Artists*, London, 1969, and reprinted in *Poems* 1949-79 (London, 1980), p. 109.
13. *All What Jazz*, 29 (see also 152). The record was cut in 1944, by which time Bechet was more regularly playing the soprano saxophone, at which he was the acknowledged, unapproachable master, and on which his power and attack frequently disconcerted all but the most determined of trumpet players.
14. Dunn, *The Happier Life*, London, 1972, 34, 'Words for Jazz Perhaps' is now available in Michael Longley's Poems 1963-1983, Edinburgh, 1985, 4-47.
15. This is unavoidably loose. The terms were created by blacks and perhaps especially by black musicians, and they seem to have been applied to the kinds of dances or even ways of walking which blacks associated with whites, and which they guyed outrageously in their own dances. But then 'strut' and 'cakewalk' became incorporated into the titles of numbers that were meant (and played) in a more straightforward manner, as, for example, 'Struttin' With Some Barbecue' and 'Cakewalking Babies'.

THE WORK OF A LEFT-HANDED MAN: ON ROY FISHER

When jazz musicians tune up they commonly ask for an A. I have a pianist friend who, on any occasion he's confronted by this question, balances a pair of lens-less horn-rimmed spectacles on the end of his nose, stares severely over them, and in a Herr Doktorish manner barks 'Any particular key?' The friend isn't Roy Fisher though I imagine he will be familiar with the joke. For all I know, he may have started it. Jazz jokes tend to become shared property, as endlessly and unquestioningly repeated as the two-bar tag on 'Buddy Bolden's Blues' or the ordering of themes in 'Panama Rag' (or any other rag, come to that). I suspect the underlying reason for this is that once you know the jokes and the routines – the rituals, even – you're considered part of the brother-and-sisterhood. This isn't to be compared to the masonic handshake, but only because jazzmen and women see themselves as either coming from or belonging to the wrong side of the tracks.

I am here talking about jazz in the UK, and the kind of jazz I have in mind is usually dubbed 'New Orleans to mainstream'. Men (mostly) and women (a few) who began to play this music during and after the Second World War came from mostly provincial backgrounds and, with a handful of exceptions, were of working-class origin. Jazz became their music because, quite apart from its intrinsic merits, it exuded an enviable air of freedom, gaiety, of being un-English, unstuffy, above all, I suspect, unshackled from the snobberies of class. And in case this should seem to be a grotesque sentimentalization, we need to recall that post-war Britain was, not surprisingly, a fairly depressing place in which to live, and that by contrast the USA, at all events as it appeared in versions supplied by technicolour Hollywood and other forms of popular culture, looked vivid with pleasures of the flesh. Jazz evoked such pleasures and in the UK it was therefore musically and, by implication, sexually, socially and politically transgressive. Jazz was the music of opposition. Jimmy Porter plays the trumpet.

Such opposition can be traced back to the 1920s, when jazz was associated with 'loose' living, with decadent bright young things, with drugs – especially cocaine, and with marches of the unemployed.[1] But twenties jazz often meant no more than the occasional 'hot' number as featured by society orchestras, or imported records played over and over again on wind-up gramophones. Very few indigenous bands played jazz. A generation later matters looked rather different. Most towns and cities now had their own jazz clubs. So, too, did most institutes of higher education. The clubs were kept going by local six- or seven-piece groups who did their best to sound like the bands with national reputations and recording contracts; from these semi-professional outfits the most gifted individuals were sometimes filched for the full-time and customarily London-based bands. These had their own bases – the 100 Club, Mac's, The Winning Post – but they also went 'on the road', playing to guaranteed full houses at clubs up and down England and even at town halls. Their movements and the comings and goings of 'personnel' were logged in the *Melody Maker*, which also carried regular reviews of new recordings and jazz concerts, often stretched to article length when concerts featured guest appearances by American jazzmen and women.[2]

Given all this, it might seem that in the 1950s jazz was a thriving business. For some, it must have been. But most of the musicians got by on comparatively little money. Moreover, the clubs themselves were usually either upstairs meeting-rooms in pubs, drill halls, or made-over hotel ballrooms. They were spartan places, often with an at best rudimentary stage, a poorly tuned piano and either a drinks licence which did not permit a late bar or, worse, but by no means unusual, no licence at all. Hence the fact that jazz jokes seem for the most part hang-dog, wryly self deprecating, even defeatist. Alan Plater caught the note perfectly in his TV play *Doggin' Around*, when he has a singer tell a visiting American pianist that her retirement was 'widely reported in the *Methodist Times*.' Not only do jazz musicians tune to A, once they are in tune they announce that it's 'near enough for jazz'.

In the course of one of his entertaining and informative Radio 3 talks with the cornettist Mel Hill, Roy Fisher remarked that 'all my life I've been left-handed', and he went on to recall that for this form of deviance he'd been caned at school.[3] Fisher was born in 1930, seven years earlier than me, but I too was caned at my midlands junior school for being 'cack-handed'. I was also made to sit on my left hand and practise writing with my other. Of course I couldn't do it. In those days we used steel-nibbed pens which had to be dunked in inkwells. My ink-globbed nib spiked and blotted each clean page, for which I received further canings. Mrs Levitt, the teacher who caned me, was convinced that if only I would persevere I would become ambidextrous. My brain would then develop on both sides and I would be a genius. Roy Fisher's teacher almost certainly shared this conviction. I am not about to claim that it turned him into a poet and jazz musician, but at the very least his early exposure to the absurdities of 'jobsworth' orthodoxy will have encouraged his recalcitrant wit. It also made him aware, as he says in the same interview, that as a left-hander he was using a pen 'against the grain', and that this valuable inhibition prevented fluency.

This may also have something to do with his lack of interest in regular metres. For although regular metres obviously enforce constraint and to that extent may hinder a fatal fluency, they can also permit an unthinking acceptance of the limits they impose, or of thinking within limits. To say this is merely to echo a twentieth century commonplace, one which has its starting point in the Poundian injunction to break the pentameter. And although opposition to this has the American Yvor Winters as one of its most formidable spokesmen, and while there is no necessary connection between formalist poetics and a conservative or reactionary cast of mind, I hardly need to defend the statement that in the 1950s, when Roy Fisher was starting out, English poetry appeared to be under the dominance of those formalists, most of them from Oxbridge, who were collectively known as the Movement. Some of them came from provincial England and for a time at least made much of their contempt for the tone of 'the centre', but in truth they were a pretty conformist lot. The fact they were genuinely interested in jazz of the 'classic' period – which covers mainstream – doesn't diminish their conformism, as Larkin's famous anathematizing of 'Pound, Parker and Picasso' makes clear. Fisher, with his early acquired and abiding interest in modern art and in 'redskin' American poetry, stands outside the Movement's fenced-off concerns.

Yet Larkin's passion for jazz can at least in part be explained as a way of licensing emotions and even a romantic yearning for extended horizons which elsewhere he mournfully or snarlingly repudiates. Hence the dosing lines of his marvellous poem 'For Sidney Bechet':

> On me your voice falls as they say love should,
> Like an enormous yes. My Crescent City
> Is where your speech alone is understood,
>
> And greeted as the natural noise of good,
> Scattering long-haired grief and scored pity.[4]

The natural noise of good is both instinctive and improvisational. The double puns of the last line oppose Bechet's music to that of trained classical musicians (known as 'long-hairs' in 1950s jazz argot) and to the fully scored music they play – music which also suggests the deep-trenched lines of Niobe's forehead.

For Larkin the voyeuristic outsider, jazz 'licenses' the rioting imagination of his partly cod Englishman: in the New Orleans somehow evoked by Bechet's music, everyone is 'making love and going shares', while 'Mute glorious Storyvilles / Others may license'. The Storyville brothels, where many of the first great jazzmen played, lost their licences in 1917.[5] Renewing license enables sexual fantasy ('License my roving hands to go'). Fisher's interest in jazz is very different, but it inevitably shares Larkin's Romantic belief in 'inspiration', which as far as jazz is concerned has to be found in improvisation. He touches on this in a long and fascinating interview with the Australian poet John Tranter, recorded in March 1989. Tranter remarks that jazz piano is an American art, and Fisher replies:

> Oh, yeah. Somebody once asked me in an interview years ago who influenced my writing and I said without thinking about it, Pee-Wee Russell, you know, the Chicago clarinet player. And I wasn't being smart. Because I learned that music, I learned it as outsider music, as music you had to go around corners to find. Music that was made *against* bourgeois traditions and academic traditions. I was studying the jazz of the twenties and thirties. And that appealed to me very much, and I could understand the way of thinking of people who didn't want to play the same thing twice ever, and who had for me – and I still admire it very much in musicians – a mixture of good old-fashioned, not too worldly wise sense of Romantic creativity. You know, tonight may be the night, this number may be the number when I astonish myself, I may hit it this time. A combination of that with an honest artisan approach – yes, I know how to begin and end a number, I know how to play in time, I know how to get my fingers on the right notes, without any 'faff' about personality and fame. There's a basic artisan level in playing a tune in time and in the right key without failing, without scaling the impossible. But at the same time you're always pitching yourself against something – you've got to invent. So I like that combination.[6]

It is of the essence of jazz improvisation that unless someone happens to have a tape recorder handy you never know whether you did 'hit it this time'. (It is entirely possible that Armstrong's studio recording of 'West End Blues' may not be as good as some of those countless times he played the number live.) But Fisher's belief in 'not too worldly wise' Romantic creativity goes hand-in-hand with his belief that as a poet he has to let the poem find its way. That is one reason 'Why They Stopped Singing', 'because/ They remembered why they had started'.[7] It is why 'I saw what there was to write and I wrote it./ When it felt what I was doing, it lay down and died under me' ('Diversions', P 55-87, 133). And it is why, in one of his most famous poems, he extols the pianist Joe Sullivan for striding 'over /gulfs of his own leaving' (52). Jazz, like the poetry Fisher wants to write, is a way of risking the unknown. But unlike such poetry, jazz – the jazz Fisher plays – has clearly imposed limits. You have to play in the right key, in tune, in time. And if you play in a band you also have to rely on others. It is here that improvisational skills come up against the need to fit in with the overall structure of the tune you are playing and the band you are playing with. And as Fisher acknowledges, such contingent factors will inevitably (mis)shape intentions. Hence *The Ship's Orchestra.*

In his interview with Tranter, Fisher says that the poem came out of a combination of dreams and a reproduction of Picasso's *Three Musicians* which he owned:

> where there's a little monk-like figure holding a clarinet, and there's bits of a fourth musician, and I did a sort of you know 'What kind of musicians are these?' And I always sympathise – I mean, I make half my living by being a member of the band that turns up for a gig and say 'Who the hell have we got on bass?' The other night I played one where the bass player was really an accordion player, or a concertina player, and he played bass like a concertina, you know, what can you do? And you walk in, and you try to persuade the people to let you get out alive and pay you. I love this.

I doubt very much whether the subject of *The Ship's Orchestra* would have occurred to anyone who was not a jazz musician. Its deadpan prose is stiffened to comic resolve by the recognition that if things can go wrong for a hired musician then they almost certainly will. This ship's orchestra never even gets to play. Such comedy goes with, is sharpened by, that self-deprecatory manner which, to repeat, is endemic to jazz. It may also go with a self-conscious provincialism. Recalling in the interview with Tranter a reviewer who had claimed that the poet's 'subject matter is, I suppose, always "the provinces"', Fisher adds 'Which is everywhere else but London and Oxford and Cambridge, and one or two rather well-to-do spots around that way. It doesn't mean much, but it affects the way you behave, and what you root for and what you snarl at'. One or two well-to-do spots around that way: now there's a jazzman's laconicism.

It therefore comes as something of a surprise to find that in *City* Fisher is prepared to adopt an almost Forsterian note of quizzical disdain:

> In this city the governing authority is limited and mean: so limited that it can do no more than preserve a superficial order. It supplies fuel, water and power. It removes a fair proportion of the refuse, cleans the streets after a fashion, and discourages fighting. With these things, and a few more of the same sort, it is content. This could never be a capital city for all its size. There is no mind in it, no regard. The sensitive, the tasteful, the fashionable, the intolerant and powerful, have not moved through it as they have moved through London, evaluating it, altering it deliberately, setting in motion wars of feeling about it. Most of it has never been seen. (*P 55-87*, 22-23)

This is so strongly reminiscent of the cadences and indeed language of *Howards End* as to suggest that Fisher's account is, consciously or not, a pastiche of Forsterian effects. (To *Howards End* may be added 'the plucky, the considerate and the sensitive' of 'What I Believe'.) I mention this only because what feels like a lapse into the pose of long-haired grief and scored pity is, I think, momentary, although it may have lodged in Donald Davie's mind when he came to believe that City somehow reveals a desire for an anti-democratic, authoritarian politics, even though Davie concludes that these alternatives to 'social democracy on the British model – mean-spirited as that undoubtedly is – are too costly in terms of human suffering for any man of humane feeling, least of all a poet, to find them real alternatives any longer'.[8]

In adding the last two words Davie plainly mourns the fact that late in the twentieth century it is not possible to put faith in the truly strong man. But there are still poets around whom I would not readily identify as men of humane feeling, even though Fisher isn't one of them. Nor would it be necessarily appropriate to substitute 'jazzman' for 'poet' in Davie's summing up.

On the other hand, Fisher's way of being a jazzman, his tolerance of contingency, is anti-authoritarian in its relish for the absurdities of happenstance, of bass-players who play the bass as though it's a concertina. After all, he was doing his best, and although I no more want to sentimentalize Fisher's regard for an 'honest artisan approach' than he himself does, he patently doesn't think it should be slighted. For once you have this artisanal approach – or to put it rather more vehemently – this mastery of craft, you can afford to welcome contingency. This is not to say that you will always be able to use it to best advantage, but if you turn your back on it you will be unable to find where it is you want to go. You will simply go 'Clanging along in A-flat' without ever 'letting the tenths look out/for their own chances' ('The Home Pianist's Companion', *P55-87*, 168).

And this of course is why Joe Sullivan is so important an exemplar to Fisher. In a deft review of *Poems 1955-1987*, John Mole remarks that 'the spirit of [Fisher's poetry], as it appeals to me, could be summed up by Earl Hines's comment (though I haven't traced a Fisher reference to Hines yet) that 'every night I like to find a different harmonic route to a certain point, and when you see me smiling you know I'm lost'.[9] Fisher is in fact an admirer of Hines. He may even be invoking The Spirit of Earl 'Fatha' when he admits to Tranter that 'If I play ballads, or 'Sophisticated Lady' or 'Body and Soul', I make quite a meal of them.... I play piano in quite a juvenile, enthusiastic fashion'. On the other hand, he does not, as he here and elsewhere says, like what he describes to Tranter as 'any kind of go-go rhythm'. For a similar reason he is not especially interested in 'single-line melody', as he tells Mel Hill. And so even though he confesses that 'I play the piano more emotionally than I write', his interest in swing doesn't at all mean that he works within bar lines or accepts the clearly defined framework of, say, two- or four-bar units. He would rather go 'chasing the horns'.

So at least Fisher tells Hill, and this suggests why, to the best of my knowledge, he does not include Teddy Wilson among his pantheon of swing pianists. For Wilson, wonderful musician though he is, works within limits rather than pushing beyond them. This may be not unconnected to the fact that Wilson is among the great accompanists, as anyone who has heard his recordings with the young Billie Holiday would surely agree. Certainly 'Miss Brown to You' and 'What a Little Moonlight Can Do', recorded in New York in 1935, are among the finest of the great singer's pre-war work, and Wilson's immaculately crisp playing, together with the almost staccato effect of his right hand, whether underpinning Holiday's voice or Roy Eldridge's trumpet, seems to me about as good as swing piano can get. But I can see that, assured, even perfect though, or perhaps because it is, such playing is definitely within limits. Nor does it feel in any way cramped by them. You could never imagine Wilson 'perilously // toppling octaves down to where / the chords grow fat again'. And there is never a chance that his piano might seem 'at risk of being/ hammered the next second into scrap' (*P 55-87*, 52). Larkin thought of Armstrong as a kind of twentieth-century Chaucer; in which case it might not be improper to think of Wilson in terms of Popeian finesse, like the spider's touch which, 'exquisitely fine!/ Feels at each thread, and lives along the line'.

Talking to Tranter, Fisher at one point remarks that critics of his work have begun to elucidate and gloss 'things which I've blundered into, habits I've blundered into, areas of material ... when I say blundered, I'm not criticising myself – I intended 'to 'blunder', I wasn't doing anything else'. To 'Blunder', the *Oxford English Dictionary* says: 'Move blindly; flounder, stumble'. To blunder is to behave in an unpremeditated way; blundering is gauche behaviour. We are back at left-handedness. More tellingly, perhaps, we can deduce from Fisher's intention to blunder the reason for his shock at Basil Bunting's reply to the younger poet's asking him whether *Brigflatts* was finished. 'The music is,' Bunting assured Fisher. But how could he have known?[10]

Fisher, whose indebtedness to American modernism is not in doubt, always wants to make for the open ground. At the same time, he guards against the risk of falling into romantic preoccupation with self (self-discovery, self-aggrandizement) which this form of making can imply, may even require. Hence, his poem-as-manifesto, 'Of the Empirical Self and for Me', which begins 'In my poems there's seldom / any *I* or *you*' (P 5-87, 125). Poetry is therefore not so much concerned with selfhood as the happenstance of occurrence. The poem may draw attention to itself, the poet should not do so. Fisher is on record as saying that 'when I do readings in large halls, they have to turn the mike up. The monotone, the low conversation style is quite intentional'.[11] The poet effaces himself from his poem. Yet at the same time Fisher is characteristically the poet whose work is prompted by his readiness to honour the fortuitous. As 'A Poem to be Watched' (182) puts it, a poem comes 'into the world/ unprepared', and, 'driven to exhibit/ over and over again/ unpreparedness', it can become a kind of showpiece, 'habitually/ unready to be caught/ born' (there is no full-stop at poem's end).

Poems about poems and poetry, the art both reflecting and reflecting on itself, is, it almost goes without saying, a marked feature of much modern American poetry, from the early masters Stevens, Moore, Williams, through Levertov, Creeley, O'Hara, Ashbery, Duncan et al. There are probably quite enough of such poems in existence by now and it could be argued that, while at first they valuably endorsed ways of making it new, they have become so expected, not to say routine, as to look and feel only too well-prepared when they enter the world. For this reason, I much prefer 'On the Neglect of Figure Composition', Fisher's wildly funny fantasy about the exhausted possibilities of heroic representative / tradition-sanctioned art. I would never dare to suggest that only a jazzman could have come up with anything at once so comic and – let us be honest – piss-taking, but I *can* report that I have jazzmen friends who think anyone interested in poetry must be due a visit by the men in white coats, while they have without exception loved 'Sketch for the First Exhibition of the New Heroic Art'.

Yet this comic masterpiece doesn't require us to identify Fisher with that most tiresome of postmodernist beliefs in the inevitable self-reflexivity of art. Although he accepts that his work is the product of what he told one interviewer is 'a rather complicated mentality', and although to the same interviewer he remarked that bad readers of a poem such as Eliot's "Prufrock' … can't float … can't just read the score, one note after another', he doesn't take the imagination to feed on itself. On the contrary Fisher is very much a poet to be identified with that modern, empirically verifiable phenomenon, the city. Fisher's particular city, Birmingham, has, it is generally agreed, prompted much of his best work, from *City* itself through to *Birmingham River*. Yet talking to Tranter, Fisher as good as says that although he's lived in the city for forty years he doesn't necessarily feel of it. 'For some reason I never really swam in the city and was an urban person, although I lived in and around the town a great deal, and was in the pubs and in the jazz clubs and in the educational system of the same place for decades on end'. He ascribes this sense of not-quite-belonging to his parents: 'my family who were working people, who seemed to have not long been brought in from the country … they didn't know anything about the country, they didn't know where they'd come from, but there was a sort of strong moral air that it would be good to get back onto farm land again'.

The sense of being somehow a stranger in the city may almost be the defining experience of city existence. You can't know the city as you can the country, not only because it lacks the views by which the country is arranged – all those fixed prospects – but because its endlessly changing vistas, its streets, alleys, thoroughfares, are a kind of discomposition, a denial of orderly vision. All this is familiar to us now. The city as a place of atomistic lives, of disrupted and disorderly narratives has been addressed by writers from Baudelaire and Dickens onwards, and has more recently received much critical and scholarly attention, especially since the discovery of Benjamin's seminal essay on Baudelaire.[12]

All the more remarkable, then, that Fisher's *City* appeared in 1961, well before that attention began to be directed towards modern writing, at all events in England. It's a perfect example of where blundering can get you. In the early 1960s *The Waste Land* was still typically written about in ways that granted it supreme authority for its evocation of spiritual malaise in the modern world, where 'world' was essentially an uninspected term. It wasn't however seen as a city poem. As for Dickens, the greatest novelist of city experience, he had famously nothing to offer 'the mature critical mind'.

One of the tenets of writing about the city is that the spectator of its scenes is inevitably an invisible flâneur. Invisible because in all probability the spectator will be unknown to those he observes as they pass him by. Flâneur because while everybody else has what Engels called 'separate purpose', the lounger's only purpose is to observe and record. Still, the very fact that the flâneur is an outsider, one who recognizes no close kinship with others in the city, can be traced to his pathology, whether as an artist or a member of the bourgeoisie. This, at least, is a familiar enough tactic of reader/critics for whom realism is the predictable artistic mode adopted by those who take for granted the adequacy of their world view. Yet it would be difficult to argue that Fisher's registering of city experience in 'For Realism' is flawed by his spectatorial assumptions. It might, however, be said that at the poem's opening the narrator draws attention to the key word's problematic status by fencing it within quotation marks. The poem starts:

For 'realism':
the sight of Lucas's
lamp factory on a summer night;
a shift coming off about nine,
pale light, dispersing,
runnels of people chased,
by pavements drying off
quickly after them,

> away among the wrinkled brown houses
> where there are cracks for them to go; . . . (*P 55-87*, 54)

Yet at poem's end, when the word returns, the quotation marks have gone:

> A conscience
> builds, late, on the ridge. A realism
> tries to record, before they're gone,
> what silver filth these drains have run. (p.55)

'Realism' is, then, acknowledged to be literary artifice, and the flâneur's knowledge of what he records is initially a matter of random observation. Although he cannot help but know something about the shift workers, it is plain that he is an outsider. To him, such workers are reduced to the near-cliché of ant-like behaviour, scurrying to 'where there are cracks for them to go'. This in part re-visits a moment in *City* where the observer remarks that

> Lovers turn to me faces of innocence where I would expect wariness. They have disappeared for entire hours into the lit holes of life, instead of lying stunned on its surface as I, and so many, do for so long; or instead of raising their heads cautiously and scenting the manifold airs that blow through the streets.
> (*P 55-87*, 26)

Such mournful acknowledgement of being outside the 'lit holes of life' is not a million miles from the occasion when Larkin hears 'The trumpet's voice, loud and authoritative, / Draw[s] me a moment to the lighted glass / To watch the dancers – all under twenty-five' – / Shifting intently, face to flushed face,/ Solemnly on the beat of happiness' ('Reasons for Attendance'). It is also one of the few places in Fisher's oeuvre where the reader is bound to reflect that the empirical self can be found, all unguarded.

But guardedness soon sets in. Hence 'realism'. Yet a deeper sense of realism requires Fisher at the poem's end to acknowledge that he may be required at least to try to record 'what silver filth these drains have run'. Davie no doubt misreads the lines when he says that Fisher has in mind the

> social conscience of the confident demographer and humanitarian administrator who has demolished acres of the inner city and rehoused their denizens in high-rise apartment-blocks on the ridge above their old dwellings, at whatever cost to the human associations that these dwellings had for them.[13]

But he is right to see that Fisher is prepared to risk taking on the role of recording at a deeper and more responsible level than mere reportage: 'what silver filth these drains have run', by moving out of the present tense, acknowledges that the place has a knowable history.[14] And these are matters which engage him in *A Furnace* and *Birmingham River.*

I can't follow him in any detail into these book-length poems because to do so would take me too far from my subject. I will however note that in the 'Introit' to *A Furnace* Fisher makes himself very much the passive recipient of the scene. He blunders into the visible evidence of city living:

> ... And the road
> from Bilston to Ettingshall begins
> beating in. Whatever
> approaches my passive taking-in,
> then surrounds me and goes by
> will have itself understood only
> phase upon phase
> by separate involuntary
> strokes of my mind, dark
> swings of a fan-blade
> that keeps a time of its own,

made up from the long
discrete moments
of the stages of the street,
each bred off the last as if by
causality.[15]

Such blundering goes with, cannot be dissociated from, the awareness of 'passive taking-in' which is yet actively alert to its own processes, those 'dark / swings of a fan-blade / that keeps a time of its own'. At first glance this can look very near to a number of moments in *The Prelude*, as for example the one where Wordsworth recalls walking

... a steep ascent
Where the road's wat'ry surface, to the ridge
Of that sharp rising glittered in the moon . . .

On I went
Tranquil, receiving in my own despite
Amusement, as I slowly passed along,
From such near objects as from time to time
Perforce intruded on the listless sense
Quiescent, and disposed to sympathy ...[16]

This too seems to be a passive taking-in, but with one crucial difference. Wordsworth's mind is emptied out, laid to rest, so that it can be properly receptive to a moment of visionary, epiphanic significance. Much if not most of English poetry – and prose – since Wordsworth has been attuned to this idea of the epiphanic, that is to the reception of an image in which is embodied a pure concentration of meaning. Even 'silver filth' may be thought of as an epiphanic image, its concentration of meaning including, as Neil Corcoran has remarked, great 'metaphoric and oxymoronic energies'.[17] These are inevitably predicated on the belief that there is a knowable, graspable world out there.

And this is so, both in *City* and any number of Fisher's poems. Yet having said this, I must at once add that Fisher's secular imagination requires him to register mental activity in a manner that queries the trust in purposiveness implicit – and sometimes explicit – in Wordsworth's egotistical sublime or for that matter in such later expressions of purposiveness as Hopkins's 'thisness'. To put it differently, and in a way that frees requirement from moral glumness, Fisher's cast of mind is, as he himself frequently avows, decidedly, if wryly, sceptical. Hence his disarming remark to Tranter, 'Apparently I do have a technique of describing bits of the world with loving care but in such language as to cast enormous doubt on whether there's anything there at all'. But, he all-importantly adds, 'I don't want to play mere language games'. And so while he avoids structuring poems in a manner that resembles 'realist' narratives, with a beginning, a middle and an end and in that order, he equally disavows the poem as existing within a closed circuit. Here, what he says of *A Furnace* is especially relevant. The poem, he tells Tranter, is 'accretive … written in a sequence which to me is musical … where you revisit themes at various times … as if it were an orchestral work, certain instrument sounds, certain bell sounds'. And so, for all that it could be described as collagist, as he remarks, there is that which distinguishes *A Furnace* from other modern poems with which it apparently claims kinship. This has most markedly to do with capturing 'a cast of mind … moods … ways of reprocessing experience and joining new experience up to old experience', given that the cast of mind of this particular poet is also the cast of mind of a musician. To examine this claim apropos of *A Furnace* would take too long. There is, however, another, shorter poem that will serve my purpose, the 'The Home Pianist's Companion'.

For all its apparently freewheeling improvisatory air, 'The Home Pianist's Companion' is most subtly organized. To say this is not, however, to suggest that it is premeditated, let alone that it has a conventional narrative structure. As its use of participles indicates, the poem depends on a sure sense of blundering – if that oxymoron can be allowed – and its themes are discoverable through a kind of musical development: of statements, of phrasing, rephrasing, restatement, modulation. It begins with what seems to be an account of dutiful piano practice: 'Clanging along in A-flat / correcting faults . . . thinking of Mary Lou, / a lesson to us all, // how she will trench and / trench into the firmness of the music / modestly'. Even here, though, the poem modulates from the semi-automatic 'Clanging along' into self-awareness – 'thinking of Mary Lou' (P55-87, 168). Mary Lou Williams (1910-81) is one of the less celebrated mainstream pianists, though Fisher's regard for her is entirely understandable. Not only did Duke Ellington call her 'perpetually contemporary', meaning that she was never content to settle into routine, but her rejection of the term 'jazz' came about because, for all her modesty, she regarded its use as 'fundamentally reductive'. In their vast, well-researched *Guide to Jazz on CD, LP and Cassette*, Richard Cook and Brian Morton note of her playing that, 'However swinging and jazz-based her solo and small-group output, Williams transcended the conventional bounds of jazz composition and performance'.[18] This is very like striding over gulfs of your own leaving.

Having introduced thoughts of Mary Lou, Fisher leaves her. The poem moves on:

thinking,
in my disorder of twofold sense,
or finding rather
an order thinking for me as I play,
of the look of lean-spoked
railway wagon wheels
clanging on a girder bridge,
chopping the daylight, black
wheel across wheel, spoke

over rim, in behind girder and out
revealing the light, withholding it,
inexorable flickers
of segments in overlap

moving in mean elongate
proportions, the consecutive
fourths of appearances,
harsh gaps, small strong
leverages, never still. (168-169)

These lines provide a good instance of the kind of writing Barthes called 'scriptible', 'where a co-operation between the reader and the author is needed to attain a meaning', and which Fisher is happy to agree with Ra Page defines his characteristic way of writing.[19] In the passage just quoted we have to co-operate with Fisher's terse notation in order to register his association of a certain style of jazz piano with the flicker of repeated, clangorous wagon wheels (an image redolent of the industrial cityscape) where 'segments in overlap' is at once the stroboscopic effect of the wheels themselves and of echoed and developing musical phrases. The lines are about ways of playing, ways of seeing, and ways of thinking. And as the poem goes on so other themes are picked up: the 'sour face / on that kind of wheel' modulates into 'the eternal/ mask of a narrow-faced cat, / its cornered, cringing intensity / moving me to distraction again'. And this distraction itself modulates by way of 'the calm / of a time just after infancy' (169) to a 'primal figure of the line, / primitively remembered, / just a posture of her, an apron' (170). The pianist follows a line of music which draws in the image of a railway line, and that line then leads to a reverie where a washing-line recalls an old woman 'gaunt, narrow-faced, closed in, / acceptable, / soon dead'. This then gathers up earlier, apparently abandoned scraps of theme, before modulating into the closing lines:

Still in the air,
haunting the fourths
of A-flat major
with wheels and a glinting cat-face;

reminding me
what it was like to be sure,
before language ever
taught me they were different,
of how some things were the same. (170)

Music is itself and yet makes possible a discovery of thought processes that are ultimately pre-linguistic. Pater thought all arts aspired to the condition of music and Fisher might agree. But he would not then agree that music is the perfect symbolist form of art. For symbolism is another expression of the epiphanic, its pure concentration depending on a Platonic belief in correspondence. 'The Home Pianist's Companion' is closer to Browning's 'A Toccata of Galuppi's', which is the greatest poem I know about what involvement in the act of playing means. And it is of course no accident that a toccata is a form of composition which has built into it a measure of improvisation. Browning, an accomplished pianist, spells out the means by which the man who plays Galuppi – he is very definitely not Browning himself – finds in the music's 'commiserating sevenths', 'dominant's persistence' and 'octave', sources for his own blundering into thought processes that take him a long way from the poem's beginning. Fisher is characteristically more oblique than Browning, or it might be better to say he is less explanatory. But no one who is not a musician could have written 'The Home Pianist's Companion'. And while the title jokily suggests a less than accomplished pianist who needs to have a 'Tutor' propped up in front of him, enabling him to follow basic chords and melodic patterns, the poem in fact pays sophisticated tribute to the power of music to get beyond the restrictions of language and contained and therefore constraining habits of thought. Fisher's way of writing is here and elsewhere closely linked to, might even be said to permit and be made possible by, his commitment to styles of jazz-piano and, thus, processes of imaginative thought that liberate him from intellectual and formal constraints within which post-war English attitudes to culture typically operate. 'The Home Pianist's Companion' is a properly recalcitrant poem, the work of a left-handed man.

2000

Notes

1. For more on this see John Lucas, *The Radical Twenties: Aspects of Writing, Politics and Culture* (Nottingham: Five Leaves Publications, 1997), chapter 4.
2. From the mid-thirties until 1956 the Musicians Union banned foreign bands from playing in the UK. Visiting musicians had to be accompanied by home grown musicians.
3. *The Fortunate Cat*, BBC Radio 3, 25-29 December 1995.
4. 'For Sidney Bechet', *Collected Poems*, ed. and intro. Anthony Thwaite (London: Faber & Faber and The Marvell Press, 1988), 83.
5. In 1917 the brothels of New Orleans lost their licences because the US government decided that the war effort would be harmed by soldiers and sailors making use of them.
6. The interview with John Tranter was recorded at Roy Fisher's Derbyshire house on 29 March 1989. It is available on Tranter's Internet magazine, *Jacket*, http//www. jacket/au/jacket01/fisheriv.html.
7. 'Why They Stopped Singing', *Poems 1955-1980* (Oxford: Oxford University Press,1980), 1.
8. Donald Davie, 'Roy Fisher: An Appreciation', *Thomas Hardy and British Poetry* (London: Routledge & Kegan Paul,1974), 172.
9. John Mole, 'The Innovative Flicker of the Piano Player', a review of Fisher's *Poems 1955-1987* in the *Poetry Review*, 79:2 (Summer 1989), pp. 27-28, at p. 27.
10. Recalling this in interview with Mel Hill, Fisher adds that he now understands what Bunting means. This does not however diminish his sense that, as Theodore Roethke says, you learn by going where you have to go. (Though paradoxically Roethke said that in a villanelle, one of the most determined of poetic forms.)
11. In an interview with Ra Page, 'People Who Can't Float', *Prop 2* (1997): 28-30, at 30.

12. There is no need to provide chapter and verse here, although attention should perhaps be drawn to Edward Timms and David Kelley's *Unreal City: Urban Experience in Modern European Literature and Art* (Manchester: Manchester University Press,1985).
13. Davie, 'Roy Fisher', 163.
14. In his interview with Ra Page, Fisher remarks that he finds the kind of writing associated with Arnold Bennett impossible to do without appearing 'patronising and pedestrian because it provides the reader with everything. See *Prop* 2, 30.
15. 'Introit', *A Furnace* (Oxford: Oxford University Press, 1986), 2-3.
16. Book IV, lines 370-80 (1805 text), in *William Wordsworth*, The Oxford Authors, ed. Stephen Gill (Oxford: Oxford University Press,1984).
17. Neil Corcoran, *English Poetry Since 1940* (Harlow: Longman,1993), 171.
18. Richard Cook and Brian Morton, *The Penguin Guide to Jazz, on CD, LP and Cassette*, new edition (Harmondsworth: Penguin,1994), 1375.
19. See *Prop* 2, 30.

REQUIEM FOR THE 20th CENTURY
ENGLAND MADE ME

Michael Baron, ed., *Larkin with Poetry*. English Association Conference Papers, 1997. ISBN 0 90023 218 8
A.T. Tolley, *Larkin at Work*, The University of Hull Press, 1997. ISBN 0 885958 622 6

The question of Larkin's Englishness, much discussed by the essayists gathered together in *Larkin with Poetry*, goes back a long way. So, too, does the question of how far he subscribed to being a little Englander. Photography, faithful 'as no art is', he famously wrote in a poem where washing lines and Hall's-Distemper Boards make a key appearance. But faithful to what? The cover photograph for the December 1963 issue of Ian Hamilton's *Review* shows the poet in overcoat and probably death-suited, leaning casually over iron railings, an umbrella held lightly enough in both hands, just open, ready to unfurl. For all I know this is a studio photograph – there is no background – its air of improvisation carefully rehearsed; and Larkin, who doesn't quite look at the camera, wears an expression at once lugubrious, severe, and conceivably on the verge of convulsive laughter. The image is a wonderful tease. This is Larkin flirting with a kind of Englishness. Ten years later he poses for the cover of a special double issue of *Phoenix*. Here, he sits on a stone plinth, his elbow resting on a square column on which is pinned a sign saying 'ENGLAND' below the shield of St George. The photograph, which was taken at Hadrian's Wall, offers the poet as a frontier guard, repelling would-be intruders. His Englishness is now decidedly more aggressive, blimpish even. He wears a hound's-tooth check jacket and there are turn-ups to his trousers. And he stares almost belligerently straight at the camera.

1964 was the year of *The Whitsun Weddings*, 1974 of *High Windows*. By the time the latter volume appeared Larkin was more or less written out. Commentators often point to 'Going, Going', which was included in *High Windows*, as evidence of what Stephen Regan in his contribution to *Larkin with Poetry* calls dejection as 'a form of cultural melancholy that issues, in part, from the end of empire and subsequent loss of power'. Tom Paulin has read this melancholy into much of Larkin's work and has linked it to lost male autonomy and repressed desires: 'angry at not being allowed to show emotion, he writhes with anxiety inside that sealed bunker which is the English ethic of privacy'.

Add to this Lisa Jardine's dismissal of the 'Little Englandism [Larkin] celebrates' from the up-to-date curricula of institutionalised studies, which, so she says, seek 'to give all our students, regardless of background, race or creed, a voice within British culture', and it might seem that Larkin is read only by a diminishing band of crusty, all-male admirers, the kind who in the last century settled down to the latest Rider Haggard, glass of gin at the ready as the sun westered over the *stoep*. It's true that James Booth, in his piece 'Philip Larkin: Lyricism, Englishness and Postcoloniality' tries to counter critics of the poet's particular Englishness by asserting that lyricism such as Larkin's is somehow outside time, but this is bunkum, as those washing lines and Distemper Boards make all-too evident. In fact, Larkin's poems are so packed with reference to everyday English habits and things, are so replete with idiom, that it's easy to imagine a future editor having to footnote just about every line. And as I can testify, teaching Larkin outside the UK means you have endlessly to explain references to – oh, to someone running up to bowl, to flat-faced trolleys, to the untransferable Truss-advertisement, and the four aways at which Mr. Bleaney plugged ... . (This last, by the way, allows Larkin to cover up one of his rare mishandlings of idiomatic phrase: you don't plug at, you plug away at.)

And yet for all Jardine's belief or hope that Larkin won't appeal to many students, he does. Not only in the UK, either. To pick at random:

in the USA, in Greece, in Romania, and in Australia, there are plenty who, for all the difficulties made by his MacNeice-like listing of daily phenomena, nevertheless love Larkin's work. It's true there's scope for misunderstanding. I recall in particular the nun in Bloomington, Indiana, who disapproved of what she felt was the 'indelicacy' of Larkin's reference in 'An Arundel Tomb' to the endless altered people marching up the aisle to see the stone effigy of earl and countess and 'Washing at their identity'. (She thought they were literally pissing on the grave.) Closer to home are the inexcusable mis-readings by critics determined to be hostile, who find in the poems evidence of Larkin the letter-writing xenophobe, racist and woman-hater. It's therefore heartening to come on Marion Lomax's fine essay, 'Larkin with Women'. She points out that among Larkin's pantheon were Christina Rossetti, Emily Dickinson and Stevie Smith, and that he emphatically didn't like them because they were any of those things which enable male writers, in Jo Shapcott's words, to categorise women poets as 'siren, eccentric, or vulnerable confessional'. It was with Emily Dickinson in mind that Larkin wrote, 'Poetry is an affair of sanity, of seeking things as they are'. And it's worth noting that washing-lines aren't often to be found in male poets' line of vision. (Personal testimony: For a very brief period at the beginning of the '60s I lodged with a poet who wouldn't allow his wife to hang out the washing when he was at work, because his study window faced onto the lawn across which the line ran and he didn't see why he should be reminded of the mundane world from which he'd shut himself away.)

Lomax provides compelling readings of 'Forget What Did', whose title she traces to Susan Coolidge's *What Katy Did* (hands up everyone who knew that) and of the much-attacked 'Deceptions', a propos of which she remarks, 'I see Larkin as someone who found it easy to sympathise with the female perspective because he understood vulnerability and the frustrations of being confronted with illusions to live up to – whether it was the macho man image he never managed to achieve because he never attracted or felt easy with the kinds of girls who were the necessary accessories to such a model – as he shows so well in 'Wild Oats' – or whether it was the woman's equivalent problem as exemplified by a poster of Sunny Prestatyn on a station platform, with the so-called 'ideal' woman who he – and the vandals who deface her – implies is 'too good for this life'.

Lomax sees off the charge of misogyny. Regan deals fairly but firmly with Booth's attempt to lift Larkin clear of history and makes a good case for the poems as being, in his words, 'responsive to the fractures and collisions in post-war English culture'. Both, however, sound a bit defensive, on the watch for a blind-side clobbering by P.C. bruisers, by those, for example, who look down on Larkin for apparently looking down on wedding couples in one of his greatest poems. It's a particular pleasure of A. T. Tolley's useful book that he shows how hard Larkin worked to communicate the experience from which the poem started: 'you couldn't be on that train without feeling all the young lives starting off ... . It was wonderful, a marvellous afternoon'. The poem eventually took 34 pages of drafting, and from 1955-1958 to complete. Prolonged labour doesn't guarantee success, but anyone who can't see that 'The Whitsun Weddings' is a masterpiece ought to be led by the groom's boy to that knacker's yard which awaits all critical orthodoxies.

1998

ACCIDENTS OF LANGUAGE

Geoffrey Hill, *The Mystery of the Charity of Charles Péguy*. London: Agenda and Deutsch, 1983.

In the issue of *Agenda* for Spring 1983 there is an essay by Geoffrey Hill which will obviously become required reading for anyone who is seriously interested in his poetry. 'Our word is our bond' is in many ways an apologia for Hill's view of poetry and, more particularly, for his sense of himself as poet. It is as dense and allusive as much of his poetry, and so closely argued that it's almost impossible to tease out individual threads without running the risk of damaging the entire fabric. Still, the risk is worth taking, if only because to do so helps with the reading of his new, long poem, in the publication of which *Agenda* had a hand.

'Our word is our bond' is, among other things, a meditation on what happens to language when it enters a poem. How much play is there in language which is not reduced to plain, denotative, logical prose? (Always supposing such a reduction to be possible.) And what does 'play' mean? Hill directs his questions against a Hobbesian view of language, which regards words as clear and unambiguous signs that identify a world of things we can confidently know. Hill's own view of the matter seems to be that the world cannot be as aggressively captured by language as Hobbes and his recent admirers assume. It has its own claims, almost its own aggressions, and these are registered through a language which is accident-prone and enables its users to discover or become aware of matters which will lie hidden from those who disdain the opportunities that figurative language puts in their way. Hobbes called metaphor the *ignis fatuus* of scientific reasoning. Hill is a grandly metaphoric poet and one who also rejoices in the accidents of pun and verbal coincidence. As he himself puts it, 'in a poet's involvement with language, above all, there is, one would darkly and impetuously claim, an element of helplessness, of being at the mercy of accidents, the prey of one's own presumptuous energy'. The play of this syntax has about it an untiring self-consciousness that is positively Jamesian. The 'one' who speaks does so on behalf of the generality of poets, is any poet. Yet he is also a particular poet. And for that poet to claim anything 'darkly and impetuously' is at one and the same time to make an almost Shelleyan bid for the primacy of imagination while accepting its possible solipsistic and error-laden basis. For those accidents, that energy, may well issue from a personality that can't be taken on trust. Indeed, as we shall see, Hill says as much: although 'one' *would* make the claim for a poet's helplessness before language, something prohibits the claim from sticking, since that would indicate a surrender to forces with which 'one' rightly feels ill at ease.

The almost inexhaustible tact of this sentence is typical of the entire essay and might, I suppose, strike some as a mere matter of tactics: ludicrous rather than ludic. Yet at one point Hill is plain enough. He gives his assent to Ransom's dictum that 'the density or connotativeness of poetic language reflects the world's density,' and he goes on to remark that certain key terms in Wordsworth's poetry – 'blind', 'gleam', 'perplexity' – 'gather their reciprocating force from this blank recognition: from the sense that without perplexity there would be no gleam and that the 'blindness' embodies them both.

Although Hill does not say so, his sense of language as something that arrives ready laden with ambiguity, and, as it were, the necessary infections of the world, is not merely anti-Hobbesian: it is anti-Arnoldian. 'Where shall we find language innocent enough' Arnold asked himself, to be able to tell the truth in 'a natural and thence irresistible manner'? The answer, as he himself seemed to feel but did not want to accept, is 'nowhere'. Language cannot be innocent, and Hill takes for granted the poet's responsibility to deny those 'adamantine affirmations' of linguistic and aesthetic theorists whose confident pronouncements 'foreclose on other possibilities'. Arnold's impossible yearning for an innocent language is one reason why he became three-parts iced-over. (It may even have helped him out of an intolerable dilemma: how, on the one hand, to wish to produce a poetry that should be 'a criticism of life', while, on the other hand, suspecting that life was altogether too much of a mess for poetry to cope with.) By contrast, Hill's chosen 'helplessness' before the dreck of language is what makes it possible for him to function as a poet.

It is true that Hill does not say this, but it can be inferred from his argument, as can an even more important point: that history itself is not to be known through theory, fact or positivist assertions, but through accident and contingency. History is not merely understood through language, history *is* language. This, I suppose, is evident enough from Hill's manner of procedure in such previous volumes as *King Log* and *Mercian Hymns*, but it feels particularly the case with his new poem. In an end-note he claims that 'Péguy, stubborn rancours and mishaps and all, is one of the great souls, one of the great prophetic intelligences, of our century,' and putting it that way suggests he admires Péguy because Péguy behaved towards his time as the poet should behave towards language. (But then Péguy was not only a poet – he was the author of *Le Mystére de la Charité de Jeanne d'Arc*.) His stubborn rancours imply a distinctively post-modern attitude to the world and in particular to history: confident only of its density, perplexity, of its having escaped from the net of theory.

Hill's poem starts in blood, absurdly. 'Crack of a starting-pistol, Jean Jaurès/ dies in a wine-puddle'. An accident of language, or was Péguy's call for Jean-Jaurès's death responsible for his murder? 'Must men stand by what they write?' Yes and no, seems to be Hill's answer to a question that possessed Yeats. But he is more concerned with trying to read history through language, and seeing it as resistant to specific answers.

> History commands the stage wielding a toy gun,
> rehearsing another scene. It has raged so before,
> countless times; and will do, countless times more,
> in the guise of supreme clown, dire tragedian.

Those oxymorons may at first seem reminiscent of Marvell in their accidental discovery of the ways in which clichés lead to truths. ('He nothing common did or mean/ Upon that memorable scene'.) But Hill is a very different poet. In his essay he remarks that 'the language a writer uses and the writer who uses the language are inextricably involved and implicated,' and he adds that 'the deepest intuitions of any creative spirit are ineluctably compounded with its inveterate stubbornness and incapacity'.

Stubbornness is not a quality that one associates with Marvell, nor can he be readily imagined as the author of a remark that is at once so chastening and aggrandising. Intuitions are contaminated by stubbornness but only stubbornness can produce them. And for Hill, Péguy is characterised by stubbornness. 'Stubbornly on guard' he says of him:

> Truth's pedagogue, braving an entrenched class
> of fools and scoundrels, children of the world,
> his eyes caged and hostile behind glass –
> still Péguy said that Hope is a little child.
>
> Violent contrariety of men and days; calm
> juddery bombardment of a silent film
> showing such things: its canvas slashed with rain
> and St Elmo's fire. Victory of the machine!
>
> The brisk celluloid clatters through the gate;
> the cortège of the century dances in the street;
> and over and over the jolly cartoon
> armies of France go reeling towards Verdun.

It would be impossible not to admire the ways in which Hill brings alive the contrarieties he identifies: the victory of the machine, which is at once the war machine, the machinery of war and the cinematograph, is made to reveal and become accountable for the physical conditions that soldiers had to endure; and by a perfect accident of language film-reel shows the fate that awaits Nivelle's army at Verdun.

History comes before us as tragic farce, at least as we may read it through the cartoon quality of early cinema. But what of that class of 'fools and scoundrels'? Not quite an old bitch gone in the teeth, a botched civilisation, but not that different either. The rasping impatience of the formulation certainly comes a long way short of Marvell's poise, and leads to the question of just whose stubborn rancour this is: Péguy's or Hill's? In an early poem Hill claimed that 'There is no bloodless myth will hold', and in this new poem it often feels as though he is out for blood. In view of the material he confronts, his rejection of a melioristic, liberal reading of history is proper enough: less proper is what occasionally feels most like a glowering, unlovely egotism, a pedagogy that lacks, say, Yeats's generous understanding of the motley history forces all of us wear. On one occasion, it is true, Hill allows for his own implication in history.

> We are the occasional just men who sit
> in gaunt self-judgment on their self-defeat,
> the élite hermits, secret orators
> of an old faith devoted to new wars.

True also, Section Eight modulates into a kind of weary tenderness for the 'Lords of life, stump-toothed, with ragged breath', who 'slowly come to use/dreams of oblivion in lieu of paradise'. Nevertheless, the poem's presiding tone is more frequently mandarin, abrasive or – well, schoolmasterly. We must

> turn away and contemplate the working
> of the radical soul – instinct, intelligence,
> memory, call it what you will – waking
> into the foreboding of its inheritance.

There is a heavy prosaicism about these lines which occurs elsewhere in the poem, which its rhythms reinforce, and which I dislike because of the way it advertises its seriousness. It too clearly has designs on the reader, as do the obtrusive half-echoes of Tate and Eliot. It is demanding to be taken as important, but ends up seeming merely self-important. In addition, the persistent games-playing with words comes across less as serendipity than as a matter of wilful labour.

> Patience hardens to a pittance, courage
> unflinchingly declines into sour rage ...
>
> the common 'dur'
> built into duration, the endurance of war;
> blind Vigil herself, helpless and obdurate ...
>
> 'Encore plus doloreux et doux'. Note how
> sweetness devours sorrow, renders it again.

I do not know what purpose is to be served by my noting these things: if it is to show how the density of history and/or its violent contrarieties must be apprehended through the accidents of language, then I have to say that as far as I am concerned the game seems solipsistic, arbitrary and tiresome. Besides, I cannot note how sweetness devours sorrow in English, because it doesn't.

Yet the poem has intensely dramatic moments, and some of them result from the fact that Hill, whose ability to write a fully sensuous poetry has never been better shown than in the moment where he evokes Péguy's dangerous dream of an *ancien régime* – 'musky red gillyvors, the wicker bark / of clematis braided across old brick' – deliberately contains such stylistic graces within a poem that strives for what he presumably regards as more important, more graceless effects. In his essay he says of Hopkins's ugly phrasings that they exemplify 'a consciousness which accepts that the determining of grace necessitates at times a graceless articulation'. In his own poem he relentlessly pursues puns and clichés for the revelations they may contain, and this inevitably requires a certain amount of 'graceless' writing. (It also leaves this reader, at least, not always sure whether a cliché is knowingly used or has slipped through unnoticed. 'Must men stand by what they write?' I look in vain for the possible exploitation of that dead phrase.) At all events, the strategy of Hill's poem seems to be deliberately pyrrhic. Whether you find this acceptable will almost certainly hinge on whether you accept the validity of his seeing history by the glimpses that a particular kind of language affords.

1983

GEOFFREY HILL'S *CANAAN*

Geoffrey Hill's new collection of poems seems to speak from a condition of exile. Hill chose to leave England in 1988 in order to take up a professorship at Boston University. He was not alone in deciding to exchange the bare and as it might seem all-but ruined groves of English academe for the more luxuriant ones watered and fed by American dollars. That same year, I remember, a well-known professor of English (who supplemented his professorial salary by undertaking a good deal of literary journalism) told me that he was being 'forced out' of England by increased pressures of work and adverse conditions. He regretted having to go, he said, but the deadly effects of Thatcherism had left him no alternative. Perhaps. My own, more sceptical view is that what 'forced' my acquaintance out of England was, not to put too fine a point on it, a mixture of greed and vaingloriousness. He was not so much protesting against Thatcher's values as endorsing them.

I must immediately add that I don't necessarily accuse Hill of such bad faith. On the other hand the 'pitch' of *Canaan* is, I suspect, in some part derived from a sense of guilt, of self-accusation, at having chosen what Peter Porter, with an earlier poet-critic in mind, wittily called 'subsidised exile'. 'Pitch' is a word Hill himself calls on in order to account for a difference he finds between the early, great, work of T.S. Eliot and the later, less considerable writing, where 'pitch' has degenerated into 'tone'. Hill makes this distinction in an essay to be found in an issue of *Agenda* (34.2) devoted to his own work. 'Dividing Legacies' is a critical account of Eliot's 1926 Clark lectures. 'I have attempted to show,' Hill says, 'that, throughout his argument, Eliot aims at pitch but, for the most part, succeeds only in tone'.

Then he goes on:

> I say 'succeeds' because tone is what people expect and suppose themselves familiar with. It was the pitch of *Prufrock and Other Observations* that disturbed and alienated readers; it was the tone of *Four Quartets* which assuaged and consoled them. That is to say, Eliot's poetry declines over thirty years from pitch into tone … .

And as an example of such tone Hill cites the lines from 'Little Gidding' in which Eliot says:' You are not here to verify, / Instruct yourself, or inform curiou sity/ Or carry report'. Who is 'you,' Hill asks. By way of an answer, he suggests Eliot takes for granted that between himself and his readers there will be a deep measure of agreement about what is found at Little Gidding and subsequently in 'Little Gidding,' and that this will have at its heart 'certain classes of ideas and expressions … rich in known habits of association, and others will be carefully excluded'. And then, having circled round the enemy, Hill swoops: 'The residual beneficiaries of *Four Quartets* have been Larkin and Anglican literary "spirituality"' Christopher Ricks has claimed that Larkin 'speaks to the human condition', but Hill will have none of it. His essay ends with a footnote (footnote 69 as it happens) which seems destined to become a key intervention in accounts of modern English poetry. 'What Larkin represents is an assumption, a narrow English possessiveness, with regard to 'good sense' and 'generous common humanity'. 'Good sense', so propertied, so keen to admit others, at a price, to its properties, strikes me as a deplorable kind of *bienseance*'.

Put all this together and it seems clear that Hill is establishing the grounds on which he can stand as a specifically English poet, one whose 'pitch' refuses to endorse the consolations of 'tone' that go with or, it may be better to say, express a certain kind of Englishness. And we may then need to remind ourselves that in *Thomas Hardy and British Poetry*, Donald Davie had accused Hardy of establishing a dominant mode for English poetry in the twentieth century, and especially for Larkin, his best-known admirer who was, Davie suggests, also his spiritual heir. What Larkin above all took from Hardy was his fatal lack of ambition – a 'disabling modesty' is how Davie phrases it – and a readiness to put up with the second best. And this is why, so Davie suggests, Larkin is the nation's unofficial poet laureate.

It is a very different kind of English poet that Hill comes before us in *Canaan*. The first poem, one of a series threaded through the collection to which he gives the collective title *'To The High Court of Parliament November 1994'* is as follows:

> Where's probity in this –
> the slither-frisk
> to lordship of a kind
> as rats to a bird-table?
>
> English – now of genius
> the eidolon –
> unsubstantial yet voiding
> substance like quicklime:
>
> privatise to the dead
> her memory:
> let her wounds weep
> into the lens of oblivion.

The collection is prefaced by an epigraph taken from passages in the Geneva Bible of 1560, at the end of which is a quotation from *Zephaniah 2:5*: 'O Canaan, the land of the Philistines, I will even destroy thee without an inhabitant'. We might say that the pitch of Hill's deliberately broken sonnet is one of near-apocalyptic discomfort. But is it? In late 1994 Parliament was preoccupied by questions of governmental sleaze and the revelations that lady Porter's Tory Westminster Council had sold off a grave-yard for £1. It may well be that finding a language adequate to the corruption at which Hill pitches is difficult; but the 'slither-frisk / to lordship of a kind / as rats to a bird-table' is surely cliché. Moreover, I hear behind it the Pound-like ending of 'For the Union Dead, 'A savage servility slides by on grease'; and even if we say that Lowell has here managed to retain pitch – which I doubt – Hill's recapitulation of such pitch inevitably lowers it to a matter of tone, of that which is 'rich in known habits of association'.

There is a further point, though one I make more tentatively. It is that here as elsewhere in *Canaan* Hill is gripped by a contemptuous anger which is disabling because random-feeling. Who *are* the 'idols of Canaan' Hill has in mind. Not professors of English, I suppose. But 'lordship of a kind' is not far from journalese, as are wounds that weep into the lens of oblivion. How, but by accretion of comminatory phrases, did we get there? In the issue of *Agenda* to which I have already drawn attention, Alan Wall claims of the opening poem's last four lines that 'this privatising of the dead England's memory, this abolition of public accountability ('there is no such thing as society' Mrs Thatcher famously said) leads us to the lens of the spectral … . This lens is surely both the ubiquitous camera that records our unrealities for us, and also the television screen that then edits them into a reality we think we recognise. This has become, for many of us, the optic through which we see the world'. I assume 'dead England' is meant to stand for the idea of a nation killed off by – by what, though? By Thatcher's children? By those who did her bidding and were duly rewarded. ('Is he one of us?') My objection against this is not that I expect poems to tell the literal truth about the state of the nation, but that here and throughout *Canaan* Hill's poetry is less exploratory than insistently condemnatory and that the condemnation feels to be routine. (Even if Wall is right about the lens of oblivion being both camera and TV he ought to ask himself how his sneer at an edited unreality – for all I know it's meant to have the 'authority' of behind it – squares with the sustained attempt of many camera-men and women to record the unedited realities of, for example's sake, Vietnam, Bosnia, Rwanda). Compared with Dryden or Pope, whom Hill doesn't draw on, or Blake, whom he does, *Canaan* is 'unsubstantial'. It's as though he expects his 'pitch' to do the work for him; and, to repeat, pitch too often becomes tone, becomes, that is, the means to elicit an expected response.

There looks to be an important exception to this. 'Churchill's Funeral' is one of two long poems in the collection. The other, 'De Jure Belli ac Pacis' is a meditation on the 1944 attempt to assassinate Hitler and the resultant execution of its perpetrators, including Hans-Bernd von Haeften, to whose memory the sequence is dedicated. I regret not being able to say anything about the poem here, but I will note that it is impelled by a contempt for contemporary Europe or as much of that as can be identified in 'speculation, fantastic pickings, late/ gold of Europa/ in her brief modish rage …' And for Hill, that seems to be much indeed. 'Churchill's Funeral' is also about what might be called declension of the soul: from the wartime ordinary heroism evoked in the opening section, to 'the brazed city' which 'reorders its own/ destruction, admits/ the strutting lords// to the temple…' in the fifth and final section. This section takes as epigraph lines from Blake's *Jerusalem*: 'every minute particular, the jewels of Albion, running down/ The kennels of the streets & lanes as if they were abhorr'd'. Blake's apocalyptic image of degradation and ruin is at extreme odds with Hill's poem's opening, which summons up Elgar's revelation of how 'one dark day in the Guildhall: looking at the memorials of the city's great past & knowing well the history of its unending charity, I seemed to hear far away in the dim roof a theme, an echo of some noble melody…' 'Churchill's Funeral' begins:

> Endless London
> Mourns for that knowledge
> under the dim roofs
> of smoke-stained glass,
>
> the men hefting
> their accoutrements
> of webbed tin, many
> in bandages,

with cigarettes,
with scuffed hands aflare,
as though exhaustion
drew them to life...

This is undoubtedly impressive, and only Hill would be able to make effective use of that word 'accoutrements', its weightedness lending an almost heraldic quality to the soldiers, those spectral, Dante-esque forms. (Yet the third stanza surely owes more than it should to Louis Simpson's great poem 'The Battle', whose last stanza runs: 'Most clearly of the battle I remember/ the tiredness of eyes, how hands looked thin/ Around a cigarette, and the bright ember/ would pulse with all the life there was within'?) Nevertheless, the 'pitch' of this opening poem feels right – that is, it feels entirely attentive, directed at its subject without desire to please or assuage readers. But from then on, increasingly, pitch becomes tone: a way of claiming authority of utterance where there is insufficient evidence for such authority. In his essay on Hill in the *Agenda* special, Jeffrey Wainwright claims that 'There are two sensibilities at work, even at war with each other in "Churchill's Funeral". One is sceptical, ironic, critical, the other feels and represents the feeling of belonging, in part sentimental, also tragic'. This is to take the intent for the deed. You can be neither properly sceptical nor tragic without far more by way of exact accounting than Hill is ready (or able?) to provide. A quick glance at *Mercian Hymns* or the best sonnets of *In Tenebrae* will show what is missing from *Canaan* and from 'Churchill's Funeral' in particular: that negotiation with English history the persuasiveness of which is derived as much from specificity as from implication. It doesn't matter that the funeral itself isn't included in the poem. But it most certainly matters that we are meant to mourn the burial of Churchillian values under the weight of present-day muck: of 'the keeper // of the dung-gate / [who tells] his own story; / so too the harlot / of many tears'. For these values are never evoked. (And what of Churchill's pre-war lauding of Mussolini, his post-war attempt to brand those on the left as betrayers of the nation?). And who for goodness' sake are the Keeper of the dung-gate and harlot? Murdoch? The tabloid press? The royals? Who knows? You have only to think of Dryden's 'MacFlecknoe' or Blake's 'London' (or for that matter the Yeats of *Responsibilities* and after) to know where *Canaan* falls short. These are high comparisons. But then Hill's poetry at its best challenges comparison with the highest.

1997

SEAMUS HEANEY AND THE POSSIBILITIES OF POETRY

At the end of his essay 'The Sense of Place', Seamus Heaney remarks that 'we are dwellers, we are namers, we are lovers, we make homes and search for our histories'.[1] Heaney has been talking especially about Patrick Kavanagh and John Montague and his audience is specifically Irish. 'The Sense of Place' was first given as a lecture in the Ulster Museum, January 1977. Presumably, then, Heaney expected his auditors to assent to his claim that 'we' are dwellers. For an English reader, however, the term 'dweller' sounds strange, almost quaint. It is difficult to think of any English writer of the past hundred years who would have been able to use it other than ironically, which is certainly not how Heaney uses it. We have in fact to go back to Wordsworth if we are to find a poet capable of affirming that 'we are dwellers' and for Wordsworth the word is both talismanic and full of tragic implications: 'Upon the forest side in Grasmere Vale / There dwelt a shepherd';[2] 'She dwelt among untrodden ways';[3] 'A single white cottage, a nest like a dove's, / The only one dwelling on earth that she loves'.[4] In all these contexts, to dwell means to have occupation and abode; it is to make a living. It offers the deepest access to identity, confirming selfhood as webbed within place and the associations of place (which may, although not necessarily, include other human beings). In short, dwelling provides for Wordsworth the reassurance of stable meanings, of the instinctive awareness of a self which is felt to be very different from the agglomeration of those selves which make up the loveless, ever-anxious crowds of the city.

It is for this reason that Wordsworth sees dwellings both as places of security and at the same time as vulnerable, threatened. Poor Susan's cottage is the haven from which she is somehow removed, as birds leave their nests. She ends in the city, part of the crowd. Michael 'dwelt' in Grasmere Vale, but his life belongs to the past; his son, Luke, leaves for the 'dissolute city'; and at the end of the poem the narrator tells us that 'The ploughshare has been through the ground/ On which the cottage stood'. As for Lucy, she is in her grave. Wordsworth's imagination is strongly drawn to a sense of the past as one of irretrievable stabilities. Dwelling is a form of resistance to what are considered to be present instabilities; as such, it is doomed. Wordsworth's accounts of the movement from the stability of dwelling to the instability and insecurity of mere 'rootless' existence are characterised by their use of passive verbs: people are acted upon. As a result, the historical and social process is mystified to the extent that it is made to appear inevitable and somehow free of human agency. Dwelling is, then, an expression of a cultural and political conservatism which is deeply paternalistic. It is noticeable, for example, that Wordsworth's dwellers are typically women and shepherds. But on one occasion at least he presents himself as a dweller, as someone, moreover, who chooses a particular place in which to dwell. At the opening of *The Prelude* Wordsworth proclaims himself free of the prison of the city:

> Now I am free, enfranchised and at large,
> May fix my habitation where I will.
> What dwelling shall receive me, in what vale
> Shall be my harbour, underneath what grove
> Shall I take up my home, and what sweet stream
> Shall with its murmurs lull me to my rest?
> The earth is all before me ... .[5]

The deliberate echo of the end of *Paradise Lost* has often enough been remarked on, but not the paradox that it implies. Where the fallen Adam and Eve go out to confront a world of bitter experience, Wordsworth sees his chosen spot of earth as a retreat from experience.

Dwelling is for him maternal, even womb-like: vale, grove, and the 'sweet stream' whose murmurs will lull him to his rest, all reveal a trust in nature as warmly receptive, sheltering.

Yet there is a further paradox in these lines. Being 'free' to 'fix' his habitation where he 'will' implies, as I have already noted, deliberate choice. Yet that choice is removed by the syntax of 'What dwelling shall receive me'. Here, it is the place, the spot of earth, which chooses him, and although the following clauses intermittently restore the activity of choice to the poet, they also allow for a feeling of mutuality, of equable transaction, which is surely deceptive, even self-deceptive. After all, dwellers *don't* by and large choose their dwelling, their occupation and abode; or, rather, the ultimate commitments that underpin the term's deepest meanings are meant to suggest a rootedness, an organic connection which is very different from free choice. Dwelling is inherited, or is what happens. If it can be chosen, that will destroy all the 'naturalness', the inevitability, which it is supposed to embody.

Wordsworth of course did choose to make his home in the Lake District. In doing so he also chose the identity of self-conscious English patriot, where such patriotism expresses itself as monarchical, Anglican and anti-egalitarian. It is therefore important to note that his later poetry is remarkably empty of any sense of community: dwelling is a spatial concept which does not imply a peopled place. This is all in sharp contrast to Shelley's way of being an English patriot, where patriotism is republican, atheistic, democratic; and where a rejection of dwelling can and does go side by side with a poetry thronged with lives. Shelley's west wind, blowing in off the Atlantic, bears the news of an achievable republican democracy. For Wordsworth, such a wind is at best 'roof-levelling'.

The phrase is Yeats's.[6] And it is inevitable that we should consider Yeats to be a dweller, even though he himself does not make use of the word. Moreover, the tower at the edge of Coole Park where he chose to live emblematises his commitment to a hierarchically ordered society, one that can accommodate a dream of the noble and the beggar-man – but not of civic virtues. Yeats has little time for those who come from counter or desk or who, in his most unqualified dismissal, 'fumble in a greasy till'.

> John Synge, I, and Augusta Gregory thought
> All that we did, all that we said or sang
> Must come from contact with the soil, from that
> Contact everything, Antaeus-like, grew strong.[7]

Even if we leave aside the dubious political posturings into which this belief in 'contact with the soil' would lead Yeats in the 1930s, there is still something almost pantomimic about his claim. Just how much contact with the soil did any of them have?

The question needs to be put, not because it can invite a literal answer, but because to ask it inevitably draws attention to the way in which Yeats mythologises actual social relations so as to produce that unlikely and surely dangerous dream of a feudalistic, 'rooted' society. Beneath all the generous-sounding proclamations of organic, natural growth, this atavistic dream glints with the cold steel of political insistence:

> And Guidobaldo, when he made
> That grammar school of courtesies
> Where wit and beauty learned their trade
> Upon Urbino's windy hill,
> Had sent no runners to and fro
> That he might learn the shepherds' will.[8]

If this is what 'traditional sanctity and loveliness' come to, then 'Whatever's written in what poets name / The book of the people' clearly requires some editorialising, even renaming. Book *for* the people would be more like it. But to say this is immediately to draw attention to what is most coercive in Yeats's high-sounding phrase. He is committing a nation to a collectivity that is known through the efforts of a particular grouping of poets. Yeats concludes 'Coole Park and

Ballylee', from which the lines quoted above come, with an apocalyptic vision:

> But all is changed, that high horse riderless
> Though mounted in the saddle Homer rode
> Where the swan drifts upon the darkening flood.[9]

An earlier acknowledgement of change had brought with it the problematic vision of terrible beauty. Now we are to understand that poets have abandoned their responsibilities to a specifically 'noble' dream of Ireland, and in the darkening flood that threatens there will be no anchorage, no roots, no dwelling. For 'darkening flood' read 'democratic politics'.

One response to this is to recall Dickens's Sir Leicester Dedlock on the opening of the floodgates and the uprooting of distinctions. Another, more generous, is to acknowledge the splendour of Yeats's myth while recognising its implausibility, as he himself did. Yet without going to the extremes of Yvor Winters, it is possible to feel that the aggrandising of friends into the new 'responsible' Ireland has about it more than a whiff of delusion. As Louis MacNeice remarks, Yeats half tricks us into forgetting that the majority of the Anglo-Irish ascendancy he so praises saw their responsibilities as extending no further than drink and horseflesh.[10]

To say this may well seem to accommodate Yeats to Heaney's account of Irish poets such as Longley, Mahon and Muldoon. 'None of these poets surrenders himself to the mythology of his place but instead each subdues the place to become an element in his own private mythology.[11] What such poets end up with is, then, 'countries of the mind'. But although this may be so, it does not dispose of all the difficulties – which would include, surely, Yeats's spirited resistance to the notion that he was merely creating an Ireland of the mind. True, he could on occasions admit that his was not so much the Ireland of his youth as an Ireland the poets had imagined, 'terrible and gay'. But it can hardly be denied that he wanted that Ireland to become reality. As Heaney himself remarks, 'Yeats bore the implications of his romanticism into action: he propagandized, specified, fund-raised, administered and politicked in the world of telegrams and anger, all on behalf of the world of vision'.[12] That was where his imagination dwelt. On the other hand, given that such imagination is bound to be appropriative, Heaney is right to distance himself from it, as he does when he wryly notes that out of the momentous meeting between Yeats and Synge 'a new country of the mind was conceived in English, the west that the poets imagined, full of tragic fishermen and poetic peasants'.[13] Patrick Kavanagh can then be adduced as the poet who rebukes Yeats's myth of 'the peasant as noble savage'.[14] But as Heaney acknowledges, in the very act of producing a different account, Kavanagh avows a discontent with an actual mode of living, and in so doing not only places himself at a distance from dwelling but from any comforting, conforming, dream of selfhood. 'From Monaghan to the Grand Canal' is the title of Heaney's essay on Kavanagh, and we might characterise his own early life as 'From Mossbawn to Belfast'. This is how he himself chooses to characterise it in the sequential movement of the opening chapters of *Preoccupations*. And this being so, we need to ask in what sense he can lay claim to being a dweller.

The answer will have to include the fact that when Heaney used the term, in 1977, he was living in Glanmore, in Eire and that he was addressing an Ulster audience. There is, then, both an element of self-justification in what he says and an appeal to a particular idea of Ireland which comes readily to him, in spite of recent historical events which had necessarily made the word 'dweller' intensely problematic, as I suppose they must continue to do. It is an idea perhaps best characterised as a dream of annealment – between country and city, Catholic and Protestant, male and female, South and North – which may have seemed realisable in the early 1960s and to which Heaney certainly seems to be temperamentally inclined, for all the terrible separations that the events of the late 1960s insistently forced on this dream.

These separations supervene upon the ones identified in his famous early poem 'Digging'. Here, Heaney both acknowledges the gap that exists between himself and his father's work – the gap between Mossbawn and Belfast, as it were – and at the same time uses the acknowledgement as a form of annealment, of commitment. If he can see his father digging he can also avow that he'll dig with his own squat pen. The avowal is necessarily self-conscious, but I do not see in this a criticism that can be levelled at the poem. Heaney cannot afford to be other than self-conscious. In the second of the Mossbawn reminiscences, 'Reading', he recalls a childhood's evening when he read aloud from a school library book:

> The oil lamp is lit and a neighbour called Hugh Bates is interrupting me. 'Boys but this Seamus fellow is a great scholar. What book are you in now, son?' And my father is likely wringing what he can from the moment with 'He's as bad as Pat McGuckin this minute.' Pat McGuckin was a notorious bachelor farmer – a cousin of ours – who was said to burn his scone like King Alfred every time he lifted a book. Years later, when *Death of a Naturalist* was published, the greatest commendation at home was 'Lord knows Pat would fairly have enjoyed this.'[15]

And in the essay 'Feeling into Words' he recalls how as a child on the road to and from school he would be told by people that 'the pen's lighter than the spade'.[16] The organisation and division of labour, Marx noted, varies according to the instruments of labour available. The difference between pen and spade is the difference between mental and manual labour. In England this now seems 'natural', because it has been for so long a part of the social process, one that began to appear in sharply defined forms at the end of the eighteenth century and then to make for recognisable and often tragic kinds of separations in the nineteenth. (*Great Expectations* and *The Woodlanders* are two of the great novels which explore key moments and elements in the process and its implications.) Such separations are so completely, 'naturally', inscribed in our social arrangements that the possibility of undoing them seems as remote as the possibility of achieving a worthwhile sense of Englishness. In the Ireland in which Heaney began writing, however, the possibilities of reconciliation and with it a new annealment felt, or could at least be plausibly presented as, realisable.

This is not to say that Heaney was so naive as to think that such possibilities were about to convert into reality. On the other hand, there is no doubt that in 'digging' and dwelling – although he does not then use the term – he can lay claim to being committed to a sense of Ireland, to the possible sharing of a cultural identity, in a way which no English poet of modern times has been able to do in relation to their own country. As for Yeats, so for Heaney, in dreams begin responsibilities. Self-consciousness is inseparable from that responsibility to a history which may become known, among other means, through digging. Digging is what archaeologists do, and Heaney's account of his fellow Irish poet John Montague makes him seem very much the poet as archaeologist.

> What is hidden at the bottom of Montague's region is first of all a pagan civilization centred on the dolmen; then a Gaelic civilization centred on the O'Neill inauguration stone at Tully-hogue. The ancient feminine religion of Northern Europe is the lens through which he looks and the landscape becomes a memory, a piety, a loved mother. The present is suffused with the past.[17]

The only twentieth-century English poets who have this specific regional sense are Edward Thomas (perhaps) and Ivor Gurney. In 'The Bare Line of the Hill'[18] Gurney registers how a landscape 'Shows Roman and / A sense of Rome hangs stil l/ Over the land'. This is unduly declarative, but the poem is saved from whimsy by its ending: 'Scabious guards the steeps, / Trefoil the slopes yield'. 'Scabious' is the original Latin word; 'trefoil' is the Anglo-Saxon version of the Latin *trifolium.*

'Reading' a landscape is nevertheless a tricky and sometimes a tricksy business. 'A sense of Rome' can quickly degenerate into history as theme park. What then disappears is any concern with history as an actual process. For all that Heaney claims Montague's poetry as 'sounding lines, rods to plumb the depths of a shared and diminished culture',[19] it is arguable that such a culture is heavily dependent on stock images and attitudes and that it thus conspires with the sense of diminishment it wishes to resist. Heaney, too, sometimes gets caught in the trap of conspiring with a number of such images and attitudes. The trap is sprung by what can fairly be regarded as a dangerous myth of dwelling, where this affirms a commitment to 'roots' and 'stability' and 'history' against those who shift about, 'Like some poor Arab tribesman and his tent'. Again I quote Yeats and again I do so deliberately. For this dream of contact with the soil turns into a regressive ruralism which must necessarily regard the city as the antitype of true civilisation.

This was how Wordsworth came to see London. Not always, it needs to be said. In book VII of *The Prelude* he is more eagerly responsive to the city's various allurements than is usually admitted. Nevertheless, it is noteworthy that in 1832, the year of the Reform Act, he wrote into the book a long passage in praise of Burke, in which he locates Burke's especial virtue in his rejection of abstract rights. Burke proclaims the majesty

> Of Institutes and Laws, hallowed by time;
> Declares the vital power of social ties
> Endeared by Custom; and with high disdain,
> Exploding upstart Theory, insists
> Upon the allegiance to which men are born –
> Some – say at once a froward multitude –
> Murmur (for truth is hated, where not loved).[20]

'Upstart Theory', that underbred affair, is obviously the product of the city, of the froward multitude clamouring for the vote. Yeats's adoption of this Burkean position is well known and is most plangently asserted in 'A Prayer for my Daughter':

How but in custom and ceremony
Are innocence and beauty born?
Ceremony's the name for the rich horn,
And custom for the spreading laurel tree.

In that section of 'The Sense of Place' which Heaney devotes to the poetry of John Hewitt, he spends some time on the long poem 'Conacre'. Hewitt questions himself, Heaney says, 'about his need to repose in the customary and ancestral world of the countryside, in spite of his urban childhood and politicized intelligence'.[21] 'Why not then seize the virtue in my luck', Hewitt muses, 'and make my theme the riveters who struck/the other day for solidarity?' But the city cannot finally engage him as deeply as 'the heathered shoulder of a hill, / a quick cloud on the meadow, wind-lashed corn'. 'I have won', he concludes, 'by grace or by intention, to delight/ that seems to match the colours mystics write/only in places far from kerb or street'.[22] Heaney introduces his account of Hewitt by reference to and quotation from 'Michael', where active nature is 'humanized and humanising'.[23] But this is to blur differences. It is difficult to see that the road from 'Michael' to 'Conacre' runs direct, because Hewitt's poem is a good deal less humanised, a good deal more picturesque, than Wordsworth's. It is, however, clear that for both poets the city can stand as cipher for the stony place barren of custom, unhallowed by time; and it is then necessary to say that the city is seen as harbouring democratic ideals and *therefore* – or so it feels – not worthy of a poet's deepest approval. At this point it is worth recalling yet again the date of 'The Sense of Place' – 1977.

In *Station Island*, published in 1984, there is a poem called 'Changes' which bears on much that has so far been said. I quote it in its entirety.

As you came with me in silence
to the pump in the long grass

I heard much that you could not hear:
the bite of the spade that sank it,

the slitherings and grumble
as the mason mixed his mortar,

and women coming with white buckets
like flashes on their ruffled wings.

The cast-iron rims of the lid
clinked as I uncovered it,

something stirred in its mouth.
I had a bird's eye view of a bird,

finch-green, speckly white,
nesting on dry leaves, flattened, still,

suffering the light.
So I roofed the citadel

as gently as I could, and told you
and you gently unroofed it

but where was the bird now?
There was a single egg, pebbly white,

and in the rusted bend of the spout
tail feathers splayed and sat tight.

So tender, I said, 'Remember this.
It will be good for you to retrace this path

when you have grown away and stand at last
at the very centre of the empty city.'

It is at once a private as well as a public poem. For although the person addressed, whom I take to be Heaney's daughter, may not be able to hear the sounds which throng to his inner ear, we can do so – that is, if we have read the earlier poems and/or 'Moss bawn'. Significantly, 'Changes' is placed after a poem called 'The Birthplace', which is in part prompted by a visit to Hardy country, and in which Heaney refers to 'the unperturbed, reliable ghost life he carried, with no need to invent'. It is as though 'Changes' carries with it its own ghost life, one that centres on dwelling, even though the pump/omphalos is now located at Glanmore rather than Mossbawn. There is also, I think, the ghost of a ghost, 'Poor Susan', faintly echoing through the connections Heaney allows to develop between pump, citadel ('any strongly fortified building or place of safety; a refuge'), the finch's nest, and the place itself.

The tone of 'Changes', as a private poem, is delicately judged. As a public poem it is an act of affirmation, a claim for continuity in spite of changes, in which dwelling is opposed to 'the empty city'. But here matters may seem less than satisfactory. Why, after all, is a city supposed to be empty? Is Heaney projecting an Irish sense of what often looks like sentimental regard for home onto his imagined future for a wandering child? The precedents exist: 'The Lake Isle of Innisfree', or Kavanagh's 'Kerr's Ass', for example:

The winkers that had no choke-band,
The collar and the reins …
In Ealing Broadway, London Town
I name their several names

Until a world comes to life –
Morning, the silent bog,
And the God of imagination waking
In a Mucker fog.

Yet although Heaney is on record as admiring Kavanagh's poem,[24] something other than 'inhabit[ing] the universe of the actual' is at work in 'Changes'.[25] *Station Island* continues that movement away from *North* which had begun in *Field Work*. And it is tempting to feel that the earlier move from Belfast, where Heaney had been a lecturer at Queen's University, to Glanmore, 'a very beautiful, secluded area in Co. Wicklow, about twenty miles from Dublin',[26] according to Neil Corcoran, where he took up the life of a freelance writer, begins to assume for him the kind of significance that Wordsworth felt would accrue to his own withdrawal from London to the Lake District: 'Now I am free, enfranchised and at large,/ May fix my habitation where I will'.

Except, of course, that Heaney's self-conscious involvement with the history of Ireland, which I have noted had been with him from his early days as a poet, might seem to make inconceivable the unalloyed Burkeanism that Wordsworth came to adopt once he had chosen his dwelling. But, then again, the move and the poems that come from it and are addressed to it might in fact make such a position appear all the more tenable, just as Wordsworth's move allowed him to relax into the betraying abstractions of his sonnet sequences, which, culminating in the 'Ecclesiastical Sonnets', finally undermine his ability to speak responsibly about England. If as matters stand it is not possible to argue this about Heaney, it is because, even allowing for the unsatisfactory opposition between dwelling and empty city, the evidence is inconclusive. I do, however, think it inevitable that we should speculate as to the cost of his involvement in the sudden, terrible openings-up of history that the late 1960s forced on him.

> Out there in Jutland
> In the old man-killing parishes
> I will feel lost,
> Unhappy and at home.

The ending of the justly admired 'The Tollund Man' in *Wintering Out* shows Heaney resistant to, or unable to align with, an unflawed, Wordsworthian joy in dwelling. Even if he continues to imagine Ireland in terms of those receptive, maternal holdings which characterise Wordsworth's sense of relationship between person and place, there are now to be read into landscape, name, region, the tragic history which the poet who wrote *Death of a Naturalist* had been able to ignore or to believe was safely buried.

> The hillside blushed, soaked in our broken wave.
> They buried us without shroud or coffin
> And in August the barley grew up out of the grave.

These are the concluding lines of 'Requiem for the Croppies', a poem which appears in Heaney's second volume, *Door into the Dark* (1969). In this volume Ireland is still predominantly identified with the female, as here, where the astonishing word 'blushed' has the ground like a bride receiving her husband. The little death blends into the greater one, and the horror of assassination yields that new life with which the soil has been impregnated. You can read this as a quite extraordinary imaginative attempt to hold onto the dream of annealment and to find a way of guarding against and perhaps denying those harsh certainties that also seem a part of Irish history (and, it must be said, virtually any history that incorporates a struggle for national identity). It thus embodies the ardent wish that Yeats breathes in 'Meditations in Time of Civil War':

> We had fed the heart on fantasies,
>   The heart's grown brutal from the fare;
> More substance in our enmities
>   Than in our love; O honey-bees,
> Come build in the empty house of the stare.

'The wet centre is bottomless' is the last line of 'Bogland', the final poem of *Door into the Dark*. But *North* exchanges the cherishable uncertainties implicit in such an image, the resistance to brutal (and perhaps brutalising) fantasies, for those certainties which Ciarán Carson and Edna Longley argue belong to the Catholic imagination, at least in so far as these endorse necessary death – death as sacrifice. The key poem is 'Punishment', and particularly its ending. Here, the poet acknowledges himself as 'the artful voyeur' of the bog girl who was ritually slaughtered for adultery and linked in the poem's structure to latter-day counterparts (girls who have gone with British soldiers), about whom Heaney says that he has

> stood dumb
> when your betraying sisters,
> cauled in tar,
> wept by the railing,
>
> who would connive
> in civilized outrage
> yet understand the exact
> and tribal, intimate revenge.

Of this ending Carson comments, 'It is as if [Heaney] is saying, suffering like this is natural; there things have always happened.... It is as if there never were and never will be any political consequences of such acts; they have been removed to the realm of sex, death and inevitability.[27] And it is with the same poem especially, though not exclusively, in mind that Edna Longley remarks that *North* 'is a book of martyrs rather than of tragic protagonists'. While this is undoubtedly true, Longley's explanation needs to be challenged. The problem, she implies, may be traced to the 'Catholic psyche … bound to immolation, and with in that immolation to savage tribal loyalties'.[28] But any outsider is likely to feel that Irish Catholics in Ulster do not have the monopoly on immolation, still less on 'savage tribal loyalties'. And if this is so, the explanation for Heaney's procedures in North is much more likely to inhere in his complex feelings about what he comes to call 'dwellers'. To try to understand how and why this should be, we need to look at the opening and closing poems of the first part of the volume.

The poems that make up the first and more remarkable part of *North* are surrounded by two poems about Antaeus. Their positioning is clearly crucial, because the volume as a whole is most carefully planned. Blake Morrison has usefully commented that the Antaeus poems function as artistic and political allegories:

> As the former they express the quarrel in Heaney between the instinctual (Antaeus) and the rational (Hercules) ... . Politically, these are poems about colonization, suggesting that dispossession is the inevitable lot of small, backward nations.[29]

Morrison fails to note, however, that the first poem is dated 1966. In other words, Heaney locates it as belonging to a time before the real Troubles began. 1966 is also, of course, the year of publication of his first volume, *Death of a Naturalist*, in which he vows to dig with his pen, and given its success, becomes known as an Irish poet and a celebrant of a place's – Catholic – history and culture. Whether he actually wrote the poem in 1966 is less important, therefore, than his wanting to identify it with that year. We are required to read 'Antaeus' as a kind of prelapsarian poem, its protagonist living, even dwelling, in a fool's paradise.

> Down here in my cave
>
> Girdered with root and rock
> I am cradled in the dark that wombed me
> And nurtured in every artery
> Like a small hillock.

But this is the fool as holy innocent: Hercules

> may well throw me and renew my birth
> But let him not plan, lifting me off the earth,
> My elevation, my fall.

History is waiting to happen but Antaeus cannot know he is to be defeated. Indeed, he denies history's inevitability and in denying this affirms an endless resistance to his threatening oppressor. He thus speaks for what he conceives to be an ultimately triumphant dream of dwelling. The other poem, 'Hercules and Antaeus', comes after those utterances of tragic awareness which make up the body of part I of *North*, including 'The Grauballe Man' and 'Punishment', and is not spoken by Antaeus but for him. Hercules, imperial antagonist, 'his mind big with golden apples / his future hung with trophies . . . has the measure / of resistance and black power / feeding off the territory'. As a result, 'Antaeus, the mould-hugger, / is weaned at last'. He has entered the terrible agony of history.

> Hercules lifts his arms
> in a remorseless V,
> his triumph unassailed
> by the powers he has shaken
>
> and lifts and banks Antaeus
> high as a profiled ridge,
> a sleeping giant,
> pap for the dispossessed.

Speaking for Antaeus, Heaney denies the vitality of that belief with which Yeats had aligned himself in 'The Municipal Gallery Revisited'. Or, rather, he implies that if contact with the soil, Antaeus-like, promises strength in art, it does so in defiance of the actualities of history. Art must then become its own consolation. 'A sleeping giant' is a comforting myth; it hints at renewal, even ultimate victory. But it is 'pap for the dispossessed', and this brutally dismissive phrase cancels the value of such hints. Martyrdom is the fatal food with which to nourish hopeless dreams, Ireland the old sow consuming her farrow.

This bleak acknowledgement of the pressures of history is challenged by the poems of part II of *North*, which in different ways register the force of particular events in Ulster and at the same time try to keep a space free for poetry. Part II ends, however, with 'Exposure', a poem that probes for the contradictory impulses and awareness that have gone into the poet's choice to fix his habitation in Glanmore:

> I sit weighing and weighing
> My responsible *tristia*.
> For what? For the ear? For the people?
> For what is said behind-backs? …
>
> I am neither internee nor informer;
> An inner émigré, grown long-haired
> And thoughtful; a wood-kerne
>
> Escaped from the massacre,
> Taking protective colouring
> From bole and bark, feeling
> Every wind that blows;
>
> Who, blowing up these sparks
> For their meagre heat, have missed
> The once-in-a-lifetime portent,
> The comet's pulsing rose.

Given that the sequence of poems which concludes part II of *North* is called 'Singing School', and that this borrowing from Yeats's 'Sailing to Byzantium' allows us to think of poetry as 'studying / Monuments of its own magnificence', it is natural to assume that 'Exposure' will be a defiant statement of the right to pursue such study, to build such monuments. And in a way it is. As Neil Corcoran has pointed out, in the phrase 'responsible *tristia*' Heaney implicitly draws an analogy with Mandelstam. '*Tristia* was the title given by its editor to one of Mandelstam's books, written out of the experience of being exiled in Voronezh, and itself echoing the title of Ovid's *Tristia*, written during his exile from Rome'.[30] Edna Longley, who is for the most part severe on *North*, admires 'Exposure' because it dramatises 'a profound self-searching', which takes Heaney 'into the moral and emotional priorities of the artist'. Heaney, she concludes, 'earns the label he gives himself – 'inner émigré', inwardly examining his emigration'.[31] I intend no disrespect to what is undoubtedly a fine poem when I say that it is difficult not to feel that Longley's praise for it seems to be partly motivated by relief that Heaney has taken himself off. At all events, it is noticeable that she does not quote the lines in which he refers to himself as 'a wood-kerne / Escaped from the massacre' (it is not Catholics who can be held responsible for most Irish massacres) and that she dismisses the second poem of the sequence, 'A Constable Calls', by saying that the ending, in which 'His boot pushed off / And the bicycle ticked, ticked, ticked', is, 'even from the child's eye view, an implausibly melodramatic time-bomb'.[32] I give it as my own conviction that anyone who knows something of the history of what has happened to Catholics in Ulster is unlikely to feel that there is much that is implausible, let alone melodramatic, in these lines. And it should be noted that they do not subscribe to the myth of a willing martyrdom. On the contrary, death is a possibility to be feared, not embraced.

I can, however, see that possibilities of melodrama overshadow later poems where Heaney is less concerned with himself as wood kerne (one of those rebels who took to the woods, when defeated, to prepare for further resistance) than with the excessive self-consciousness that 'responsible *tristia*' can come to be. For here the poet can choose, at least intermittently, to relax his hold on history. Or rather, history can again turn towards custom and ceremony. And it has then to be remarked that Longley's identification of one aspect of Heaney's imagination as predominantly Catholic misses the ways in which he pursues and nourishes those elements in his thinking which most harmoniously chime with Burke and Yeats, neither of them Catholic, but both of them deeply committed to social and political visions whose keywords are order, rootedness, custom. Such visions are therefore necessarily fed and, they would argue, authenticated by a language which is itself ceremonious. Style, a form of address which has its own shaping powers, is part of that custom which vindicates order. It may not be proper to align Heaney unambiguously with this procedure, but it is fair to suggest that there seems to be a powerful element at work in his imagination which yearns for an orderliness that can blend into assuagement.

When Heaney began writing, the possibilities of bringing nearer the reality of such assuagement must have seemed more than merely alluring. But the history of the past twenty years must surely mean that, although the allure is as strong as ever, the possibilities of realisation have diminished. Given this, it is not surprising that Heaney should retreat into the alternative possibilities of an inner freedom which the Joyce who is invoked in section XII of 'Station Island' recommends. Here, his revenant tells Heaney

> That subject people stuff is a cod's game,
> infantile, like your peasant pilgrimage.
>
> You lose more of yourself than you redeem
> doing the decent thing. Keep at a tangent.

But Joyce's essentially civic, satirical voice is not really one that Heaney can accommodate, any more than we can imagine him giving unqualified assent to Poldy Bloom's remark that 'A nation is the same people living in the same place', because this cancels the grave weight of history which for Heaney is involved in dwelling, in custom and ceremony. In other words, Heaney's choice of dwelling may be construed as a retreat into a strategy for shaping an imaginative sense of identity to be achieved through a reading of the past which, if it is in one sense 'bottomless', is also, now, necessarily made mysterious. Alternatively, I suggest that in fixing his habitation Heaney has hoped to fix for himself endless negotiable readings of history and of the social processes that both make and are made by history while nevertheless clinging to the dream of annealment which one reading of history – a pre-1968 reading – makes especially possible, even if later events suggest that it may be achievable only as a dream of dwelling.

This is not to say that Heaney was necessarily wrong in making that choice of dwelling that allowed him to become an 'inner émigré'. Edna Longley's praise for his surrender to the 'immediate and painful' is an endorsement of those Keatsian qualities on which Helen Vendler bases her admiration of Heaney's achievement, and which he very remarkably reveals at all stages of his career. But such endorsement carries its own ideological charge, one that identifies true poetry in terms of negative capability, and then caricatures alternatives as a form of irritable reaching after fact, a propagandist insistence on certainties. A particularly blatant form of this occurs in a recent essay by John Kerrigan, which champions Longley's account of Heaney in order to damn Tom Paulin's work. Taking particular exception to *Fivemiletown*, Kerrigan presents it as sterile, shrill and (naturally) unceremonious. Paulin opts for 'choppy, short lines, too often arbitrary in verse breaks and gangling in syntax (a paragraph in praise of Tomlinson should be inserted here)'.[33] However distantly, this type of criticism echoes Coleridge's Burkean complaint to his friend Poole that the French have 'rejected all the *cements* of language'. As at the end of the eighteenth century, so at the end of the twentieth. But *Fivemiletown* does not so much dismantle the bricks of language as show how they are used to assemble a culture. This is a civic, responsible, way of exploring the history of a particular place, which necessarily includes the history of its language. (Paulin explains in a note that Fivemiletown was once named Mount Stewart, after its founder, 'the Jacobean planter Sir William Stewart ... . It is now so called because it is five Irish miles from the nearest villages, Clogher, Brookeborough and Tempo'.) But for Kerrigan, poetry must resist such deconstructive, decreative tendencies. Paulin's previous volume *Liberty Tree,* which was certainly more affirmatory, more committed to the celebration of possible assuagements, is therefore used as a stick with which to beat *Fivemiletown*. There, apparently, the 'Hardyan restraints' of 'stanzaic form' provided for at least an 'unwieldly coherence'.[34] In view of the fact that no more than four or five of the poems of that volume can be said to be written in 'stanzaic form', and that none of them is among *Liberty Tree's* major achievements, it is difficult to decide whether Kerrigan has actually read the volume, or is relying on a dim memory of Paulin's having written a much-praised study of Hardy's poetry. No matter. *Liberty Tree* has 'formal structures'.[35] Not so *Fivemiletown*. And the abandonment of these structures, so the argument goes, has disastrous consequences.

Since Kerrigan offers very little by way of evidence for his assertions, it is not easy to know what he has particularly in mind. However, if we insert into the argument a stanza of Tomlinson, as Kerrigan more or less enjoins us to do, we can at least see what Paulin will not have had in mind. This comes from 'On the Hall at Stowey':36

> Five centuries – here were (at the least) five –
> In linked love, eager excrescence
> Where the door, arched, crowned with acanthus,
> Aimed at civil elegance, but hit
> This sturdier compromise, neither Greek, Gothic
> Nor Strawberry, clumped from the arching-point
> And swathing down, like a fist of wheat,
> The unconscious emblem for the house's worth … .

That this is a shapely enough stanza cannot be denied. But likewise it can hardly be denied that its language, clogged by the fussy punctuation, the pedant's pointing, is dully fixed on the ceremonious endorsement of what it describes. That this is in any way serious historical poetry seems to me doubtful. Is the fist of wheat there to represent fecundity or as something to bash the peasantry with? Merely to ask the question is to recognise the impossibility of expecting the lines to yield up anything more than a stale smell of Burke and buckram.

Here, by contrast, are some lines from the title-poem of Paulin's volume, which Kerrigan quotes in order to damn them:

A church and a creamery,
the trope of villages
on the slow road to Enniskillen
where they made a stramash
of the Imperial Hotel
two days before
our last prime minister
was whipped to Brize Norton
at smokefall.

Of this, Kerrigan remarks that

> the imagery is stale and coercive (do those communities want to be 'troped'?), violence diffuses its thrills unfocussedly, cut free from what bombing *is* as surely by 'stramash' as by some euphemism in a communiqué, and the glance towards Eliot 'at smokefall', echoed from some dimly remembered spat in the *London Review of Books*, decodes too easily into the notion that British prime ministers equal Anglicanism plus colonialism (subtle, that 'Imperial' Hotel), and are in Ireland … a bad thing.[37]

This is entirely to ignore the fact that here as elsewhere in the volume Paulin presents sexual and linguistic differences as problematic, shaping forces. It is also to suppose that we are to identify with the speaker of the poem and thus the weary flippancy of 'stramash'; and to suppose this is entirely to misunderstand the poem's narrative strategy, its presentation of a particular consciousness trapped within a language. It is also worth saying that the use of Eliot's 'smokefall' has nothing essential to do with 'dimly remembered' spat and much to do with a remark in the introduction to Paulin's *Faber Book of Political Verse,* where he speaks of Eliot's ambition 'to express a unifying conservative vision … . In 'Little Gidding' he imagines a cultural consensus where the English people are at last united "in the strife which divided them"'.[38] But difference or *différence* (Paulin needs to use the Derridean word, as he does in 'Rosetta Stone', because it chisels away at the linguistic processes which go into the cementing of a history) prevents this unifying vision. It is a matter, then, not of whether the reference to the Imperial Hotel is subtle, but of whether naming it instances, as it surely does, a recognition of forces that ravage though they do not necessarily finally destroy the dream of annealment, of assuagement, of all that Heaney most generously intended when, speaking as an émigré, he told his Ulster audience that 'we are dwellers'.

1992

Notes

1. Seamus Heaney, 'The Sense of Place', *Preoccupations: Selected Prose, 1968-1978*, London: Faber and Faber, 1980, 148-9.
2. William Wordsworth, 'Michael', *William Wordsworth: Selected Poems*, ed. Walford Davies, London: Dent, 1975, 63.
3. Wordsworth, 'She dwelt among untrodden ways', ibid., 46.
4. Wordsworth, 'The Reverie of Poor Susan, ibid., 1.
5. William Wordsworth, *The Prelude*, 1805 edition, 9-15.
6. W. B. Yeats, 'A Prayer for my Daughter', *W. B. Yeats: Selected Poetry*, ed. A. Norman Jeffares, London: Macmillan, 1974, 100.
7. Yeats, 'The Municipal Gallery Revisited', ibid., 193.
8. Yeats, 'To a Wealthy Man who promised a Second Subscription to the Dublin Municipal Gallery if it were Proved the People Wanted Pictures', ibid., 54-5.
9. Yeats, 'Coole Park and Ballylee, 1931', ibid., 151.
10. See Louis MacNeice, 'The Irish Background', *The Poetry of W. B. Yeats*, London: Faber and Faber, 1967, 46-57.
11. Heaney, 'The Sense of Place', *Preoccupations*, 148.
12. Heaney, 'Yeats as an Example?', ibid., 100.
13. Heaney, 'The Sense of Place', ibid., 135.
14. Heaney, 'From Monaghan to the Grand Canal', ibid., 124.
15. Heaney, 'Mossbawn', ibid., 21-2.
16. Heaney, 'Feeling into Words', ibid., 42.
17. Heaney, 'The Sense of Place', ibid., 141.
18. Ivor Gurney, 'The Bare Line of the Hill', *Collected Poems*, ed. P. J. Kavanagh, Oxford: Oxford University Press, 1982, 121-2.
19. Heaney, 'The Sense of Place', *Preoccupations*, 141.
20. Wordsworth, *The Prelude*, 1850 edition, II, 526-32.
21. Heaney, 'The Sense of Place', *Preoccupations*, 146.
22. Ibid.
23. Ibid., 145.
24. See ibid., 141, where Heaney quotes 'Kerr's Ass'.
25. Ibid., 140.

26. Neil Corcoran, *Seamus Heaney*, London: Faber and Faber, 1986, 31.
27. Quoted in Edna Longley, "'Inner émigré' or 'artful voyeur?': Seamus Heaney's *North*', *Poetry in the Wars*, Newcastle upon Tyne: Bloodaxe Books, 1986, 154.
28. Ibid.
29. Blake Morrison, *Seamus Heaney*, London: Methuen, 1982, 58-9.
30. Corcoran, *Seamus Heaney*, p. 125.
31. Longley, "'Inner émigré' or 'artful voyeur?'", *Poetry in the Wars*,
32. Ibid., 157.
33. John Kerrigan, 'From Parable Island to Steel City', *Poetry Durham* 17 (Winter 1987-8): 34.
34. Ibid., 33.
35. Ibid.
36. Charles Tomlinson, 'On the Hall at Stowey', *Seeing is Believing*, London: Oxford University Press, 1960, 40-2.
37. Kerrigan, 'From Parable Island to Steel City', *Poetry Durham*, 17.
38. Tom Paulin (ed.), Introduction to *The Faber Book of Political Verse*, London: Faber and Faber, 1988, 28.

SPEAKING FOR ENGLAND

Shortly after the Fall of the House of Thatcher the *Guardian* newspaper carried an article by Howard Brenton called 'The Art of Survival'. Brenton claimed that at a time when 'some kind of evil' was stalking the land many writers at least were describing and accounting for the state of the nation's soul. Among them were Amis (Martin), Rushdie, Bleasdale, Kureishi, Churchill (Caryl) and Brenton himself. Some of these may turn out to have staying power as well as having written to the moment. On the other hand, given the 'evils' that might be thought to have made their appearance in Scotland and Northern Ireland during the 1980s, the names not on Brenton's list tell us a great deal about his own depressingly limited sense of what matters. And if he were to counter by saying that for the purpose of his article he was concerned exclusively with England – which of course he *daren't* say but which is transparently the case – then the name that ought surely to have appeared at the top of his list is that of Tony Harrison.

This is not to suggest that Harrison would find himself in agreement with the hectic, technicolour quality of Brenton's prose. It is, however, to argue that many of the sonnets from *The School of Eloquence* explore the underlying 'condition of England' which is also given painful, decisive utterance in *v.*, that excoriating Elegy in a City Graveyard. This is why Richard Eyre's television film of Harrison reading the latter poem to an invited audience was bound to cause a furore. In the last analysis it was the nation itself which became the invited audience. *Anyone* could switch on and listen to this foul-mouthed spokesperson for two, divided, cultures giving voice to the possibly irreconcilable tensions that existed – and exist – not only within him (the skinhead as poet, the poet as skinhead), but within England. It gave the lie both to the government's pretence to speak for the nation and to that wider orthodoxy which endlessly claims to be at once representative and authoritative. And on television, at that. There was the rub. When at the last Conservative Party Conference the egregious Kenneth Baker dubbed the BBC the 'Bolshevik Broadcasting Corporation' it was BBC TV he was really gunning for. And beyond the BBC were the Independent Channels, in particular Channel Four. Baker has edited a couple of Faber anthologies and claims to be a poetry lover, but it is difficult to imagine him being at ease with Harrison's poetry. And though it would be good to think that, had he watched the programme, *v.* would have disturbed him for the right reasons, it is far more likely that it would have upset him because its eloquent ability to speak for 'the tongue-tied', could hardly be put down as ill-formed rant. This was the work of a poet with formidable technical resource, even panache. Nor could it be waved away as the outpourings of a London-based trendy leftie. For this poet was from working-class Leeds and clearly knew, intimately, the kinds of lives his poem evoked. Of course, these are the right reasons for being upset by the poem, but this can hardly be admitted by a Conservative Minister for Education. Which is why the TV performance of *v.* had an importance that requires further comment.

Throughout the 1980s the government made plain its detestation of TV as a medium. Beneath all the clichés about 'the freedom to choose' was the reality of the Tory party's determination to sanitise our screens, to wipe them clean of the filth of opposition. It wasn't only the IRA which was to be denied 'the oxygen of publicity'. E.P. Thompson was not allowed to deliver the Richard Dimbleby Lecture because as a CND supporter and brilliant rhetorician he might do lasting damage to the official welcoming of Cruise to Britain. Attempts to provide independent reporting or assessment of the Falklands War were denounced as 'unpatriotic' by hysterical back-benchers. These bully-boy tactics worked. For the most part TV's masters became, not its programme heads, but the government of the day. The reporting of the Miners' Strike was so one-sided that viewers were left in ignorance of the fact that the provocation for most of the violence began not with the miners but with the police. I was in Greece for most of that time and saw uncut film of the gleeful, 'come and get us' police tactics, none of which was shown in England. (The Greek students – and not just students – were understandably bewildered by it all. 'It's like the time of the Colonels,' they said. 'It's like a police state'.) Then again, when Channel Four broadcast a series about the Greek Civil War, revealing the deviousness of Britain in helping to restore the monarchy to Greece and so scupper the hopes of precisely those Greeks who had fought with the allies to defeat the Nazis, government spokespersons were quick to call the series misleading and Lord Annan was wheeled on to explain that it should neither be re-run nor exported to Greece because it might confuse the Greeks, who we were assured had been solidly in favour of the British intervention. (This was news to all of my friends in Athens.) And recently, in a debate about the virtue of 'balanced' programmes, the same Annan argued in the House of Lords that if Channel Four could show *Death on the Rock*, the government was surely entitled to put *its* case about what really happened to the IRA suspects whom the S.A.S. gunned down in Gibralter? It apparently didn't occur to Annan that *Death on the Rock* was the *only* programme that queried – and virtually destroyed – the official account of that squalid incident.

We need to recall these examples of the government's would-be control of TV. because to do so helps us to understand why the broadcasting of *v.* was such an important intervention and why the like of the *Daily Mail* and Mrs Whitehouse were inevitably incensed that it should be broadcast at all, albeit at a comparatively late hour. *v.* did more to anatomise the 'state of the nation's soul' than most of the writers on Brenton's list. Besides, the poem was dangerous just because it could reach so many people. Brenton and Churchill write plays which for the most part speak to the converted. This may not be their fault, but it limits their usefulness. Not only that: the plays are performed in a space which is itself exclusive. As a working-class Labour voter remarked in my hearing, 'Theatre's not for the likes of us'. *v.* may not be for the likes of all, but it does have a good deal to say for and about 'the tongue-tied's fighting'.

Here, however, a qualification is needed. The voices of Harrison's poems are more or less exclusively male. I am not sure whether this is a criticism, but it does draw attention to a fact which the Miners' Strike revealed to the miners' wives: that working-class culture is predominantly masculinist in its accredited forms of utterance.

> These Vs are all the versuses of life
> from LEEDS v. DERBY, Black/White
> and (as I've known to my cost) man v. wife,
> Communist v. Fascist, Left v. Right,
>
> class v. class as bitter as before,
> the unending violence of US and THEM,
> personified in 1984
> by Coal Board MacGregor and the NUM,
>
> Hindu/Sikh, soul/body, heart v. mind,
> East/West, male/female, and the ground
> these fixtures are fought out on's Man, resigned
> to hope from his future what his past never found.

This typically packs in a great deal, but my own re-readings of *v.* have left me convinced that whatever hope for reconciliation the poem may gesture towards, its real energies are in the versuses; and that its attempt to knit up male/female towards the end when Harrison journeys 'home to my woman', feels merely dutiful. At all events, it lacks the passion and energy of the encounter between skinhead and poet. Given that the 'skin' turns out to be the poet's *alter ego* this is, perhaps, inevitable, but it may also explain why in the sonnet sequence, *The School of Eloquence*, the father figure seems an altogether more substantial presence than the mother.

This is a point to which I shall return. First, though, I want to say more about that energy. 'So right, yer buggers, then! We'll occupy/

your lousy leasehold Poetry'. These are the opening words of the second of two sonnets called 'Them & [uz]'. They are dedicated to 'Professors Richard Hoggart & Leon Cortez'. Hoggart, the working-class boy from Leeds, became famous with the publication of his book *The Uses of Literacy* which is, among much else, a by-now canonical account of working-class culture and the tensions felt by those who like Hoggart – and Harrison – are educated out of it. Leon Cortez is or rather was a comedian, self-styled 'professor', whom I recall hearing regularly on radio in the immediate post-war period. His standard routine featured a comic, Jewish-working-class resumé of the plots of Shakespeare's plays. ('So this geezer 'amlet, 'e goes up to his muvver an' 'e sez…'). Like Harrison and Hoggart, Cortez is not one of 'us', a point made with epigrammatic terseness in the other sonnet of the pair, where a schoolmaster remarks 'We say [^s] not [uz], T.W.!' That shut my trap./ I doffed my flat a's (as in 'flat cap')/ my mouth all stuffed with glottals …' Much of the force of these lines comes from the rhyming of working-class argot for mouth, 'trap', with the parodic 'flat cap'. In other words, the poem knowingly presents the clash between 'Them and [uz]' in terms that look as though 'they' can be accommodated to comic routine and as such become a defence mechanism against deeper feelings of hurt or anger. But then the mouth stuffed up with glottals has 'great lumps to hawk and spit out … *E-nun-ci-ate!*' And there, the comic gives way to a controlled violence that may include a measure of self-hate but which is more valuably directed at the system itself responsible for those divisions to which the poems' title draws attention.

Elsewhere, Harrison makes his reader join in this entirely serious game of having to choose a manner of enunciation. For example, in the justly famous 'Book Ends' (and if that poem isn't one by which the 1980s will have to know itself I don't know what is), Harrison sits in sullen communication with his newly-widowed father.

> The 'scholar' me, you, worn out on poor pay,
> only our silence made us seem a pair.

Not as good for staring in, blue gas,
too regular each bud, each yellow spike.

A night you need my company to pass
and she not here to tell us we're alike!

Your life's all shattered into smithereens.

Back in our silences and sullen looks,
for all the Scotch we drink, what's still between's
not the thirty or so years, but books, books, books.

The isolated line 'You life's all shattered into smithereens' eloquently catches the gap between father and son which the self-conscious rhyme on 'between 's' serves to reinforce rather than close. But literally the most telling evidence of the gap comes on the rhyme 'gas/pass'. For of course it's only a rhyme if you haven't doffed your flat a's. 'Books', education, sunder the would-be rhyme words. I have read this poem aloud on a number of occasions and *always* the decision about whether to enunciate the rhyme or not comes as a moment of pure embarrassment. I imagine that most people reading these words will have been educated to pronounce 'pass' with a long 'a'. Try reading 'Book Ends' if you want to experience something of the strength of Harrison's argument about them and us – an argument which is, of course, precisely articulated through his great technical skills, especially when it comes to rhyme. Who else, after all, would fit together 'Stroked nylon crackled over groin and bum/like granny's radio stuck on Hilversum'. Here, part of the comic brio, the sheer unexpected rightness of the thing, depends on the fact that Radio Hilversum broadcast jazz and other *outré* music and as such wasn't at all the kind of thing granny might be expected to have switched to. The comic improprieties of the rhyme go in both directions.

That couplet comes from 'Allotments', a poem to be found in *The Loiners*. Already in his first full volume Harrison had found the subject and style that he has subsequently made uniquely his own. It was 'mucky' stuff: back-alley sex, working-class deviancy, the adventures of 'The White Queen' in Africa (colonialism and homosexuality: 'O he could move / Like an oiled (slow-motion) racehorse at its peak, / Outrageous, and not gently, tame, or meek – '). But as that echo of a famous line of Wyatt's makes plain, Harrison is a very literary poet. Whether *The Loiners* was meant to *épater les bourgeois*, as Blake Morrison claimed, I don't know. But the volume can hardly be read as an *echt* version of life among the proles. It's altogether too knowing, too truculently delighted in its own making, to be taken as an example of the documentary realism – earnest, often artless – associated in the 1960s with Sillitoe, Barstow and others. If there is a debt it is surely to Lowell? Harrison's tightly-wrought couplets, with their hammering iambs, often sound very close to the poet of *Lord Weary's Castle*; and two of the poems from *The Loiners*, 'Ginger's Friday' and 'The Pocket Wars of Peanuts Joe', can almost be read as rhubarbarian versions of 'Man and Wife' and '"To speak of Woe that is in Marriage"' (from *Life Studies*).

But although Harrison is a more than able *pasticheur*, *The Loiners* is original, not only in its subject-matter (with the possible exception of Tony Connor, no other published poet of the time had the ability and experience to speak for 'the tongue-tied'), but in its formal inventiveness. Add to his skill at rhyme Harrison's use of a variety of formal metres, from tetrameters through to hexameters, and even to septennaries, and it is obvious that *The Loiners* is in no sense prentice work.

> Sunday Scotsman Northwards, autumn all rusting up;
> My fifth *Light Ale* is swashing in its BR plastic cup.
> Coming back to England; there's no worse way than this
> Railroad North from London up to *Worstedopolis*.
> Britannia, Old Mother Riley, bending down to pray,
> The railway line's the X-Ray of her twisted vertebrae.

'The Death of the PWS Man' from which these lines come is, in fact, a *tour-de-force* of rancid, over-the-top observation: the free-wheeling thoughts of a beer-soaked brain:

> The rot sets in at Retford and the stations beyond;
> Coffles of coupled, rusty coaltrucks chalkmarked COND.
> But at each abandoned station shunned like a suicide
> There's that loveliest of flourishers, the purple *London Pride*.
> Though why the 'proud' metropolis should monopolise weeds
> Beats me, when we've got millions more all over mucky Leeds,
> Springing up wherever life is teetering on the brink
> Like pensioned-off yours truly's pickled in his drink.
> With a bit of help off Bitter, I can do it on my own.
> They can stuff their pink *Somalgins* and their *Phenobarbitone*.

The relish that went into the making of these lines is reminiscent of Auden's trochaic octameters in 'Get there if you can and see the land that you were proud to own'. And like that poem this includes a relish for the parodic. To get the seven stresses into each line often requires stretching or distortion of normal speech sounds; but this seems to be deliberate. Once Harrison has established his template in the poem's opening lines – and this he does scrupulously – he can afford to make us work to fit each line to the pattern. So with 'The rot sets in at Retford and the stations beyond', 'stations' has to be pronounced as a three-syllable word for the sake of the metre, and this emphasises a southern drawl, presumably meant to be heard as a parody of 'poshness' by the drunken traveller as he journeys home to Leeds. Similarly, 'Coffles of coupled, rusty coaltrucks chalkmarked COND' not only has great fun with alliteration and gobbly near-assonance, it also requires a sudden and hefty pause after 'rusty'. Scan the line, and you will come up with something like this: 'Cóffles of coúpled, rústy cóaltrúcks chálkmarked CÓND'. Again, you can get seven stresses into 'Though why the "proud" metropolis should monopolise weeds' only if you throw the stress on 'monopolise' forward from the second to the third syllable. To do this means you have to go back from a stumbled run at the line and approach it again, with due caution.

Since those early days Harrison has seldom allowed himself such comic excess, such exuberance, and when it does reappear, it tends to be in the plays rather than the poetry, as in the poulter's measure of *The Big H*, his television verse drama for schools (and everyone else) with its 'Inner Voice of Herod': 'Make way for ranting Herod, The Anti Christ Kid King / who cringes every Christmas when the Noels start to ring. / Make room for me King Herod your Inner Mr Hyde / who'd rid himself of Jesus by unleashing genocide'. But this is exceptional. By and large Harrison has limited himself to the iambic pentameter, almost it seems as an act of faith: a pledge to be true to his 'roots'. At all events, in the second of two sonnets, 'Lines to my Grandfathers', he says: 'I strive to keep my lines direct and straight, / and try to make connections where I can – '; and as a way of implying connection he ends the sonnet by remarking of the prized possession of one grandfather, 'the knuckleduster's now my paperweight'. But the connection is insecure.

That it should be so leads to a further point. The ending of Harrison's poem inevitably recalls the ending of Seamus Heaney's 'Digging': 'Between my finger and thumb/ The squat pen rests./ I'll dig with it.' Heaney is trying to establish a continuity between what he can do with his craft and what his father had done with the spade by which he made a living for himself and his family. But as Neil Corcoran has remarked (in his study *Seamus Heaney* [Faber, 1986]), this is a willed continuity:

> In 'Feeling into Words', Heaney speaks of this poem as if it is an illustration of the 'proverbial' wisdom of a saying remembered from his childhood, 'the pen's lighter than the spade'. In fact, however, this is the wisdom of an agricultural labourer who knows the heaviness of the spade, and knows that there is something easier as a way of life: the word 'lighter' in the saying opens a huge gap between the worlds

> of manual work and education. That gap is narrowed in 'Digging' to the single blank line before its final stanza; and the analogy, far from acknowledging the pen's lightness, in fact wants to make it 'squat' and heavy again.

Corcoran is right to call the analogy a strained one. Harrison on the other hand doesn't enforce a connection between his 'rude, unlettered' grandfather's knuckleduster and his own life as a poet. Knuckleduster to paperweight doesn't press a connection at all. It can even be read as pointing a disconnection: what was once for real is now a *kitsch* object. It is this possible disconnection, and the other fears and guilts that go with it, which has much to do with the matter of Harrison's work.

For this reason the issue of connection between educated poet and working-class family, especially the father, is one that preoccupies Harrison to the point of obsession. Hence, perhaps, the desire to keep his lines 'direct and straight'. It's as though he believes only such lines can speak to the family he has in some sense outgrown, can indeed reach straight back to a shared past. Whether the lines are in fact able to perform such a function is a moot point, but there is anyway another problem: the lines are not always direct and straight. On the contrary, they can be so buckled as to de-rail the unwary traveller/reader. Sometimes this is a matter of syntax, sometimes of grammar. To take just one example: for the life of me I can't see what the repeated 'that' is doing in the line 'That's why when I've heard George Formby that I've wept' ('Punchline'). But the major problem has to do with the metre.

Harrison occasionally shortens or lengthens his customary pentameter by a foot. He presumably does so in order to break what might otherwise feel to be a threatening monotony or too great mellifluousness, much as we are told that Dryden – and more sparingly Pope – made functional use of the alexandrine in order to interrupt the movement of their heroic couplets, or to draw attention to some weighty reflection or … or … . Well, all right, though to my ear at least the game is rarely worth the candle, for Dryden, for Pope, or for Harrison. And yet I am less concerned with such moments than with ones where the metre seems to lie uneasily athwart the rhythm of a line to the confusion of both. As here, for example.

> Almost the time for ghosts I'd better scram.
> Though not given much to fears of spooky scaring
> I don't fancy an encounter with mi mam
> playing Hamlet with me for this swearing.

The first line is an almost regular pentameter (the substitution of trochee for iamb in the opening foot is a standard device). The second line has twelve syllables and either its first or second foot is anapaestic (depending on whether you stress 'not'); the third line opens with an anapaest and has to take stresses on the words 'an' and 'with' (admittedly light but they're needed to fulfil the pulse of the pentameter); and the fourth line – the fourth line seems to me a total mess. Given that the previous lines have established their opening feet as anapaestic, it feels natural to put the line's initial stress on the first syllable of Hamlet. But if you do so the next stress has to fall on 'with', the next 'for' and to complete the pattern you have to make a spondee out of 'swearing'. Chaos! So you go back and re-construct the line beginning with a stress on the opening syllable. Now the line falls into an acceptable pattern. 'Pláying Hámlet wíth me fór this swéaring'. Except that in the process it has become a pure trochaic line. I could go on. How many stresses has the following for example: 'or as reunion for dead parents soon recedes'. And in the line 'A matter of mere time and it will swallow', isn't 'mere' shifted from its expected place in order to smooth the metre, and for the same reason isn't 'it will' there instead of Harrison's habitual, colloquial 'it'll'? And when he writes 'I look out for known landmarks', isn't 'known' metrical padding? (What would an unknown landmark be?). All these examples, which I could multiply, come from v., and in view of my conviction that Harrison is customarily so exact in keeping his lines if not 'direct and straight' then at least metrically well ordered, I'm at a loss to explain these lapses except by taking the fairly desperate route of what used to be called 'imitative fallacy'. That is, because the poem's subject is rough, coarse, even deliberately crude, the form in which it is written has to match the roughness of the matter. I don't really believe this, but it does lead to another charge often brought against Harrison, and one I want to confront.

Harrison is accused, by Craig Raine among others, of making too much of a fuss about working-class deprivation, of loss, of suffering. Blake Morrison points out the difference between the two poets – for Raine also comes from a northern working-class background – when he remarks that whereas Raine 'presents his parents as participants in a colourful drama of small-town life, Harrison treats his as emblems of class and cultural underprivilege. And where Raine's tone is free of resentment, Harrison's bears grudges and (socialist) anger'. This is well said, although despite commentators preferring Raine's tone it's possible to feel that resentment might be of occasional use to him. But then the fact is that, yes, Harrison's parents are 'emblems' in the poet's dramatic presentation of class and underprivilege. I have no more means of knowing whether the father of his great sonnet is 'really' Harrison senior than I can tell whether Walter Morel is 'really' D. H. Lawrence's father. I don't doubt that there are connections between the two, but as Harrison is an immensely gifted playwright it probably makes good sense to see in the tensions, connections and disconnections between father and son a working through of *typical* issues. As such, the sequence will survive the local occasion of its writing and remain a definitive account of the struggle to articulate the rottenness of the most class-conscious nation in the world.

Whether this will be true of *v.* is more open to doubt. I have hinted that, powerful as *v.* is, it is very much of its moment. I now suggest that those ungainly passages to which I have alluded are what make it a poem of the 1980s in a manner that may in the end prove limiting. If I am right about this, it is because the poem as a whole testifies to a deliberate uncouthness which, for all Harrison's insistence on being a poet, suggests that he is sometimes distrustful of both craft and title. This is not to be wondered at. For reasons too complex to tease out in the present context, the predominantly masculinist expression of English working-class culture is markedly uneasy with the very idea of poetry. 'Poet', 'Poetry'. These are deeply contaminated words (as they don't seem to be in analogous Welsh, Irish or Scottish contexts). '*Ah've told yer, no more Greek'... / So don't speak Greek. Don't treat me like I'm dumb*'. The skinhead who mouths these words in v. speaks for all those who instinctively recognise they are excluded from a culture that will never accept them or their kind. His chosen response to this is, then, one of aggressive, male, rejection of what rejects him.

If this is understandable it is also deeply depressing and may explain why in *v.* Harrison feels he has no option but to savage 'poetry' itself. I hope it is not sentimental, therefore, to welcome the more recent 'Cypress & Cedar' for its suggestion of a new departure. The smell of cypress is identified with dark, rank, forbidding forces, cedar with the sweet, the sensual, the generous. In the end, however, cedar 'is the smell coming off my pencil as I write'. The last line of this lovely, graceful poem suggests that to be a poet is less a matter of enforcing oppositions than of celebrating complementaries.

1991

NEW POLYOLBIONS

I

In 1962 A. Alvarez prefaced his influential anthology, *The New Poetry*, with the remark that he wasn't trying to give examples of every kind of poetry then being written in Great Britain. His intention was 'to represent what I think is the most significant work of British poets who began to come into their own in the fifties'. Then, in an introduction which soon became notorious, as much for its provocative sub-title 'Beyond the Gentility Principle' as for its argument, he protested at what he took to be the fundamental weakness of much of the home-grown product.

> Sometime in the twenties Thomas Hardy remarked to Robert Graves that *vers libre* could come to nothing in England. 'All we can do is write on the old themes in the old styles, but try to do a little better than those who went before us.' Since about 1930 the machinery of modern English poetry seems to have been controlled by a series of negative feed-backs designed to produce precisely the effect Hardy wanted.[1]

Eleven years later Donald Davie returned to this charge in his book, *Thomas Hardy and British Poetry*. 'The poems I am to discuss in the following pages,' Davie says, 'have been chosen to illustrate a thesis: that in British poetry (as not in American) the most far-reaching influence, for good and ill, has not been Yeats, still less Eliot or Pound, not Lawrence, but *Hardy*'.[2] It will be noted that whereas Alvarez had limited Hardy's harmful influence to English poetry, Davie is prepared to go the whole hog: it is now *British* poetry which has suffered from Hardy's 'surrender' to the second-rate, his disabling modesty, his fatal lack of ambition – for as the book proceeds Davie accuses Hardy of all these sins and more besides, and of passing them on to his fucked-up heirs.

Another nine years – we are now in 1982 – and Blake Morrison and Andrew Motion bring out the *Penguin Book of Contemporary British Poetry*.[3] The stars of this anthology, at all events if you go by number of poems chosen, are the Irishman, Seamus Heaney and Douglas Dunn, a Scot. Dunn's literary debt to Larkin is, the editors say, 'crucial'; and by then, of course, everyone knew that Hardy was Larkin's favourite poet. In the *Oxford Book of Twentieth Century English Verse,* 1973, Larkin had given Hardy more space than any other poet. In the introduction to his reprinted first volume, *The North Ship*, he had credited Hardy with curing him of Celtic fever; and in numerous interviews he made plain that the poet Hardy had no rival in his affections. As for Heaney, although Morrison and Motion mention Lowell and Hughes as poets to whom he stood in debt, his very next volume, *Station Island*, pays open homage to Hardy; and his most recent one, *Seeing Things*, seems to me heavily, perhaps even fatally, dependent on him. At all events I don't see how you can read these lines (from 'Settings' XV) – 'I watched the sentry's torchlight on the hoard. / I stood in the door, unseen and blazed upon"[4] – without recalling 'The Self-Unseeing,' especially since earlier in the poem Heaney has referred to the 'Rembrandt-gleam' which is so often a pre-condition for visionary moments in Hardy's prose as well as his verse. (In fairness I should add that there are also blatant echoes of Lowell, though the lists that fill so many lines of so many poems in *Seeing Things* come from Larkin.) In other words, Hardy clearly affects the work of a poet who, as soon as the Morrison/Motion anthology appeared, dissociated himself from it in a verse letter to the editors, pointing out that as the carrier of an Irish passport, and as someone who identifies with Irish culture and history, he has no wish to be labelled British.

Two points of some importance emerge from what I have so far said. Alvarez, Davie, Larkin, Morrison and Motion are all of them English and all are men. With the exception of Larkin, they claim to be anthologising and speaking about *British* poetry, yet the poetry they are chiefly concerned with is that produced by *English* poets, or poetry that can be accommodated to a specifically English tradition which is said to originate with Hardy. And this, which Alvarez and Davie to be a bad thing, will explain why English poetry has for much of the twentieth century been, they say, second-rate. Davie quotes with approval from the introduction to Sidney Bolt's anthology, *Poetry of the Twenties,* where, in Davie's words, Bolt argues 'that the precedents offered by Hardy were inadequate to accommodate and register the horrific experiences' of poets who had returned to England after the Great War.

> The critical question was whether new themes did not demand new forms, and here the influence of Hardy was conservative. Advising the young Graves that '*vers libre* would come to nothing in England' he added: 'all we can do is to write on the old themes in the old styles, but try to do a little better than those who went before us.' The implication that the old styles were linked to the old themes is clear and whether or not they recognised the fact, the themes of these poets were too new to be accommodated by minor modifications of the style they inherited. As a result, the honesty which they had in common sometimes exposed the limitations of their verse.[5]

Leaving aside that weasel word 'sometimes' and the fact that Bolt's argument is little more than an attempt to shave some whiskers off the Leavisian thesis about *New Bearings in English Poetry*, we have surely to notice that Davie's endorsement of Bolt's words means that his own position is closely aligned with Alvarez's, no matter how Davie might want to contest this. To see why, I have only to quote the following sentences from 'Beyond the Gentility Principle'.

> I am not suggesting that modern English poetry, to be really modern, must be concerned with psychoanalysis or with the concentration camps or with the hydrogen bomb or with any other of the modern horrors. I am not suggesting, in fact, that it *must* be anything. For poetry that feels it has to cope with pre-determined subjects ceases to be poetry and becomes propaganda. I am however, suggesting that it drop the pretence that life, give or take a few social distinctions, is the same as ever, that gentility, decency, and all the other social totems will eventually muddle through.
>
> What poetry needs, in brief, is a new seriousness. I would define this seriousness simply as the poet's ability and willingness to face the full range of his experience with his full intelligence; not to take the easy exits of either the conventional response or choking incoherence.[6]

This may not at first blush seem to require a formal innovativeness, but Alvarez makes clear it does by placing at the head of his anthology poems by John Berryman and Robert Lowell, including a passage from 'Homage to Mistress Bradstreet' and some of Lowell's *Life Studies.* New styles of architecture must accompany a change of heart – are, indeed, the register for that change.

Anyone introducing an anthology of new poetry is of course almost certain to argue that it's needed because the times are changing. Hence, the most recent anthology of note, Bloodaxe's *The New Poetry*,[7] which came out last year, and whose editors, Michael Hulse, David Kennedy and David Morley, though they are all English men, nevertheless offer many more poets for inspection than Alvarez, with his eighteen, and Morrison and Motion, with their twenty, of whom five were women. (Alvarez had room for none, not even Elizabeth Jennings.) The Bloodaxe anthology includes no fewer than fifty-five poets – including seventeen women – and is said to represent what the editors believe 'to be the best poetry written in the British Isles in the 1980s and early 1990s'. Given that at least six of the poets were born and live in Eire this cannot be the literal truth; but the editors are determined to be as pluralist as possible in their choices. They open their 'Introduction' with the unfortunate claim that 'Every age gets the literature it deserves' and that in our age 'in the absence of shared moral and religious ideals, common social or sexual mores or political ideologies, or any philosophy on the conduct of life, plurality has replaced monocentric totemism'.[8] Theirs is a determinedly politically correct, post-modern anthology, although they end their introduction by identifying an element common to the 'best poetry' of the moment.

> It is a poetry which understands that before it is moral, representational or empirical, it is above all *sceptical*; whose defining presences are, consequently, most often to be found in John Ashbery, W. H. Auden, Elizabeth Bishop and Derek Mahon; and which represents an exhilarating re-discovery of the freedom of the imagination.[9]

Quite how this can be squared with the claim with which the paragraph begins, that 'The work collected here documents poetry in the British Isles at last responding to the imperatives of the times', is not easy to understand; and it is still less easy to grasp how an age which is notable for the absence of shared ideals can also be said to have imperatives. But what does seem clear is that, according to the Bloodaxe editors, the best of the new British poets have freed themselves from the crippling legacy with which Hardy hobbled earlier generations. These poets walk arm-in-arm with a quartet of poets whose work is now customarily claimed as – well, as American or Irish and gay or lesbian: oh, then, quintessentially post-modernist.

II

I shall return to this, but before I do I want to do belated justice to Hardy, by uncoupling him from the remark which, while it has led to his sanctification by numbers of reactionary writers and critics, has more usually damned him, as the words of Alvarez and Davie make plain. Not only them, either. In Hugh Kenner's *The Sinking Island*[10] England is identified as the home of lost causes and bad faith: In particular, the literary establishment is to be condemned for abandoning high Modernism in favour of the easy read, of pandering to the semi-literate. Larkin, above all, is to be blamed for somehow making a virtue of philistinism, and behind Larkin is you know who. Now there is something very odd about this. After all, Hardy the poet, the declared enemy of modernism, is also Hardy the novelist, about whose fictions many books have been written, nearly all of them claiming him for a radical vision and, inevitably, an accompanying formal radicalism. John Goode's brilliant study of the novels is called *Thomas Hardy: The Offensive Truth*.[11] Can this really be the same writer as the poet who seems so anxious not to offend, so ready to endorse a formal and by implication contentual conservatism? In an attempt to answer this question and to clear Hardy's reputation of the limiting 'modesty' of which, as we have seen, he is so regularly accused, I want to go back to the incident which, if not its starting point, is the one most often referred to as proof positive of Hardy the reactionary.

'Sometime in the twenties'. We can improve on Alvarez's airy vagueness. The fateful meeting with Robert Graves took place in August, 1920. In that month Graves and his then wife, Nancy, cycled down to Max Gate in order to meet the poet whom Graves, in common with other poets of his generation, hugely admired. Hardy's references to the visit are brief. On August 5th he writes to his friend, Florence Henniker, to tell her that 'A poet & his wife – two quite young people – are going to descend upon us on bicycles this month, & stay a night – so they tell us. But as she lately had a baby it seems rather a wild project of theirs. Their scheme is to bicycle from Oxford into Devon'.[12] As far as I know that is his only reference to the visit. But to Graves it meant a great deal. He devotes no fewer than six pages of *Good-bye to All That* to recalling it, and as his account includes the conversation in which Hardy is credited with those remarks to which later commentators trace the malaise of much subsequent English poetry, this meeting of the poets occupies a momentous place in the history of English literature in the twentieth century. It therefore comes as a shock to discover from Martin Seymour-Smith's biography, Robert

Graves: *His Life and Works* (1982) that Graves's account of the visit, 'based on notes he made at the time and written up in a hurry, is proof he wanted to show his love for Hardy, but was inaccurate, careless and managed to sound patronising – and failed to convey the warmth he felt. Nevertheless, his meeting with the old poet deeply affected him. He was most of all impressed with Hardy's disdain for critics, his loyalty to his friends and his dislike of *vers libre*'.[13] Graves's self-criticism doesn't, however, occur in *Good-Bye to All That*. It was made, many years later, to his biographer. In his introduction Seymour-Smith says that he has greatly depended on Graves's confidences, and these must surely include the betraying admission of 'inaccuracy' about the notes recording Graves's visit to Hardy. And we have then to remind ourselves that much in *Good-Bye to All That* was fiction – fiction that sometimes hurt and bewildered friends who were mentioned in its pages. So much so, that in the second edition Graves was forced into a number of retractions. Since then, Paul Fussell, in *The Great War and Modern Memory*, has unearthed other fancies or inventions in a book which earlier and less cautious commentators took for truth.[14]

This brings me to the nub of the matter. I don't believe Hardy ever made the remarks with which he has been saddled. It seems far more likely that Graves invented them and gave them to Hardy because that way his own loathing of modernism could be credited with an authority he himself lacked. Once you examine the evidence, this becomes obvious. Why after all in August 1920 should Hardy have dismissed vers libre? It can hardly be said that England was by then awash with it, or that it looked to be the fashion of the hour. At all events, I can find no evidence that the magazines of the moment were much preoccupied with it, at either a theoretical or practical level. Two years later, however, *The Waste Land*, that canonical text of free verse, was published, and in the same year Graves made his first attack on modernism, in an essay called 'Of English Poetry'. He returned to the battle of 1925, when he published *Contemporary Techniques of Poetry*. Here, he dismisses virtually all contemporary poets. Only Hardy and Robert Frost are exempt, because they alone understand poetry's traditional skills. We should note that by then Graves had met Pound and taken an instant dislike to him. Their meeting – in 1922, that key year – convinced Graves, so he later told Eliot, that 'I could never regard [Pound] as a poet,' and in his infamous Clark lecture of 1954, 'These Be Your Gods, O Israel,' he reveals a loathing for Pound which borders on the pathological. 'It is an extraordinary paradox that Pound's sprawling, ignorant, indecent, unmelodious, seldom metrical *Cantos*, embellished with esoteric Chinese ideographs – for all I know, they may have been traced from the nearest tea-chest – and with illiterate Greek, Latin, Spanish and Provencal snippets (the Italian and French read all right to me, but I may be mistaken) are now compulsory reading in many ancient centres of learning.' But anything is to be expected of a man who, so Graves reveals, was 'plump, hunched, soft-spoken and ill-at-ease, with the limpest of handshakes'. Pound, it will be apparent, was scarcely a man at all. He was certainly not an Englishman, not with that limp handshake. No wonder, then, that 'Imagism never caught on here. It seemed both precious and metrically undisciplined'.[15] The echo of Hardy's supposed dismissal of *vers libre* is, we must surely feel, too close for comfort.

And this is bound to strike us even more powerfully as soon as we note that Hardy took a very real interest in Pound's poetry. He sent Pound a kind note about *Homage to Sextus Propertius* and even made what Pound described as 'one impracticable and wholly invaluable suggestion' about altering the title. But then, as Hardy's biographer Michael Millgate remarks, Hardy was always keen 'to catch the sound of new and distinctive voices' in poetry.[16] Hence, his praise for Charlotte Mew's 'The Farmer's Bride' which, while it isn't in free verse, is certainly in irregular and shifting metres; hence his unfailing interest in developments in contemporary French and German poetry, and hence the fact that he copied out in his Notebook for 1917 the closing lines from 'The Love Song of J. Alfred Prufrock', by which he was clearly fascinated. (In passing I should add that Tom Paulin has pointed out to me that you can find images in late Hardy poems which owe something to *The Waste Land*.) And though in an undated entry in his notebook for 1910-12 Hardy writes 'the problem is to express *new*, & profound ideas in a perfectly sound & classical style,' an entry for 1912 has this:

> [*On New & original forms of Literature & Art*]. [Not 'change for the sake of a change' (F. Harrison) but -] A style grows to perfection. Nothing more can be done in it. And no mere device for change, no irreverence or impatience, but a necessity of artistic development pushes poets – artists into new channels of expression, new forms.[17]
> *Times,* on F. Harrison 'Among My Books' 10.10.12

In short, given the clear evidence of his hospitable reception of new work, it is simply not believable that Hardy would have made the remarks that have been used to convict him of exerting a baleful influence on later English poetry. If Graves was able to get away with putting his own prejudices into Hardy's mouth it was simply because by the time he came to write *Good-Bye to All That* Hardy was in his grave. He couldn't therefore challenge Graves's fictions as, say, Siegfried Sassoon could and did. And if subsequent critics have been content to accept Graves's account it is because they have taken too little note of Hardy's practice, his innovativeness, the sheer range of opportunities he offers to such very different poets as, to name a few, Auden, Dylan Thomas, Thom Gunn, Tom Paulin, as well of course as Larkin, Heaney and Douglas Dunn, just as these same critics have not really taken the measure of Pound's remark *à propos* of Hardy's collected poems, 'Now *there* is a clarity. There is the harvest of having written 20 novels first'.[18]

Pound's praise, brief as it is, shows that he found in Hardy something of inestimable value when he came to write *Hugh Selwyn Mauberley*. (That this hasn't been noticed is, I suspect, because we are habituated to thinking that Gautier must be a major influence behind Pound's poem and that Hardy, the well-known traditionalist, couldn't have been.) And from the list of poets mentioned above it will be clear that I think Hardy has been a wonderfully enabling force for later poets, all of whom can be thought of as beyond 'the Gentility Principle' – for although Alvarez had Larkin principally in his sights when he wrote his essay/introduction, the charge can't be made to stick. Whatever may be said against Larkin, the poet who wrote 'Essential Beauty' and 'This Be the Verse' can hardly be accused of gentility. And while Davie's accusations of Larkin's 'lowered sights' and 'putting up with the second-rate' undoubtedly have more substance, they cannot fairly be traced back to Hardy. Detach Hardy from Graves's account of what he was supposed to have said and the radical importance of those poems gathered together in 'Moments of Vision' becomes clear – as Davie himself well knows, because in his essay 'Hardy's Virgilian Purples''[19] he has not only written the greatest single essay on Hardy's poetry that I know, but has explained why the poems he there discusses can in no sense be thought of in terms he applies to Larkin and whose origins apparently lie in Hardy's failure of ambition. But anyway, to say of the poet who wrote *The Dynasts* that he lacked ambition is at best perverse; and there seems to me to be little sense in asserting that the author of 'The Convergence of the Twain,' 'Channel Firing' and 'There Came a Great Calm' was prepared to put up with second best, whether that is meant as formal criticism or as indicating Hardy's compliance with prevailing *mores*. (I name three poems more or less at random but it would be easy to supply a very long list of poems whose extraordinary technical panache, even daring, is not necessarily the most remarkable thing about them.) Hardy, it must be plain, cannot be blamed for the subsequent failures of English poetry.

This brings us to the important question of why Alvarez and so many commentators after him have found it convenient to accuse Hardy of setting twentieth-century English poetry on a minor road leading to nowhere in particular. The answer it to be found in those self-proclaimed admirers of Hardy who began to emerge in the period after the second world war, and for whom he could be seen as a blessedly 'simple' writer promising escape from modernity into the rustic joys of a 'timeless' Wessex, an England untroubled by those issues that were bound to seem to anyone writing in the early 1960s as of pressing immediacy, and that became even more urgent following the events of

1968, whose traumatising effect on Donald Davie he has himself acknowledged. Alvarez was, of course, right to want to get beyond the gentility principle; and Davie was right in wanting to oppose that habit of putting up with second best – in a word the cultural and political defeatism – which he powerfully diagnoses in *Thomas Hardy and British Poetry*. (And, more recently, in *Under Briggflatts*.)[20] But, as I have suggested, both are wrong in identifying such gentility, such defeatism, with Hardy. And they are even more wrong in thinking the failures they diagnose to be *British* failures, which therefore require Alvarez to find an antidote in the poetry of such Americans as Lowell and Berryman, and Davie to insist that the example of Ezra Pound must operate as the necessary corrective for all he dislikes. And this is not to deny the value of the best work of any of these poets, but to suggest that the examples they needed were nearer to hand.

III

Here, then, we need to remind ourselves that *The New Poetry* first appeared in 1962. Alvarez's choice of poets ranges from R. S. Thomas (born 1913) to John Fuller, who was born in 1937, and whose first volume had not even been published when *The New Poetry* came out. I intend no disrespect to Fuller when I note that he fits perfectly within that very gentility principle against which Alvarez sets his face. On the evidence of the handful of poems Alvarez chooses to print, Fuller is a writer to whom it's too easy to attach such epithets as polished, witty, urbane – the kinds of terms which damn with faint praise. It is of course possible that Alvarez wanted to conclude *The New Poetry* with such poems in order to write Q.E.D. to his thesis: Fuller is the embodiment of that gentility from which *British* poetry is supposed to suffer. But it is then necessary to remark that when in 1956 Robert Conquest had brought out *New Lines*, an anthology inviting its readers to establish 'Movement' poets as the centrally important poets of their generation, a tactic which, to judge from reviews and subsequent commentary, was remarkably successful, it was answered by another anthology, *Mavericks*. This included work by, among others, Dannie Abse, Anthony Cronin and Jon Silkin, none of whom Alvarez chooses to represent in *The New Poetry*, although none of them is noticeably inferior to several poets whose work he does include. Silkin in particular seems an odd omission – until we note that not only was he anti-Movement, he was also powerfully identified with a non-London, even anti-London centre of poetic energy based first at Leeds, where he was for a while Gregory Fellow and where he began his famous Northern House pamphlets, and subsequently Newcastle, where he took his equally famous magazine *Stand*. (*Stand* had been appearing since 1952.) And while he was still at Leeds he had a powerful influence on younger poets, especially James Simmons and Tony Harrison.

It might of course be said that Alvarez couldn't have known much about the new energies connected with Silkin's Leeds, but this won't wash. If I, as a postgraduate student and later young lecturer at Reading knew what was happening in those years, then Alvarez, who was poetry reviewer for the *Observer* as well as a ubiquitous literary journalist, could hardly not have known. For it wasn't only Leeds that was beginning to challenge those loathed voices of 'gentility.' I can't here do more than note that to myself and I am certain, therefore, to others, the London-Oxford axis didn't seem all that interesting or important, and that we felt the true provincialism to belong to that contented, insular assumption which took for granted that *English* and, then, *British* poetry could be accommodated under the collective soubriquet of gentility.

Leave England out of it for the moment. In 1955 W. S. Graham had published *The Nightfishing*, which, for all its rhetorical excesses, was obviously a work of great originality. Yet Alvarez has nothing to say about Graham. Perhaps he saw him as a follower of the discredited neo-apocalyptics and of Dylan Thomas, the poet they revered, although Thomas did not return the compliment. And yes, it's true, Graham does owe something to Thomas. But he is also very obviously a Scottish poet, a fact he would never have contested, any more than Thomas would have doubted that he was Welsh. Neither, however, would have wanted to be called British. The traditions out of which those poets came were at once more local and more internationalist: American and European. *British*, by contrast, is a term of peculiar containment. I don't know any *English* poet who thinks of him/herself as *British* – that is a term reserved for those provincials, the Scottish, Welsh and Northern Irish. And of course they perfectly well understand that the term is one to resist.

Resistance is, therefore, a perfectly proper stance – a proper pleasure – for poets who don't want to be *British* and who either aren't *English* or who want to side-step the implications of what *Englishness* all too often means. Here, for example, is the poet Herbert Lomas writing unironically in *The London Magazine*:[21] 'English poets ... know themselves ethnically English deep down; they love their psychological soil and subsoil; they feel poignantly what Pound calls the *patria*'. And if they don't know and feel these things? Then they are surely bound to detest the dreary complacencies by means of which generalisations about 'English poetry' or 'British poetry' are arrived at by those who have virtually no awareness of what is going on beyond the small circles in which they move and which are, they comfort themselves by murmuring, 'essentially English'. These are the ones Auden had in mind when he spoke in 'A Summer Night' of 'Our metaphysical distress/ Our kindness to ten persons'.

It may be objected that the Auden who wrote those lines would himself eventually gravitate to a position where kindness to ten persons was as far as he was prepared to go. Certainly, by the 1960s Auden was sheltering behind the creepered walls he had earlier wanted down. But beyond them was, if not a gathering multitude, then a growing number of writers who couldn't be contained on or by the college lawn. They included – to take an instructive example – Gael Turnbull. A doctor by profession, Turnbull had moved south from his native Scotland in the 1950s and soon began the Migrant Press, a one-man mimeographed enterprise that made available to writers within the UK the work of poets from elsewhere, especially America. Because of Turnbull, George Oppen and William Carlos Williams became known here. In addition, Turnbull knew Basil Bunting, who approved of his poems. He championed the work of Charles Tomlinson at a time when Tomlinson needed all the help he could get. Perhaps because of this, Tomlinson dedicated his Penguin selection of *Criticism of William Carlos Williams* to Turnbull. And Turnbull is also the dedicatee of Roy Fisher's Poems 1955-1980. (Naturally Alvarez had nothing to say about Fisher.) We have here an important nexus of poetic voices, and in a fuller account I would want to show ways in which much that was best, most challenging, in the poetry of the 1960s and 70s was dissolved by the corrosive acid of the Arts Council literary board under its appalling chairman, Charles Osborne. Here, I can say only that any serious history of English poetry of the period 1960-1980 will have to take into account the importance of small independent presses – especially perhaps the Fulcrum Press – and the disreputable role of funding bodies and *soi-disant* spokes-persons for 'literary matters' in stifling these presses.[22]

The result was that by the early 1980s a very few people seemed to be controlling poetry in England – as Kenner had great fun in pointing out. Craig Raine, Andrew Motion, Blake Morrison – their power was out of all proportion to any real sense they had of the value as well as the variety of poetry being produced within the UK. And this was how it obviously struck others. For something new, energising, and of real importance could be seen to be happening. Resistance to this coterie meant that the London/Oxford axis simply ceased to be of much significance in determining what poetry was published, read, and enjoyed. New journals appeared, others suddenly became of importance, not least because they carried work by writers of other than British nationality. *The Honest Ulsterman*, the Manchester-based *Poetry Nation Review, Poetry Durham, Joe Soap's Canoe, The Rialto* (published from Norwich), Huddersfield's *Wide Skirt* and Hull's *Bête noire*, the Scottish *Verse* and revived *Edinburgh Review* – these and more beside began to make known work by new poets who spoke in voices which had nothing to do with that little England so regretted by Alvarez and Davie, yet which they saw as definitive. Built into these journals was a theoretically-sharpened criticism, often conducted by way of interviews and reviews as well as articles, which brought into the open such questions as the authority/authenticity or otherwise of the poet's voice, narrative strategies, formal considerations, and which offered perspectives on non-UK poetry. New or newly empowered publishing houses began to bring out collections of these poets' work, among them Carcanet from Manchester, Peterloo from Cornwall, Smith/Doorstep from South Yorkshire, Liverpool's Spike Books and Headland, and – the greatest success story of them all – Neil Astley's Bloodaxe, which has turned Newcastle into an extraordinary centre for poetry, especially when you think that the city is also home to *Stand* and that Durham's Pig Press is just down the road.

4

This then brings me back to Bloodaxe's multi-voiced anthology of *The New Poetry*, although I should perhaps add that Astley's anthology of the poets his house publishes, *Poetry with an Edge*,[23] is an equally good indication of the sheer variety of poetry now being written. I suggested that the end of the introduction seemed to forget its beginning, and that the three anthologists cannot on the one hand speak of a post-modernist world characterised by an endless polyphonia and on the other of the 'imperatives of the times'. It is of course a commonplace of the post-modernist condition that all the old certainties, the major narratives of history are gone, and that we are unable to construct a narrative we can know to have meaning. But as John Needham has rightly noted, 'To suggest ... that a loss of belief in the 'master' narrative entails a loss of belief in the 'local' narratives, is like saying that since we can't satisfactorily locate our galaxy in the universe then we can't find our way around the block'.[24] I do not know which 'imperatives' Messrs Hulse, Kennedy and Morley have in mind and which they think their chosen poets are addressing; but I do know that whatever quibbles I may have about individual choices and omissions, their anthology in its very variety, its inclusion of such poets of Afro-Caribbean origins as Fred D'Aguiar, Jackie Kay, Grace Nichols and David Dabydeen, of Sujata Bhatt, of Geoff Hattersley, Ian MacMillan and Simon Armitage, of Eavan Boland, Liz Lochhead, Carol Ann Duffy and Paula Meehan, of Sean O'Brien, Matthew Sweeney and Ian Duhig – this anthology, this variety, sinks for ever the notion of English-stroke-British which took for granted that consensus could be achieved through a particular tradition given primacy over others even as it was reviled for its inadequacies. The Bloodaxe anthology, in its multifariousness, its readiness to acknowledge the value of heterodox utterance, does not so much persuade me we live in a post-modern society as that those of us who carry British passports do not have to think of ourselves, if we ever did, as defined by terms that Alvarez, Davie, and their followers regard as exhausting the available possibilities.

To say this is not to say that I regard poetic value as merely arbitrary. On the contrary, I agree with Adam Cerniawski that 'we cannot at will increase the supply of poets by organising favourable conditions'.[25] Still, it is apparent that the best poetry now emerging is energised and replenished by and from sources, voices, experiences once thought marginal to that older idea of cultural orthodoxy which so often passed for Englishness but which, far from being marginal, ought instead to be central to our own sense of social and cultural identity. The site of this identity is not pastoral England, that place where 'simple' Hardy was located, but the city. The city sustains heteroglossial utterance, and while this necessarily challenges authority, it nevertheless thrives on dialogue, on rival voices discovering each other in a peopled place: 'As through a child's rash happy cries / The drowned voices of its parents rise / In unlamenting song'. Hardy, whose poetry is thronged with other voices, would have understood the importance of this.

1995

Notes

1. A. Alvarez, *The New Poetry*, Harmondsworth: Penguin, 1962, 17.
2. Donald Davie, *Thomas Hardy and British Poetry*, New York: Oxford University Press, 1972, 3.
3. Blake Morrison and Andrew Motion, eds, *The Penguin Book of Contemporary British Poetry*, Harmondsworth: Penguin, 1984.
4. Seamus Heaney, 'Settings XV,' *Seeing Things*, London: Faber, 1991, 71.
5. Davie, 131.
6. *The New Poetry*, 23ff.
7. Michael Hulse, David Kennedy and David Morley, eds, *The New Poetry*, Newcastle: Bloodaxe, 1993.
8. Ibid., 16.
9. Ibid., 28.
10. Hugh Kenner, *The Sinking Island*, London, 1989.
11. John Goode, *Thomas Hardy: The Offensive Truth*, Oxford: Blackwell, 1988.
12. *The Collected Letters of Thomas Hardy*, ed. R. Little and M. Millgate, Oxford: Clarendon Press, 1978, 241.
13. Martin Seymour-Smith, *Robert Graves: His Life and Works*, London: Hutchinson, 1982, 87.
14. Paul Fussell, *The Great War and Modern Memory*, Oxford: Oxford University Press, 1975, cf. esp. 203-220.
15. Robert Graves, 'These Be Your Gods, O Israel,' *The Crowning Privilege,* Harmondsworth: Penguin, 1955, 144.
16. Michael Millgate, *Thomas Hardy*, Oxford: Oxford University Press, 1982, 534.
17. *The Personal Notebooks of Thomas Hardy*, ed. R. H. Taylor, London, 1978, 214.
18. See Douglas Brown, *Thomas Hardy*, London: Longmans, 1954, 145.
19. "Hardy's Virgilian Purples,' *Agenda: Thomas Hardy Special Issue*, London, Spring/Summer 1972.
20. Donald Davie, *Under Briggflatts: A History of Poetry in Great Britain* 1960-1988 (Manchester: Carcanet, 1989.

21. *The London Magazine* 33 (Feb/March 1994).
22. A start has been made in two essays, by Eric Mottram and R. J. Ellis, which can be found in a recent collection, *New British Poetries: The Scope of the Possible*, ed. J. Hampson and P. Barry (Manchester: Manchester University Press, 1993).
23. Nigel Astley, ed., *Poetry with an Edge*, Newcastle: Bloodaxe, 1988.
24. *PNR* 19.5 (1993): 27-28.
25. *Bête noire* 14/15 (1993): 216.